American Ways

An Introduction to
American Culture

THIRD EDITION

Maryanne Kearny Datesman

JoAnn Crandall

Edward N. Kearny

Longman

Dedicated to Lisa Kearny and Joseph Keyerleber

American Ways: An Introduction to American Culture, Third Edition

Pearson Education, 10 Bank Street, White Plains, NY 10606

Editorial director: Laura Le Dréan
Senior development editor: Lucille M. Kennedy
Vice president, director of production and design: Rhea Banker
Production supervisor: Christine Edmonds
Senior production editor: Jane Townsend
Vice president, marketing: Kate McLoughlin
Senior manufacturing buyer: Dave Dickey
Photo research: Dana Klinek
Text design: Wendy Wolf
Electronic production supervisor: Kim Teixeira
Text font: 11.5/13 Adobe Garamond
Cover design: Elizabeth Carlson
Cover art: *Sunday Morning on the Docks*, by Judson Smith (1880–1962). Reprinted by
    permission of Smithsonian American Art Museum, Washington, D.C. / Art Resource, NY.
Photo and illustration credits: See page 296.

American Ways reviewers:
Gena Bennett, Marietta City Public Schools, Marietta, GA: **Susan Gelder**, Mt. Hood
Community College, Gresham, OR; **Casey Peltier**, George Mason University, Fairfax, VA;
Luis M. Quesada, Miami Dade Community College, Hialeah, FL; **Tom Riedmiller**,
University of Northern Iowa, Cedar Falls, IA; **Kathy Sherak**, San Francisco State University,
CA; **Barbara Smith-Palinkas**, University of Southern Florida, Tampa, FL

Note: At time of publication, the web sites listed in this text were active.

Library of Congress Cataloging-in-Publication Data
Datesman, Maryanne Kearny.
    Amercan ways: an introduction to American culture / by Maryanne Kearny Datesman,
JoAnn Crandall, and Edward N. Kearny.—3rd ed.
        p. cm.
    ISBN 0-13-150086-4
    1. English language—Textbooks for foreign speakers. 2. United States—Civilization—
Problems, exercises, etc. 3. Readers—United States. I. Crandall, Jo Ann. II. Kearny,
Edward N. III. Title.
    √PE1128.D347 2005 c.2
    428.6'4—dc22

                                                    2004025216

ISBN: 0-13-150086-4

Printed in the United States of America
14 15 V001 14 13 12

CONTENTS

TO THE TEACHER

What is "culture"? There are many definitions. Some would define it as the art, literature, and music of a people, their architecture, history, religion, and traditions. Others might focus more on the customs and specific behavior of a people. We have chosen to use a sociological definition of *culture* as *the way of life of a group of people, developed over time and passed down from generation to generation*. This broad definition includes every aspect of human life and interaction. However, it would be impossible to cover every facet of American culture in a single book. We have, therefore, taken a values approach to our discussion, focusing on the traditional mainstream values that have attracted people to the United States for more than two hundred years. After explaining how these traditional values developed, we will trace how they influence various aspects of American life.

Why a book on American culture? There are many reasons. Those of us who have worked with foreign students in American universities or who have taught English to students both here and overseas repeatedly encounter questions about life in the United States. These students are frequently confused or even mystified about American values, attitudes, and cultural patterns. Even those students who have mastered enough English to take courses in an American university often find that they do not understand the cultural rules well enough to be successful as students. Many of these rules can be understood only within the broader context of American cultural patterns.

It is not only students who need the kind of information presented in this book. Foreign businesspeople, visiting scholars or government officials, and even tourists find their time in the United States more satisfying when they understand the values that underlie American behavior patterns and institutions. Newly arrived immigrants and refugees adapt more easily to their new home when given a systematic introduction to their new country and its inhabitants.

For all of these reasons, *American Ways* is suitable for a wide audience. It has been used as a text in a number of programs for foreign students, including intensive English programs, short summer courses in the United States for foreign high school and college students, both quarter and semester courses at American universities, government programs for foreign visitors, and classes for immigrants. It has also been used in many different settings outside the United States, both as a text for students and as a reference guide—for U.S. Peace Corps volunteers, for example, and others who are teaching American culture.

What do we really learn when we study other cultures? First and foremost, we learn about our own. Until we are confronted by a different way of doing things, we assume that everyone does things the same way that we do, and thus our own culture—our values, attitudes, behavior—is largely hidden from our view. When we spend time analyzing another culture, however, we begin to see our own more clearly and to understand some of the subtleties that motivate our behavior and our opinions. By reading *American Ways*, students can begin to understand themselves and their own cultures better. To enhance this understanding, each chapter in the book is followed by a series of exercises. Some of these exercises are specifically designed to encourage students to think about their own values or patterns of behavior and to compare them with what they are learning about or experiencing in American settings. We have also included a number of exercises to encourage students to interact with and talk with Americans. In these exercises we have provided a set of carefully structured questions that students can ask Americans. The answers they receive will help students form a composite picture of American beliefs and practices as they relate to education, business, government, sports, recreation, and so on.

Some of the chapter exercises provide students with an opportunity to explore more fully an idea that has been presented or to discuss ideas with other students. You may wish to assign different exercises to different students or to small groups of students and then ask them to share their findings and opinions with the class. If possible, small groups should include students from different countries so that in addition to learning about American culture and their own, they are also learning about other cultures.

Perhaps this is the real goal of a course about culture: to help us become more sensitive to cultural differences, and more accepting of them. However, there will always be aspects of another culture that we may not like, no matter how much we understand it. The objective of this book is not to persuade others to approve of life in the United States, but rather to help them understand it more fully.

About the Third Edition

In revising the content of this book, we concentrated on updating events that have occurred since the second edition was published in 1997. The issues surrounding multiculturalism continue to be of great importance as the cultural diversity of the United States continues to increase. Indeed, estimates are that by the mid-2000s, the United States will be *majority minority*. That is, the majority of Americans will be from minority groups. The traditional group of white Americans of European descent will be in the minority. Already this is the situation in the largest school systems in the country. It is becoming increasingly more difficult to describe the American culture, and it is uncertain whether the traditional mainstream culture will continue to be the dominant culture in the future. In the third edition of this book, the basic conceptual framework of *traditional* values remains the same. However, it is not clear how future generations will interpret or change them. Chapter 12 has been completely rewritten to focus more clearly on what is happening to traditional American values and on the challenges the United States faces after the terrorist attacks of September 11, 2001.

Originally we envisioned this book primarily for use in English language courses designed to prepare students to study in American universities. We believe students in those courses need experience presenting information and voicing their personal opinions to others; they should be encouraged to make both oral and written reports and participate in debates and formal discussions. We have written many exercises that suggest appropriate topics and activities. The third edition also includes other exercises that can be used to help students become more effective in American universities. For example, some exercises provide instruction on how to identify and organize academic information into main ideas and supporting details; others focus on skimming and scanning. There is also much more attention to vocabulary in this edition, including some exercises on collocation. Answers to the exercises, additional teaching tips, and graphic organizers can be found in the Teacher's Manual.

We have been delighted to hear from many teachers about creative ways they have used *American Ways*—not only in courses that introduce American culture, but also in courses focusing on cross-cultural communication, listening/speaking, reading/writing, academic preparation, and even literature. Teachers have used the values framework to design courses where students could explore ways in which the values appear in American literature or current events, for example, focusing on materials the teacher developed from other sources and presented in addition to the text.

The Book at a Glance

Purpose

- To increase students' awareness and understanding of the cultural values of the United States, their own country, and, we hope, other countries

- To provide interesting cross-cultural activities for small group and class discussions, and topics for oral presentations, research, and writing projects

Level

High intermediate to advanced. The vocabulary level is in the range of 3,000 to 4,000 words, with emphasis on the Academic Word List.* (See page 285.) Grammatical structures are not controlled, although an effort has been made to avoid overly complex patterns.

Content

Information about traditional basic American values, where they came from, and how these values affect various institutions and aspects of life in the United States, for example, religion, business, government, race relations, education, recreation, and the family.

Types of Exercises

Pre-reading activities, vocabulary work (including collocation exercises), comprehension questions on both main ideas and details, topics for discussion, values clarification, questions for Americans, suggestions for research and oral reports, ideas for pair work and group projects, proverbs, people watching and experiments, understanding polls and the media, Internet activities, writing topics, and suggested books and movies.

Use of Text

- To orient students to American culture

- To foster cross-cultural communication

- To promote reading, writing, and discussion

---

* For details on the development and evaluation of the AWL, see Coxhead, Averil (2000) A New Academic Word List. TESOL Quarterly, 34(2): 213–238.
For more information about the AWL and how to use it, visit the Internet site
http://www.vuw.ac.nz/lals/research/awl/

- To encourage conversation

- To serve as a conceptual framework and accompany other cultural materials focusing on literature, the media, current events, and so on

About the Authors

Maryanne Kearny Datesman is the author of several ESL reading texts. She has taught ESL and administered programs at Western Kentucky University and American University, and she has taught also at Georgetown University. In Kentucky, she established and administered a private language school and directed programs for refugees. She was co-founder of Kentucky TESOL and is a former president of WATESOL.

JoAnn (Jodi) Crandall is a professor of education at the University of Maryland Baltimore County. At UMBC she has co-directed the master's program in ESOL/Bilingual Education and directed the interdisciplinary Ph.D. program in Language, Literacy and Culture. She is a former president of TESOL and AAAL (American Association for Applied Linguistics) and a frequent speaker at national and international conferences.

Edward N. Kearny is professor emeritus of government at Western Kentucky University. He earned his Ph.D. in government from American University in 1968. He also holds a bachelor's degree in economics and a master's degree in psychology, and he has written a number of books and articles on American politics.

Acknowledgments

Our great appreciation goes to Elizabeth Coppolino for helping us with the permissions, and to Lisa Kearny for contributing creative ideas for exercises and activities that would be fun to do. We also want to thank all the editors at Pearson for their considerable efforts and contributions: Laura Le Dréan, Dana Klinek, Jane Townsend, and particularly the faithful Lucille Kennedy. We would also like to thank Averil Coxhead at the School of Language Studies, Massey University, Palmerston North, New Zealand, for allowing us the use of the Academic Word List. We wish to acknowledge the comments and encouragement we have received from many colleagues who have used this book in a wide range of settings all over the world. We would also like to thank the students we have worked with over the years for sharing their insights and perceptions of the United States with us and, in the process, helping us to better understand our own American culture.

M. K. D.
J. A. C.
E. N. K.

American mosaic: beyond the "melting pot"

CHAPTER 1

INTRODUCTION: UNDERSTANDING THE CULTURE OF THE UNITED STATES

Culture hides much more than it reveals, and strangely enough what it hides, it hides most effectively from its own participants. Years of study have convinced me that the real job is not to understand foreign culture but to understand our own.

Edward T. Hall (1914–)

BEFORE YOU READ

Preview Vocabulary

A. **Every chapter of** *American Ways* **contains many words from the Academic Word List (AWL).* Notice the AWL words in italics as you work with a partner to discuss the following questions.**

1. If a country has great *ethnic diversity*, would you expect to find many people who speak different languages and have different customs?

2. Could planning a visit to another country *motivate* someone to learn a foreign language?

3. Should *immigrants* be required to learn the language of their new country before they become citizens?

4. How could you learn about the customs and *traditions* for a holiday in another country?

---

*See page 285 for an explanation of the AWL and how to use it. Some of these words are key to understanding the chapter reading.

5. If there are more people in the United States who speak English than Spanish, which is the *dominant* language in the United States?

6. Is the climate of a country a *significant factor* in the daily lives of the people? Why?

B. There are five AWL words in the quotation by Edward T. Hall at the beginning of the chapter. Read the quotation and find the words with the following meanings. Write each word next to its meaning.

_____ 1. made someone think that something is true

Reveals 2. shows something that was hidden

_____ 3. ideas, beliefs, and customs

_____ 4. work

_____ 5. people who are taking part in an activity

Preview Content

A. Before you read the chapter, think about what you know about the "culture" of a country. Work with a partner and answer the questions.

1. What is the culture of a country? If someone asked you to describe your country's culture, which of these would you mention?

art   dance   holidays

beliefs   food   houses

cities   geography   literature

climate   government   music

customs   history

Anything else? _____

2. Do you agree with the quotation by Edward T. Hall? Do people really not understand their own culture? What aspects of a country's culture are the hardest to understand?

B. Look at the pictures, charts, and graphs in this chapter, and read the headings. Then predict three topics you think this chapter will discuss.

1. _____

2. _____

3. _____

Life in the United States

1   People are naturally curious about each other, and when we meet people from different countries, we want to know many things:

- What is life like in their country?
- What kind of houses do they live in?
- What kind of food do they eat?
- What are their customs?

2   If we visit another country, we can observe the people and how they live, and we can answer some of these questions. But the most interesting questions are often the hardest to answer:

- What do the people believe in?
- What do they value most?
- What motivates them?
- Why do they behave the way they do?

3   In trying to answer these questions about Americans, we must remember two things: (1) the immense size of the United States, and (2) its great ethnic diversity. It is difficult to comprehend the size of the country until you have tried to travel from one city to another. If you got in a car in New York and drove to Los Angeles, stopping only to get gas, eat, and sleep, it would take you four or five days. It takes two full days to drive from New York to Florida. On a typical winter day, it might be raining in Washington, D.C., and snowing in New York and Chicago, while it is warm enough to swim in Los Angeles and Miami. It is not difficult to imagine how different daily life might be in such different climates, or how lifestyles could vary in cities and towns so far apart.

4   The other significant factor influencing American life—ethnic diversity—is probably even more important. Aside from the Native Americans who were living on the North American continent when the first European settlers arrived, all Americans came from foreign countries—or their ancestors did. (Incidentally,[1] some Native

ROB ROGERS reprinted by permission of United Features Syndicate, Inc.

Americans are still members of separate and distinct Indian nations, each with its own language, culture, traditions, and even government.) In the 1500s, Spain established settlements in Florida, California, and the Southwest, and France claimed large territories in the center of the North American continent. But from the 1600s to the birth of the United States in 1776, most immigrants were from northern

---

[1] **incidentally:** by the way

Europe, and the majority were from England. It was these people who shaped the values and traditions that became the dominant, traditional culture of the United States.

A Nation of Immigrants

5   In 1815, the population of the United States was 8.4 million. Over the next 100 years, the country took in about 35 million immigrants, with the greatest numbers coming in the late 1800s and the early 1900s. Many of these new immigrants were not from northern Europe. In 1882, 40,000 Chinese arrived, and between 1900 and 1907 there were more than 30,000 Japanese immigrants. But by far the largest numbers of the new immigrants were from central, eastern, and southern Europe. The new immigrants brought different languages and different cultures to the United States, but gradually most of them assimilated[2] to the dominant American culture they found here.

6   In 1908, a year when a million new immigrants arrived in the United States, Israel Zangwill wrote in a play,

> America is God's Crucible,[3] the great Melting-Pot where all the races of Europe are melting and re-forming. . . . Germans and Frenchmen, Irishmen and Englishmen, Jews and Russians—into the Crucible with you all! God is making the American!

7   Since Zangwill first used the term *melting pot* to describe the United States, the concept has been debated. In Chapter 8 we consider this issue in more detail, and trace the history of African Americans as well. Two things are certain—the dominant American culture has survived, and it has more or less successfully absorbed vast numbers of immigrants at various points in its history. It has also been changed over time by all the immigrant groups who have settled here.

8   If we look at the immigration patterns of the 1900s, we see that the greatest numbers came at the beginning and at the end of the century. During the first two decades of the twentieth century, there were as many as 1 million new immigrants per year, so that by the 1910 census, almost 15 percent of all Americans had been born in another country. In 1921, however, the country began to limit immigration, and the Immigration Act of 1924 virtually closed the door. The total number of immigrants admitted per year dropped from as many as a million to only 150,000. A quota system was established that specified the number of immigrants that could come from each country. It heavily favored immigrants from northern and western Europe and severely limited everyone else. This system remained in effect until 1965, with several exceptions allowing groups of refugees from countries such as Hungary, Cuba, Vietnam, and Cambodia into the United States.

9   The immigration laws began to change in 1965 and the yearly totals began to rise again, from about 300,000 per year in the 1960s to over a million per year in the 1990s. By the end of the century, the United States was admitting more immigrants than all the other industrialized countries combined. In addition to the legal immigration, estimates were that illegal immigration was adding more than a half a

---

[2] **assimilated:** became part of a country or group and were accepted by other people in it
[3] **crucible:** a container in which substances are heated to a very high level

million more per year. Changes in the laws that were intended to help family reunifications [4] resulted in large numbers of non-Europeans, creating another group of new immigrants. By the late 1900s, 90 percent of all immigrants were coming from Latin America, the Caribbean, and Asia.

10   In the twenty-first century, the numbers of new immigrants have begun to approach the percentages of the early twentieth century. By the year 2000, more than 11 percent of all Americans were foreign born, born in another country. Some states had even higher percentages of foreign-born residents:

- California, over 26 percent
- New York, over 20 percent
- New Jersey, Florida, and Nevada, each over 15 percent
- Arizona, Illinois, and Texas, each over 12 percent

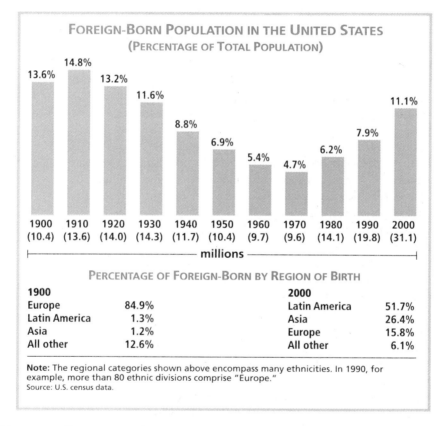

FOREIGN-BORN POPULATION IN THE UNITED STATES
(PERCENTAGE OF TOTAL POPULATION)

1900	1910	1920	1930	1940	1950	1960	1970	1980	1990	2000
13.6%	14.8%	13.2%	11.6%	8.8%	6.9%	5.4%	4.7%	6.2%	7.9%	11.1%
(10.4)	(13.6)	(14.0)	(14.3)	(11.7)	(10.4)	(9.7)	(9.6)	(14.1)	(19.8)	(31.1)

—————— millions ——————

PERCENTAGE OF FOREIGN-BORN BY REGION OF BIRTH

1900		2000	
Europe	84.9%	Latin America	51.7%
Latin America	1.3%	Asia	26.4%
Asia	1.2%	Europe	15.8%
All other	12.6%	All other	6.1%

Note: The regional categories shown above encompass many ethnicities. In 1990, for example, more than 80 ethnic divisions comprise "Europe."
Source: U.S. census data.

11   The twenty-first-century immigration patterns are continuing to change the color and the ethnic mix of the American population. First, the percentage of white Americans of European descent [5] is growing smaller. Few Europeans are immigrating to the United States now, and many of those who came in the early 1900s have died. Their descendants have married Americans with ancestors from other countries, and many of these second- and third-generation immigrants no longer think of themselves as Irish or German or English.

---

[4] **reunifications:** the joining of the parts of something together again
[5] **descent:** family origins, especially in relation to the country where one's family came from

12   Second, more than half of all the new immigrants are from Latin America, resulting in large concentrations of Spanish speakers around the country, particularly in California, Florida, Texas, Arizona, and other southwestern states. Hispanics now represent the largest minority in the United States, larger than the number of African Americans. Recognizing the influence of this new minority, in 2001 President George W. Bush became

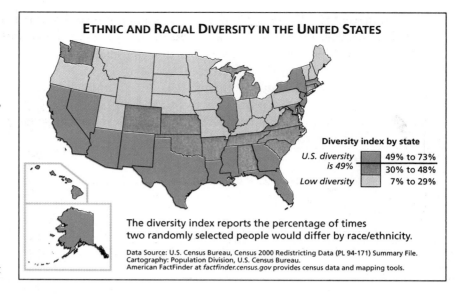

ETHNIC AND RACIAL DIVERSITY IN THE UNITED STATES

Diversity index by state

U.S. diversity is 49%
49% to 73%
30% to 48%

Low diversity
7% to 29%

The diversity index reports the percentage of times two randomly selected people would differ by race/ethnicity.

Data Source: U.S. Census Bureau, Census 2000 Redistricting Data (PL 94-171) Summary File.
Cartography: Population Division, U.S. Census Bureau.
American FactFinder at *factfinder.census.gov* provides census data and mapping tools.

the first president to give his weekly radio speech in Spanish, in honor of Cinco de Mayo[6] (May 5), a festival celebrating Mexican heritage.[7] Later that year, the White House website began to include Spanish translations of presidential news.

13   The immigrants from Asian countries are also contributing to the new American mix. Today, more than one-quarter of all first-generation immigrants are from Asia. As the minority, nonwhite population of the United States continues to grow, the white majority grows smaller.

Cultural Pluralism in the United States

14   One of the critical questions facing the United States today is what role new immigrants will play in their new country. To what degree will they choose to take on the traditional American values and culture? How much will they try to maintain their own language and cultural traditions? Will they create an entirely new culture based on some combination of their values and those of the traditional American culture?

15   Historically, although the children of immigrants may have grown up bilingual and bicultural, for a number of reasons many did not pass on their language and culture. Thus, many grandchildren of immigrants do not speak the language of the old country and are simply American by culture. However, in parts of the country with established communities that share a common language or culture, bilingualism[8] and biculturalism continue. This is particularly true in communities where new immigrants are still arriving. In California, for example, the test for a driver's license is given in thirty different languages. In general, cultural pluralism[9] is more accepted in the United States today than it was in the first half of the twentieth century, and many of the school systems have developed bilingual programs and multicultural curricula.

---

[6] **Cinco de Mayo:** a traditional Mexican holiday that honors the Mexican army's victory over an invading French force at Puebla, Mexico, in 1862
[7] **heritage:** the traditional beliefs, values, and customs of a family, country, or society
[8] **bilingualism:** the ability to speak two languages equally well
[9] **cultural pluralism:** the principle that people of different races, religions, and political beliefs can live together peacefully in the same society

16   The census of 2000 recognized the increase in the diversity of the American population. There were many racial and ethnic categories to choose from, and for the first time it was possible to select more than one category.*

montgomery

CENSUS 2000 SUMMARY: DIVERSITY OF THE AMERICAN POPULATION		
SUBJECT	**NUMBER**	**PERCENT**
RACE		
Total population	281,421,906	100.0
One race	274,595,678	97.6
White	211,460,626	75.1
Black or African-American	34,658,190	12.3
American Indian and Alaska Native	2,475,956	0.9
American Indian	1,865,118	0.7
Alaska Native	97,876	0.0
Both American Indian and Alaska Native	1,002	0.0
American Indian or Alaska Native, not specified	511,960	0.2
Asian	10,242,998	3.6
Asian Indian	1,678,765	0.6
Chinese	2,432,585	0.9
Filipino	1,850,314	0.7
Japanese	796,700	0.3
Korean	1,076,872	0.4
Vietnamese	1,122,528	0.4
Other Asian category	1,061,646	0.4
Two or more Asian categories	223,588	0.1
Native Hawaiian and Other Pacific Islander	398,835	0.1
Native Hawaiian	140,652	0.0
Samoan	91,029	0.0
Guamanian or Chamorro	58,240	0.0
Other Pacific Islander category	99,996	0.0
Two or more Native Hawaiian or Other Pacific Islander categories	8,918	0.0
Some other race	15,359,073	5.5
Two or more races	6,826,228	2.4
Two races including Some other race	3,001,558	1.1
Two races excluding Some other race, and three or more races	3,824,670	1.4
Two races excluding Some other race	3,366,517	1.2
Three or more races	458,153	0.2
HISPANIC OR LATINO		
Total population	281,421,906	100.0
Hispanic or Latino (of any race)	35,305,818	12.5
Mexican	20,640,711	7.3
Puerto Rican	3,406,178	1.2
Cuban	1,241,685	0.4
Other Hispanic or Latino	10,017,244	3.6
Not Hispanic or Latino	246,116,088	87.5
RACE AND HISPANIC OR LATINO		
Total population	281,421,906	100.0
One race	274,595,678	97.6
Hispanic or Latino	33,081,736	11.8
Not Hispanic or Latino	241,513,942	85.8
Two or more races	6,826,228	2.4
Hispanic or Latino	2,224,082	0.8
Not Hispanic or Latino	4,602,146	1.6

Source: U.S. Census Bureau, Census 2000 Summary File 1, Matrices P3, P4, PCT4, PCT5, PCT8, and PCT11.

---

*For the 2000 census, people were allowed to check as many ethnic and racial categories as they wished. This chart is the U.S. government's presentation of the very complicated census information that resulted. The chart reflects the difficulties in determining ethnic and racial identities of Americans. For further information, visit the government website www.census.gov.

17   On the one hand, many Americans try to maintain their ethnic heritage and their cultural traditions. On the other hand, the number of interracial marriages is increasing, and the majority of young people believe it does not matter which race they marry. Some have called this the "Tiger Woods effect," referring to the U.S. golfer who became at the same time the first African American and the first Asian American to win the Masters Golf Tournament. Tiger Woods says he is "Cablinasian"—a mixture of Caucasian (white), black, Indian, and Asian. By the middle of the century, the nation will probably no longer have a white majority; some say the color of most Americans will be more like beige, or light brown, as a result of the mixing of races and ethnic groups. Already, many of the nation's largest cities are "majority minority." This means more than half of the population are members of minority groups.

"Cablinasian" Tiger Woods with his parents

18   In the United States, people have become very sensitive to the language used to describe racial and ethnic groups, and they try to be politically correct, or "P.C." For example, some black Americans prefer the term *African-American* instead of *black* to identify with their African heritage. The terms *Native American* and *American Indian* are both used by those native to the North American continent. Some Spanish speakers prefer to be called *Latinos* (referring to Latin America) instead of *Hispanics* (referring to Spain), while others prefer to be identified by their country of origin (*Cuban-American* or *Cuban*, *Chicano*, *Mexican-American* or *Mexican*, etc.). Since the census uses a variety of terms, we will also use the terms *white*, *Native American* or *American Indian*, *black* or *African-American*, and *Hispanic* or *Latino*.

19   In spite of all this diversity, there is still a tie that binds Americans together. That tie is a sense of national identity—of being an American. Incidentally, when citizens of the United States refer to themselves as Americans, they have no intention of excluding people from Canada or Latin American countries as residents of the American continents. There is no term such as *United Statesians* in the English language, so people call themselves *Americans*. Thus, what is really a language problem has sometimes caused misunderstandings. Although citizens of Latin American countries may call the people in the United States *North Americans*, to many people in the United States this makes no sense either, because the term *North American* refers to Canadians and Mexicans as well as citizens of the United States. (NAFTA—the North American Free Trade Agreement, for example, is a trade agreement among Canada, the United States, and Mexico.) The word *American*, then, is used in this text as the nationality of the people who live in the United States of America.

Making Generalizations About American Beliefs

20   What, then, can we say about Americans? What holds them together and makes them feel American? Is it possible to make generalizations about what they believe? It is, but we must be cautious about generalizations. As we talk about basic American beliefs, we must remember that not all Americans hold these beliefs, nor do all Americans believe these things to the same degree. The ways in which some Americans practice their beliefs may also differ, resulting in a great variety of lifestyles. What we attempt to do is to define and explain the traditional, dominant cultural values that have for so many years attracted immigrants to the United States.

Immigrants who have just been sworn in as new American citizens

21   Throughout this book we will be drawing on the wisdom of a famous observer of the American scene, Alexis de Tocqueville. Tocqueville came to the United States as a young Frenchman in 1831 to study the American form of democracy and what it might mean to the rest of the world. After a visit of only nine months he wrote a remarkable book called *Democracy in America*, which is a classic study of the American way of life. Tocqueville had unusual powers of observation. He described not only the democratic system of government and how it operated, but also its effect on how Americans think, feel, and act. Many scholars believe that he had a deeper understanding of traditional American beliefs and values than anyone else who has written about the United States. What is so remarkable is that many of these traits of the American character, which he observed nearly 200 years ago, are still visible and meaningful today.

22   Another reason why Tocqueville's observations of the American character are important is the time when he visited the United States. He came in the 1830s, before America was industrialized. This was the era of the small farmer, the small businessman, and the settling of the western frontier. It was the period of history when the traditional values of the new country were being established. In just a generation, some forty years since the adoption of the U.S. Constitution, the new form of government had already produced a society of people with unique values. The character traits Tocqueville describes are the same ones that many Americans still take pride in today. He, however, was a neutral observer and saw both the good and the bad sides of these qualities.

23   This is a book about those traditional basic American beliefs, values, and character traits. It is not a book of cold facts about American behavior or institutions,[10] but rather it is about the motivating forces behind the people and their institutions. It is about how these traditional basic beliefs and values affect important aspects of American life: religion, business, work and play, politics, the family, and education.

---

[10] **institutions:** large organizations, especially ones dedicated to public service

24   We invite you to participate in this book. We will describe what many Americans think and believe, but you will have an opportunity to test these descriptions by making your own observations. As you read about these traditional basic values, think of them as working hypotheses[11] which you can test on Americans, on people of other nations, and on people of your nationality. Compare them with your own values and beliefs and with what is most important in your life. Through this process, you should emerge with a better understanding not only of Americans, but also of your own culture and yourself. It is by studying others that we learn about ourselves.

AFTER YOU READ

Understand Main Ideas

Academic English organizes information into main (or most important) ideas and supporting details. That is, there are usually three or four major points presented, and the rest of the information serves to explain or support these main ideas:

- First main idea
  Supporting details

- Second main idea
  Supporting details

- Third main idea
  Supporting details

When reading academic English or listening to a lecture, it is important to recognize the main points. The introduction focuses your attention on the topic. Then the main points are presented, and the conclusion reminds you of one or more central ideas. Noticing the headings in a text will help you figure out the main points the writer is presenting.

Check the predictions that you made on page 2 before reading the chapter. Then answer these questions about the main ideas.

1. What are two important factors that affect life in the United States?

2. What is the heading for the section that discusses the history of immigration in the United States?

3. What is cultural pluralism?

---

[11] **hypotheses:** ideas that are suggested as an explanation for something, but that have not yet been proven to be true

4. What is the main idea of the section headed *Making Generalizations About American Beliefs*?

5. What relationship is there between the quotation at the beginning of the chapter, the introduction (first two paragraphs), and the conclusion (paragraphs 23 and 24) of the reading?

Understand Details

Write *T* if the statement is true and *F* if it is false according to the information in the chapter.

_____ 1. One factor affecting lifestyles in the United States is the different climates.

_____ 2. American Indians all speak the same language.

_____ 3. The dominant American culture was established by immigrants who came from southern Europe.

_____ 4. Throughout the history of the United States, more immigrants have come from English-speaking countries than any other countries.

_____ 5. Zangwill believed that immigrants would lose their native cultures and become something different when they came to the United States.

_____ 6. All immigrants want to assimilate to the U.S. culture completely; they have no desire to maintain their own culture.

_____ 7. U.S. immigration policy has stayed the same for the last 100 years.

_____ 8. The English language has no adjective for *United States* and therefore uses the term *American* to refer to its people.

_____ 9. It is not possible to make generalizations about what Americans believe because they are so different.

_____ 10. Many of the characteristics of Americans which Alexis de Tocqueville observed in the 1830s are still true today.

Improve Your Reading Skills: Scanning

In order to become a good reader in English, your reading speed and techniques should vary according to your purpose. For example, you may look down a page (or over several pages) to find a particular piece of information—a number, a date, a place, or the time a movie begins. This type of *reading for a specific fact is* called **scanning**.

Read the questions below. Scan the reading to find the specific information you need to answer each question.

1. Which states have the largest numbers of immigrants?

   _____

2. In what year did Alexis de Tocqueville come to visit the United States?

   _____

3. In 1910, what percentage of the U.S. population was foreign born?

   _____14.8%_____

4. What was the total U.S. population according to the 2000 census?

   _____

5. In what year did Israel Zangwill write a play in which he used the term *melting pot*?

   ⁽⁶⁾ _____ In 1980 _____

6. What does *Cablinasian* mean, and who made up this word?

   _____

Talk About It

Work in small groups and choose one or more of the following topics to discuss.

1. How would you compare the size and ethnic diversity of your country with that of the United States? What are some of the challenges that size (large or small) and diversity (great or limited) present to a country?

2. Should a country have immigration quotas based on country of origin? Should immigrants become citizens? Should countries allow "guest workers" (people who work there temporarily)?

3. How would you describe the average person in your country and what he or she believes?

4. Do you think people all over the world are basically the same or basically very different?

Build Your Vocabulary

Use Context Clues There are several types of context clues that will help you guess the meaning of words you do not know. By looking at the words around an unfamiliar word, you may be able to figure out its meaning. See the four kinds of context clues on the next page. In the examples, the vocabulary words are in boldface. The context clues are in italics.

1. The word may be defined in the sentence. Sometimes the definition is set off by commas or dashes. Other times it is not.

   EXAMPLE: There is still a tie that binds Americans together. That tie is a sense of national **identity**—*of being an American.*

   EXAMPLE: A **quota** system was established that *specified the number of immigrants that could come from each country.*

2. There may be a synonym used in the same sentence.

   EXAMPLE: Native Americans belong to *separate* and **distinct** Indian nations, each with its own language, culture, and even government.

3. There may be a comparison or contrast with a word (or a phrase) more familiar to you.

   EXAMPLE: As the **minority**, nonwhite population of the United States continues to grow, the white *majority* grows smaller.

4. The sentence may give an example that helps you figure out the meaning.

   EXAMPLE: Tocqueville, however, was a **neutral observer** and *saw both the good and bad sides of these qualities.*

A. Use the context clues to figure out the meaning of the boldfaced words in the sentences above. Then write the correct word next to its definition.

_____quota_____ 1. a limit on the number allowed

_____minority_____ 2. a group of people whose race is different from that of most people in a country

_____neutral observer_____ 3. someone who observes without expressing an opinion

_____identity_____ 4. the qualities a group of people have that make them different from other people

_____distinct_____ 5. clearly different or separate

B. Now fill in the blanks with some of the boldfaced words above to complete the paragraph.

What qualities give people a national _____? Do they have to
                                             1
have characteristics that are _____ from those of other countries?
                                   2
The people who are part of a _____ group may feel they have a set
                                  3
of characteristics that differ from those of the majority in their country.

More AWL Words Test your knowledge of these additional AWL words in the reading by doing the puzzle below. First match the AWL words with their definitions. Then find the AWL words in the puzzle and circle them. Words may run horizontally, vertically, diagonally, or backwards.

__d__ 1. aspect

__f__ 2. category

____ 3. concept

__k__ 4. debate

____ 5. establish

____ 6. estimate

____ 7. hypothesis

____ 8. incidentally

__a__ 9. institution

____ 10. survive

__c__ 11. unique

____ 12. vary

a. a large organization, especially one dedicated to public service

b. to start something that will continue

c. to be different

d. one part of an idea that has many parts

e. to continue in spite of difficulties

f. group of things that all have the same qualities

g. to judge by calculating and guessing

h. one of a kind

i. an idea

j. an explanation not yet proven

k. a discussion of different opinions

l. by the way

① an established organization
② a place where take care of people

```
N N F B E S T A B L I S H F L
S I S E H T O P Y H O D B A V
M M L U N I Q U E V Z U I Z I
R E C E Y D E M P T R A B L U
I P U C Q G G M H V E J J Z N
W V S U R V I V E I Z G G O Y
Y L L A T N E D I C N I I R E
I I M R K T T N Z O S T O T E
Q Y V X M S B T M G U G A W T
D F Y K X A O Y O T E M M F A
A S P E C T O E I T I N N E B
H N P R O P Y T A T K I U X E
U V S U N K S C S S E K X A D
I D G O D N V E V A R Y K N V
Z F V R I T P E C N O C U J W
```

Understand Prefixes Recognizing the meaning of a prefix, a group of letters added to the beginning of a word (or its root), will also help you guess the meaning of a new word. For example, the prefix *re-* means *again* (*reunification*) and the prefix *mis-* means *wrong* (*misunderstand*).

Each of the boldfaced words in the sentences below has a prefix. Identify the prefix and write its meaning. Use a dictionary, if necessary.

EXAMPLE: Before the 1960s, the majority of immigrants to the United States were Europeans, but changes in immigration laws resulted in large numbers of **non-Europeans**.

Prefix: ___non___ Meaning: ___not___

1. Estimates were that in addition to legal immigration, **illegal** immigration was adding more than a half a million more people per year.

   Prefix: ___il___ Meaning: ___not___

2. In some parts of the country with established communities that share a common language or culture, bilingualism and **biculturalism** continue. Cultural pluralism is more accepted now than in the first half of the twentieth century, and many of the school systems have developed bilingual programs and **multicultural** curricula.

   Prefix: ___bi___ Meaning: ___two___

   Prefix: ___multi___ Meaning: ___many___

3. People may migrate to another location in order to find work. While many people **immigrate** to the United States each year, very few Americans choose to **emigrate** to another country to live.

   Prefix: ___im___ Meaning: ___doing a verb.___

   Prefix: ___e___ Meaning: ___//___

4. In the census of 2000, there were nineteen racial categories to choose from. The number of **interracial** marriages is increasing . . . and the majority of young people believe it does not matter which race they marry.

   Prefix: ___inter___ Meaning: ___between___

Word Partners Certain words and phrases tend to go together in English, for example, *ethnic diversity* or *traditional values*. This is called **collocation**. Learning these word partners will increase your ability to use new words correctly and help you express yourself as native speakers do.

Read the sentences below. Then match the adjectives on the left with their noun partners on the right. Use the collocations to complete the sentences.

_c_	1. established	a. immigrants
_g_	2. significant	b. culture
_b_	3. neutral	c. communities
____	4. industrialized	d. pluralism
_a_	5. legal	e. hypotheses
_e_	6. dominant	f. countries
_d_	7. cultural	g. factor
____	8. working	h. observer

1. In parts of the country with <u>**established communities**</u> that share a common language, bilingualism continues.

2. Tocqueville was a ___3b_____ who saw both the good and bad sides of the American character traits.

3. Ethnic diversity is a ___e 6._____ affecting American life.

4. Think of the traditional values in this book as _____8 2_____ that you can test against your own observations.

5. The United States now takes in more ___5a_____ each year than all other _____ combined.

6. When several cultures exist together successfully in a society, there is _____7 d_____.

7. The _____ in the United States is becoming less white in the twenty-first century.

Ask Americans

Interview several Americans of different ages (if possible) and ask them to complete the following statements. If there are no Americans to interview, you can ask other international students or your classmates.

1. Americans are _____.
2. They like _____
3. They don't really like _____.
4. They act _____.
5. Most Americans believe in _____.
6. The United States is a country where _____.
7. The average American is _____.
8. Americans today are worried about _____.
9. The most important thing in life to most Americans is _____.

Think, Pair, Share

Think about the following questions, and write down your answers. Then discuss your answers with a partner and share your answers with another pair of students.

1. How would you define *culture*? Look at several dictionaries to find definitions and read the first paragraph of the introduction to this book.

2. What do you think are the most important aspects of your native culture?

3. Complete the statements in the previous exercise (*Ask Americans*) about your own country and share your answers. For example: People from my country are _____.

Understand Polls

Conducting opinion polls is very popular in the United States. A newspaper, a magazine, a TV station, or a professional polling organization asks a representative group of Americans several questions to determine what their opinions are about a given topic. The pollsters choose men and women of different ages, occupations, and races in the same proportion that these groups are found in the population. Sometimes, however, a random sample is taken which picks people by chance.

Polls are especially popular around election time because everyone wants to know which candidate is ahead in the race and what the voters think about the key issues of the campaign. There are three well-known polling organizations that measure public opinion on a variety of topics: Louis Harris and Associates, the Roper Organization, and Gallup International Research Institutes.

There have been a number of polls on the topic of sport-utility vehicles (SUVs) in the United States. SUVs are extremely popular with Americans, even though they are more expensive to drive because they generally do not get good gas mileage. Polls show that one reason for their popularity is that owners of SUVs feel that they and their families are safer in these large vehicles than they would be in other cars. However, studies have shown that SUVs may roll over more easily and may therefore be more dangerous than people originally thought. The Advocates for Highway and Auto Safety organization asked the Harris polling organization to survey attitudes about the safety of SUVs and other vehicles. One of the questions was "The next time you purchase a new vehicle, would you like to see information posted on a window sticker about the likelihood of a rollover, or would you not like to see that information on a window sticker?"

HOW KEY GROUPS FEEL ABOUT THE IDEA OF POSTING INFORMATION ON THE WINDOWS OF ALL NEW CARS INDICATING THE LIKELIHOOD OF THE VEHICLE TO ROLL OVER			
	Favor	**Oppose**	**Not Sure**
	%	%	%
NATIONWIDE	83	14	3
By Region			
South	88	9	3
East	86	12	2
Midwest	79	17	4
West	77	18	5
By Race/Hispanic			
Non-Latino Black	93	6	1
Latino	91	8	1
Non-Latino White	80	16	4
By Gender			
Women	87	8	5
Men	79	19	2
By Annual Household Income			
$25,000 or less	90	8	2
$25,001–$50,000	83	13	4
$50,001–$100,000	82	15	3
$100,000 and over	71	23	6
By Vehicle Ownership			
SUV	84	12	4
Pick-up truck	83	15	2
Other passenger car	83	13	4
Van	82	15	3

Source: Survey of the Attitudes of the American People on Highway Safety, conducted for Advocates for Highway and Auto Safety by Louis Harris Research Group, Inc., June 2004

Examine the poll results and answer the following questions.

1. Who thinks it is more important to have the rollover information on a window sticker—men or women?

2. According to this poll, do you think people who own SUVs are much more concerned about rollovers than those who own other vehicles?

3. Are Americans who live in the West more or less interested in rollover stickers than people who live in the South?

4. Which ethnic/racial group appears most concerned about the danger of rollovers?

5. Which socioeconomic group appears the least concerned—those who make the least money, or those who make the most?

Many Americans who own SUVs have a lifestyle that is child-centered. In his book, *The Clustered World: How We Live, What We Buy, and What It All Means About Who We Are*, Michael J. Weiss describes sixty-two distinct American lifestyles, or clusters of behavior. The cluster with the highest percentage (3 percent) is called "Kids & Cul-de-Sacs."

> *It's not uncommon for parents to put in fifty miles a day carpooling their kids to after-school karate classes, piano lessons, and soccer practices. Residents are twice as likely as average Americans to own minivans and sport-utility vehicles. For leisure, these Americans are more likely than the general population to throw barbecues, watch videos, and play board games. . . . A typical Saturday night involves pizza and videos with the kids.*

KIDS & CUL–DE–SACS LIFESTYLE

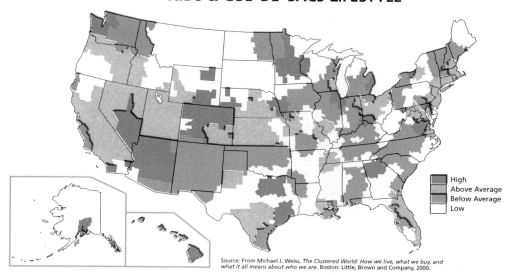

High
Above Average
Below Average
Low

Source: From Michael J. Weiss, *The Clustered World: How we live, what we buy, and what it all means about who we are.* Boston: Little, Brown and Company, 2000.

People Watching

Different countries have different rules for personal space, that is, when people touch, how close they stand when they are speaking to one another, how close they sit, how they behave on elevators, etc. The rules for personal space sometimes differ according to how well people know each other. They are usually not consciously aware of these rules, but they may become very uncomfortable if the rules are broken and their space is entered without permission. You can discover the rules by observing people interacting and also by testing or breaking the rules to see how other people respond.

Conduct two experiments about personal space. Follow these steps.

1. Read the rules for personal space below.

2. Make your own observations of people. Write your observations in a journal. It may be helpful to work in pairs: One person tests the rules while the other observes and records what happens.

3. Experiment with the rules. Write the responses you receive.

4. If you are not in the United States and if you do not have an opportunity to observe Americans, you may still learn from these experiments by watching people in your own country or by observing Americans in movies or TV shows.

People in line try to avoid touching each other.

First Rule: When they are in a crowd, Americans have a bubble of space around their bodies which is about an inch thick. This bubble of space must not be broken by a stranger. If American strangers touch each other accidentally, they mutter an apology such as "Pardon me," "Excuse me," "Oh, I'm sorry," or just "Sorry."

Observation: Watch people in a crowd, standing in line, waiting in a group, or passing on a street or in a hallway. Who is touching whom? What does their relationship appear to be? What happens when people touch accidentally? How does the person touched respond? What does the one who has broken the other's bubble do? Record gestures, facial expressions, emotional responses, and words exchanged.

Experiment: See how close you can stand to someone in a crowd without touching him or her. Try breaking someone's bubble of space with a very light touch of your elbow or arm. What is the person's response? (*Warning*: This may provoke an angry response!)

Second Rule: When standing in elevators, Americans usually face the door, speak quietly, and try to avoid touching one another. If a stranger enters an elevator where there is only one other person, he or she will stand on the opposite side of the elevator. As more people get on the elevator, they occupy the corners first and then try to disperse themselves evenly throughout the available space.

Observation: Observe people in elevators. Which direction are they facing? If you are alone in an elevator and someone comes in, where does that person stand? As more people enter the elevator, where do they stand? Do the people talk to one another? How loudly do they speak? Do strangers touch? What happens in a crowded elevator when someone in the back has to get off?

Experiment: Get on an elevator where there is only one person and stand next to that individual. What is the person's reaction? In an elevator where there are a number of people, turn and face the group with your back to the door. How do the people react? Have a conversation with someone in a crowded elevator and don't lower your voice. How do you think people feel about this? Note their facial expressions.

People in an elevator avoid eye contact.

Use the Internet

Harris Polls are usually scientific polls, but they also conduct informal weekly polls online. These informal weekly polls only reflect the views of the people who happen to visit their website and answer the poll questions. You can participate in their weekly poll.

Visit the Harris Polls website at www.harrisinteractive.com and click on the *Weekly Poll* link. Then answer the question and see how others voted.

A. **Choose one of the following writing topics. Then write a short composition about it. To organize your thoughts, use a graphic organizer to write down your ideas before you begin your composition.**

EXAMPLE: If you were describing the American Kids & Cul-de-Sacs lifestyle (see page 19), your graphic organizer might look like this.

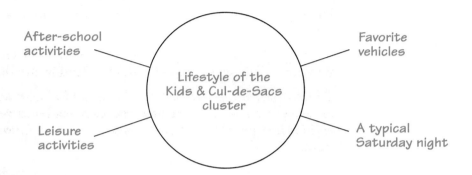

After-school activities

Favorite vehicles

Lifestyle of the Kids & Cul-de-Sacs cluster

Leisure activities

A typical Saturday night

1. Think about why SUVs are popular with Americans who have a Kids & Cul-de-Sacs lifestyle. Reread the poll on page 18. Would you want to own an SUV? Explain why or why not.

2. How do you and your family spend leisure time together?

3. Where are three places that you would want to take someone visiting from another country?

4. Choose a folktale from your culture. Retell the folktale in English and explain why you think this tale is representative of your culture.

 B. **Use the Internet to look for information about your country's or another country's census or population characteristics. Use a search engine such as www.google.com or www.yahoo.com to help you find information. Be sure to include the URL (the uniform resource locator), which is the address of the website. Do the following searches and write a report about what you find.**

1. census + _____ (a country)

2. "population characteristics" + _____ (a country)

Note: You must use quotation marks (" ") when one of the terms you are searching for has more than one word.

Books to Read

Sherwood Anderson, *Winesburg, Ohio*—Published in 1919, this literary masterpiece explores the hidden passions of ordinary lives in a small American town.

John F. Kennedy, *A Nation of Immigrants*—President Kennedy, himself the grandson of Irish immigrants, discusses how old immigrant traditions mix with the new experiences of immigrants starting life over in America.

O. E. Rölvaag, *Giants in the Earth: A Saga of the Prairie*—The classic story of a Norwegian pioneer family's struggles as they try to make a new life on the American frontier.

Henry David Thoreau, *Walden*—A classic account of Thoreau's experiment of simple living in a cabin on the shore of Walden Pond in the 1840s.

Michael J. Weiss, *The Clustered World: How we live, what we buy, and what it all means about who we are*—Drawing on census data, market surveys, and interviews, the author explores how people spend their time and money in America and throughout the world.

Movies to See

La Bamba—Based on the true story of Ritchie Valens, a young 1950s rock and roll singer who rose to fame from poverty and brought the Latin American influence to his hit songs.

School of Rock—A "wanna-be" rock star in need of cash pretends to be a substitute teacher at a prep school and tries to turn his class into a rock band.

Seabiscuit—The true story of an undersized racehorse whose surprising victory lifted the spirits of a nation trapped in the Great Depression of the 1930s.

Spellbound—A documentary that follows several children and their families as they prepare for and compete in the national spelling contest.

The Terminal—An eastern European immigrant who is not permitted to enter the United States decides to take up temporary residence at a JFK airport terminal.

Immigrants seeking a new life in the "Land of Opportunity"

CHAPTER 2

TRADITIONAL AMERICAN VALUES AND BELIEFS

We hold these truths to be self-evident, that all men are created equal, that they are endowed by their Creator with certain inalienable rights, that among these are Life, Liberty and the pursuit of Happiness.

The Declaration of Independence (1776)

BEFORE YOU READ

Preview Vocabulary

A. **Here are some key AWL words in this chapter. Look at their definitions. Put a check next to the words you already know.**

_____ 1. *individual* one person, considered separately from the group

_____ 2. *achieve* to succeed in getting the result you wanted

_____ 3. *benefit* something that gives advantages or improves life in some way

_____ 4. *reliant* being dependent on someone

_____ 5. *constitution* a set of basic laws and principles that a democratic country is governed by

_____ 6. *ethical* relating to principles of what is right and wrong

_____ 7. *resources* a country's land, minerals, or natural energy that can be used to increase its wealth

_____ 8. *status* social or professional rank or position in relation to others

_____ 9. *welfare* money paid by the government to people who are very poor, sick, not working, etc.

_____ 10. *foundation* a basic idea or principle

B. **Work with a partner. Complete each question with a word from the preceding list. Then answer the questions.**

1. Why would the _____ of a country forbid titles of nobility? (titles such as "princess" or "sir")

2. If there are no titles of nobility, how does a society recognize people with high social _____?

3. Which do you think is more important to Americans, the well-being of the group or the _____status_____?

4. What do immigrants have to do to _____achieve_____ success in their new country?

5. What are some of the natural _____foundation_____ found on the North American continent?

6. What _____benefit_____ does a person get from being self- _____?

7. When would it not be _____ to compete with someone?

8. What country provided the language and the _____constitution_____ for the political and economic systems of the United States?

9. What problems might cause a person to need _____welfare_____?

C. **Read the quotation from the Declaration of Independence at the beginning of the chapter, and find the words with the following meanings. Write each word next to its meaning.**

_____ 1. the act of trying to achieve something in a determined way

_____ 2. easily noticed or understood; obvious

_____ 3. that cannot be taken away from you

_____ 4. given a good quality

Preview Content

A. **Before you read, preview the chapter by looking at the illustrations and reading the headings and the captions under the pictures. Work with a partner and discuss these questions.**

1. What is the main idea of the quotation at the beginning of the chapter?
2. What are some of the reasons people want to come live in the United States? Use this graphic organizer to write down your ideas. Are any of these ideas similar? If so, draw lines connecting them.

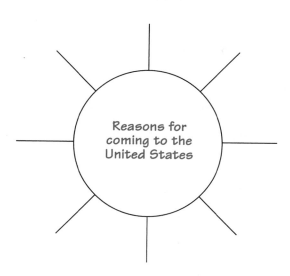

3. What is the "American Dream"? (Hint: Give a one-sentence summary of the ideas you wrote for question #2.)
4. What do you think Americans believe is the best thing about their country?

B. Think about what values and beliefs could be important to Americans. Work with a partner, and make three predictions about what you will read. Write your predictions here.

1. _____
2. _____
3. _____

The Context of Traditional American Values: Racial, Ethnic, Religious, and Cultural Diversity

In the twenty-first century, the United States probably has a greater diversity of racial, ethnic, cultural, and religious groups than any other nation on earth. From the beginning of the history of the United States there has been diversity—Native Americans throughout the North American continent, Spanish settlers in the Southwest and in Florida, French missionaries and fur traders along the Mississippi River, black slaves brought from African countries, Dutch settlers in New York, Germans in Pennsylvania, and of course the British colonists, whose culture eventually provided the language and the foundation for the political and economic systems that developed in the United States.

2   Most early Americans recognized this diversity, or pluralism, as a fact of life. The large variety of ethnic, cultural, and religious groups meant that accepting diversity was the only practical choice, even if some people were not enthusiastic about it, or were even threatened by it. However, in time, many Americans came to see strength in their country's diversity. Today, there is more recognition of the value of cultural pluralism than at any other time in the history of the United States.

NEW WORLD COLONIES IN 1750

Source: http://web.uccs.edu/~history/index/151maps.html.

3   When we examine the system of basic values that emerged in the late 1700s and began to define the American character, we must remember this context of cultural pluralism. How could a nation of such enormous diversity produce a recognizable national identity?

4   John Zogby, an American pollster who surveys public opinion, says that what holds the United States together is that "we all share a common set of values that make us American. . . . We are defined by the rights we have. . . . Our rights are our history, why the first European settlers came here and why millions more have come here since."

5   Historically, the United States has been viewed as "the land of opportunity," attracting immigrants from all over the world. The opportunities they believed they would find in America and the experiences they actually had when they arrived nurtured this set of values. We will examine six basic values that have become traditional American values. Three represent traditional reasons why immigrants have been drawn

to America: the chance for individual freedom, equality of opportunity, and material wealth. In order to achieve these benefits, however, there were prices to be paid: self-reliance, competition, and hard work. In time, these prices themselves became a part of the traditional value system.

Individual Freedom and Self-Reliance

6   The earliest settlers came to the North American continent to establish colonies which were free from the controls that existed in European societies. They wanted to escape the controls placed on many aspects of their lives by kings and governments, priests and churches, noblemen and aristocrats.[1] To a great extent, they succeeded. In 1776, the British colonial settlers declared their independence from England and established a new nation, the United States of America. In so doing, they defied[2] the king of England and declared that the power to govern would lie in the hands of the people. They were now free from the power of the kings. In 1787, when they wrote the Constitution for their new nation, they separated church and state so that there would never be a government-supported church. This greatly limited the power of the church. Also, in writing the Constitution they expressly forbade titles of nobility to ensure that an aristocratic society would not develop. There would be no ruling class of noblemen in the new nation.

7   The historic decisions made by those first settlers have had a profound[3] effect on the shaping of the American character. By limiting the power of the government and the churches and eliminating a formal aristocracy, the early settlers created a climate of freedom where the emphasis was on the individual. The United States came to be associated in their minds with the concept of *individual freedom*. This is probably the most basic of all the American values. Scholars and outside observers often call this value *individualism*, but many Americans use the word *freedom*. It is one of the most respected and popular words in the United States today.

8   By *freedom*, Americans mean the desire and the right of all individuals to control their own destiny without outside interference from the government, a ruling noble class, the church, or any other organized authority. The desire to be free of controls was a basic value of the new nation in 1776, and it has continued to attract immigrants to this country.

9   There is, however, a price to be paid for this individual freedom: *self-reliance*. Individuals must learn to rely on themselves or risk losing freedom. Traditionally, this means achieving both financial and emotional independence from their parents as early as possible, usually by age eighteen or twenty-one. It means that Americans believe they should take care of themselves, solve their own problems, and "stand on their own two feet." Tocqueville observed the Americans' belief in self-reliance in the 1830s:

> They owe nothing to any man, they expect nothing from any man; they acquire the habit of always considering themselves as standing alone, and they are apt to[4] imagine that their whole destiny is in their own hands.

---

[1] **aristocrats:** people who belong to the highest social class
[2] **defied:** refused to obey someone or do what was expected
[3] **profound:** important and having a strong influence or effect
[4] **are apt to:** have a natural tendency to do something

10   This strong belief in self-reliance continues today as a traditional basic American value. It is perhaps one of the most difficult aspects of the American character to understand, but it is profoundly important. Most Americans believe that they must be self-reliant in order to keep their freedom. If they rely too much on the support of their families or the government or any organization, they may lose some of their freedom to do what they want.

11   Often adult children return home to live with their parents because of economic conditions or a failed marriage. Parents are usually happy to help out, but most members of the family expect this to be a short-term arrangement. When people are dependent, they risk losing freedom and they may also lose the respect of their peers.[5] Even if they are not truly self-reliant, most Americans believe they must at least appear to be so. In order to be in the mainstream of American life—to have power and/or respect—individuals must be seen as self-reliant.

12   Although Americans provide a lot of financial support to people in need through charities or government programs, they expect that help to be short-lived. Eventually, people should take care of themselves. Although receiving financial support from charity,[6] family, or the government is allowed, it is generally not admired. Some people believe that such individuals are setting a bad example, which may weaken the American character as a whole. The sight of beggars on city streets and the plight[7] of the homeless may inspire sympathy but also concern, for the same reason.

Equality of Opportunity and Competition

13   The second important reason why immigrants have traditionally been drawn to the United States is the belief that everyone has a chance to succeed here. Generations of immigrants, from the earliest settlers to the present day, have come to the United States with this expectation. They have felt that because individuals are free from excessive political, religious, and social controls, they have a better chance for personal success. Of particular importance is the lack of a hereditary[8] aristocracy.

New immigrants on Ellis Island at the turn of the century

14   Because titles of nobility were forbidden in the Constitution, no formal class system developed in the United States. In the early years of American history, many immigrants chose to leave older European societies because they believed that they had a better chance to succeed in America. In "the old country," the country from

---

[5] **peers:** people who are the same age or have the same type of job, rank, etc.
[6] **charity:** an organization that gives money, goods, or help to people who are poor, sick, etc.
[7] **plight:** a bad, serious, or sad condition or situation
[8] **hereditary:** can be passed from an older to a younger person in the same family

which they came, their place in life was determined largely by the social class into which they were born. They knew that in America they would not have to live among noble families who possessed great power and wealth inherited and accumulated over hundreds of years.

15   The hopes and dreams of many of these early immigrants were fulfilled in their new country. The lower social class into which many were born did not prevent them from trying to rise to a higher social position. Many found that they did indeed have a better chance to succeed in the United States than in the old country. Because millions of these immigrants succeeded, Americans came to believe in equality of opportunity. When Tocqueville visited the United States in the 1830s, he was impressed by the great uniformity of conditions of life in the new nation. He wrote,

> *The more I advanced in the study of American society, the more I perceived that . . . equality of condition is the fundamental fact from which all others seem to be derived.*

16   It is important to understand what most Americans mean when they say they believe in equality of opportunity. They do not mean that everyone is—or should be—equal. However, they do mean that each individual should have an equal chance for success. Americans see much of life as a race for success. For them, equality means that everyone should have an equal chance to enter the race and win. In other words, equality of opportunity may be thought of as an ethical rule. It helps ensure that the race for success is a fair one and that a person does not win just because he or she was born into a wealthy family, or lose because of race or religion. This American concept of "fair play" is an important aspect of the belief in equality of opportunity.

17   President Abraham Lincoln expressed this belief in the 1860s when he said,

> *We . . . wish to allow the humblest man an equal chance to get rich with everybody else. When one starts poor, as most do in the race of life, free society is such that he knows he can better his condition; he knows that there is no fixed condition of labor for his whole life.*

18   However, the price to be paid for this equality of opportunity is competition. If much of life is seen as a race, then a person must run the race in order to succeed; a person must compete with others, even though we know not everyone will be successful. If every person has an equal chance to succeed in the United States, then many would say that it is every person's duty to try. Many Americans enjoy matching their energy and intelligence against those of others in a contest for success. People who like to compete are often more successful than others, and many are honored by being called *winners*. On the other hand, those who do not like to compete and those who are not successful when they try are sometimes dishonored by being called *losers*.

Shaking hands may be a polite acknowledgment of your competitor, as well as a greeting.

19   The pressures of competition in the life of an American begin in childhood and continue until retirement from work. Learning to compete successfully is part of growing up in the United States, and competition is encouraged by strong programs of competitive sports provided by the public schools and community groups. Competitive sports are now popular with both men and women.

20   The pressure to compete causes Americans to be energetic, but it also places a constant emotional strain on them. When they retire (traditionally at age sixty-five), they are at last free from the pressures of competition. But then a new problem arises. Some may feel useless and unwanted in a society that gives so much prestige[9] to those who compete well. This may be one reason why older people in the United States sometimes do not have as much honor and respect as they have in other, less competitive societies. In fact, generally speaking, any group of people who do not compete successfully—for whatever reason—do not fit into the mainstream of American life as well as those who do compete and succeed.

Material Wealth and Hard Work

21   The third reason why immigrants have traditionally come to the United States is to have a better life—that is, to raise their standard of living. For the vast majority of the immigrants who came here, this was probably the most compelling reason for leaving their homeland. Because of its incredibly abundant natural resources, the United States appeared to be a land of plenty where millions could come to seek their fortunes. Of course, most immigrants did not "get rich overnight," and many of them suffered terribly, but the majority of them were eventually able to improve upon their former standard of living. Even if they were not able to achieve the economic success they wanted, they could be fairly certain that their children would have the opportunity for a better life. The phrase "going from rags to riches" became a slogan[10] for the "American Dream." Because of the vast riches of the North American continent, the dream came true for many of the immigrants. They achieved material success and many became very attached to material things. Material wealth became a value to the American people.

22   Placing a high value on material possessions is called *materialism*, but this is a word that most Americans find offensive. To say that a person is materialistic is an insult. To an American, this means that this person values material possessions above all else. Americans do not like to be called materialistic because they feel that this unfairly accuses them of loving only material things and of having no religious values. In fact, most Americans do have other values and ideals. Nevertheless, acquiring and maintaining a large number of material possessions is still of great importance to most Americans. Why is this so?

23   One reason is that material wealth has traditionally been a widely accepted measure of social status in the United States. Because Americans rejected the European system of hereditary aristocracy and titles of nobility, they had to find a substitute for judging social status. The quality and quantity of an individual's material possessions became an accepted measure of success and social status. Moreover, as we shall see in later chapters, the Puritan work ethic associated material success with godliness.

---

[9] **prestige:** the respect and importance that a person, organization, or profession has
[10] **slogan:** a short, easily remembered phrase used in advertising or politics

24   Americans have paid a price, however, for their material wealth: *hard work*. The North American continent was rich in natural resources when the first settlers arrived, but all these resources were undeveloped. Only by hard work could these natural resources be converted into material possessions, allowing a more comfortable standard of living. Hard work has been both necessary and rewarding for most Americans throughout their history. Because of this, they came to see material possessions as the natural reward for their hard work. In some ways, material possessions were seen not only as tangible[11] evidence of people's work, but also of their abilities. In the late 1700s, James Madison, the father of the American Constitution, stated that the difference in material possessions reflected a difference in personal abilities.

25   As the United States has shifted from an industry-based economy to one that is service- or information-based, there has been a decline in high-paying jobs for factory workers. It is now much more difficult for the average worker to go from rags to riches in the United States, and many wonder what has happened to the traditional American Dream. As the United States competes in a global economy, many workers are losing their old jobs and finding that they and their family members must now work longer hours for less money and fewer benefits. When the economy weakens, everyone suffers, and there are greater numbers of the working poor—those who work hard but have low-paying jobs that do not provide a decent standard of living and may not provide health insurance.

26   Most Americans, however, still believe in the value of hard work. Most believe that people should hold jobs and not live off welfare payments from the government. There have been many efforts to reform the welfare system so that people would not become dependent on welfare and stop looking for jobs to support themselves. Limitations have been put on the number of years a family can remain on welfare, but the system still has many problems. One of the most critical problems is the cost of health care in the United States and the fact that many employers no longer offer health insurance to their employees. It is often the children who suffer most, particularly in families of the working poor. Another issue is government benefits to immigrants and immigrant children; many of these families are living in poverty.

The American Dream

27   John Kenneth White, in *The Values Divide: American Politics and Culture in Transition*, observes that in spite of all the changes in the nation's population, economy, and culture, the behaviors and values of Americans have remained remarkably constant:

> *Americans still love their country and believe that they can accomplish almost anything. A recent poll found 91 percent who agreed with the statement, "Being an American is a big part of who I am." Only 11 percent said they would like to emigrate elsewhere. . . . Frenchman Clotaire Rapaille captured this unique aspect of American patriotism: "America is not a place. It is a dream."*

---

[11] **tangible:** concrete, able to be touched

28   In understanding the relationship between what Americans believe and how they live, it is important to distinguish between idealism and reality. American values such as equality of opportunity and self-reliance are ideals that may not necessarily describe the reality of American life. Equality of opportunity, for example, is an ideal that is not always put into practice. In reality, some people have a better chance for success than others. Those who are born into rich families have more opportunities than those who are born into poorer families. Inheriting money does give a person a decided advantage. Race and gender may still be factors affecting success, although there are laws designed to promote equality of opportunity for all individuals. And, of course, new immigrants continue to face challenges unique to their situation.

29   The fact that American ideals are only partly carried out in real life does not diminish their importance. Most Americans still believe in them and are strongly affected by them in their everyday lives. It is easier to understand what Americans are thinking and feeling if we can understand what these basic traditional American values are and how they have influenced almost every facet[12] of life in the United States.

30   The six basic values presented in this chapter—individual freedom, self-reliance, equality of opportunity, competition, material wealth, and hard work—do not tell the whole story of the American character. Rather, they should be thought of as themes[13] which will be developed in our discussions on religion, family life, education, business, and politics. These themes will appear throughout the book as we continue to explore more facets of the American character and how they affect life in the United States.

To some, owning a beautiful house means they have achieved the American Dream.

---

[12] **facet:** one of several parts of someone's character or a situation
[13] **themes:** main subjects or ideas in a piece of writing, speech, or movie

Understand Main Ideas

1. **Check the predictions you made on page 27 before reading the chapter.**

In Chapter 1, we looked at the relationship between the introduction and the conclusion, and at how the headings signaled the main ideas. The outline below shows the structure of Chapter 2: the introduction (A), the three sections containing the six traditional values (B, C, D), and the conclusion (E). The numbers under each heading show the main ideas of each section.

2. **Reread paragraph 5 of the introduction section on pages 28–29. What does this paragraph tell you about the structure of the reading? Work with a partner to complete the outline. (Part of it is done for you.)**

    A. Introduction: The Context of Traditional American Values: Racial, Ethnic, Religious, and Cultural Diversity

        1. The United States has great diversity, but it also has a national identity.

        2. What holds the United States together is a common set of

        _____.

    B. Individual Freedom and Self-Reliance

        1. The early settlers came to the North American continent for individual freedom—the most basic of all the American values.

        2. The price for individual freedom is _____.

    C. _____

        1. Immigrants have always come for equality of opportunity—the belief that everyone should have an equal chance to _____.

        2. _____.

    D. _____

        1. Immigrants have traditionally come for material wealth—the chance for a higher standard of _____.

        2. _____.

E. Conclusion: _____

    1. Many Americans believe that, with hard work, their dreams of success can _____.

    2. Even though many of the traditional values are ideals that may not describe the reality of American life, they still influence _____

_____.

Understand Details

Choose the best answer to complete the sentences about the chapter.

_____ 1. Early settlers came to the North American continent and established colonies mainly because they wanted to be free from
    a. the power of kings, priests, and noblemen.
    b. the influence of their families.
    c. the problems of poverty and hunger.

_____ 2. There are no titles of nobility in the United States today because
    a. no one likes aristocrats.
    b. the church does not allow it.
    c. they are forbidden by the Constitution.

_____ 3. The price that Americans pay for their individual freedom is
    a. self-reliance.
    b. competition.
    c. hard work.

_____ 4. The American belief in self-reliance means that
    a. receiving money from charity, family, or the government is never allowed.
    b. if a person is very dependent on others, he or she will be respected by others.
    c. people must take care of themselves and be independent, or risk losing their personal freedom.

_____ 5. The American belief in equality of opportunity means that
    a. all Americans are rich.
    b. Americans believe that everyone should be equal.
    c. everyone should have an equal chance to succeed.

_____ 6. In the United States, learning to compete successfully is

     a. part of growing up.
     b. not seen as healthy by most people.
     c. not necessary, because Americans believe in equality.

_____ 7. Traditionally, immigrants have been able to raise their standard of living by coming to the United States because

     a. Americans value money more than anything else.
     b. there were such abundant natural resources.
     c. the rich have shared their wealth with the poor.

_____ 8. Americans see their material possessions as

     a. having nothing to do with social status.
     b. the natural reward for their hard work.
     c. showing no evidence of a person's abilities.

_____ 9. A belief in the value of hard work

     a. developed because it was necessary to work hard to convert natural resources into material goods.
     b. developed because the immigrants who came here had a natural love of hard work.
     c. has never been a part of the American value system because people have so much.

_____ 10. In reality, such American ideals as equality of opportunity and self-reliance

     a. do not exist because there is no equality in the United States.
     b. are always put into practice in the United States and truly describe American life.
     c. are only partly carried out in real life, but are still important because people believe in them.

Talk About It

Work in small groups and choose one or more questions to discuss.

1. Americans believe strongly in self-reliance and the freedom and independence of the individual. What are the advantages and disadvantages of being very independent? Which is more important to you, pleasing your family or having the freedom to do what you want?

2. If Americans had to pick one aspect of their country that they are most proud of, over 90 percent would choose freedom. What aspect of your country are people most proud of? How does that quality affect life there?

3. Is it healthy for a person to want to compete? Which is more important in a society—competition or cooperation? Which do you value more? Why?

Improve Your Reading Skills: Scanning

Read the questions below. Scan the chapter to find the specific information you need to answer each question.

1. What three types of freedoms were the early settlers seeking?

2. What happened in 1776?

3. What does *plight* mean?

4. Who wrote *The Values Divide: American Politics and Culture in Transition*?

5. In what year was the Constitution of the United States written?

6. What do Americans mean by the word *freedom*?

7. Who said, "Americans still love their country and believe that they can accomplish almost anything"?

8. Why didn't a hereditaty aristocracy develop in the United States?

9. Who was James Madison and what did he say in the late 1700s?

10. Who said, "We . . . wish to allow the humblest man an equal chance to get rich with everybody else"?

Build Your Vocabulary

More AWL Words Test your knowledge of these additional AWL words in the reading by completing the crossword puzzle on the next page.

accumulate	decade	ethic	promote
adult	diminish	financial	shift
authority	eliminate	fundamental	unique
concept	energy	global	
convert	enormous	maintain	

Across

2. being the only one of its kind
4. an idea of how something should be done
5. to become smaller or less important
9. of central and underlying importance
10. a period of ten years
13. the physical and mental strength that makes you able to be active
14. to gradually get more and more money, possessions, or knowledge over a period of time
15. to move from one place or position to another
16. extremely large in size or amount

Down

1. the power you have because of your official position
3. to get rid of something completely
4. to change from one form, system, or purpose to a different one
6. to make something continue in the same way
7. a general idea or set of moral beliefs that influences people's behavior and attitudes
8. relating to the whole world
9. relating to money
11. a fully grown person or animal
12. to help something or someone advance and be successful

Use Context Clues Review the four kinds of context clues on pages 12 and 13 in Chapter 1. Use context clues in these sentences to choose the best meaning for the boldfaced words.

_____ 1. In 1776, the British colonial settlers declared their independence from England and established a new nation, the United States of America. In so doing, they **defied** the king of England and declared that the power to govern would lie in the hands of the people.

   a. They killed the king and members of his court.
   b. They refused to recognize the king's power to govern them.

_____ 2. By *freedom*, Americans mean the desire and the right of all individuals to control their own **destiny** without outside interference from the government, a ruling class, the church, or any other organized authority.

   a. They wanted to control their own future lives.
   b. They wanted to control their Constitution.

_____ 3. To say that a person is **materialistic** is an insult. To an American, this means that this person values material possessions above all else.

   a. The person loves things.
   b. The person fears being poor.

_____ 4. John Kenneth White observes that in spite of all the changes in the nation's population, economy, and culture, the behaviors and values of Americans have remained remarkably **constant**.

   a. The behaviors and values have stayed the same.
   b. The behaviors and values have changed.

_____ 5. Because of its incredibly **abundant** natural resources, the United States appeared to be a land of plenty where millions could come to seek their fortunes.

   a. There were many natural resources.
   b. There were very few natural resources.

Word Partners There are many verb + noun object collocations, or word partners, in English.

EXAMPLE: *achieve independence*
Americans expect their adult children to *achieve independence* and support themselves.

Read these word partners. Then complete the sentences that follow with the correct verb + noun object collocation.

   face challenges
   seek their fortunes
   provide a decent standard of living
   surveys public opinion
   control their own destiny

1. John Zogby is an American pollster who _____

   _____.

2. By *freedom*, Americans mean the desire and the right to _____

   _____.

3. Millions came to the United States to_____

   _____.

4. The working poor have low-paying jobs that do not _____

   _____.

5. Of course, new immigrants continue to _____

   _____.

Some English words can collocate, or partner, with only a few words; others have a great many collocations. For example, the verb **survey** has relatively few collocations with nouns:

>   survey (public) opinion
>   survey a group of people (teachers, voters)

When **face** is used as a verb, it has many collocations. It usually means confronting someone or something that is difficult or unpleasant:

>   face the facts, reality, the truth, the consequences
>   face the problem head-on, face the music
>   face an opponent, a rival, another sports team
>   face a challenge

The verb **seek** also has many collocations. It often means *to look for something you need* or *to ask someone for advice*:

>   seek shelter, sanctuary, comfort, help, advice, counseling
>   seek your fortune, a better life, an opportunity
>   seek a solution to a problem or seek a compromise
>   seek the truth, seek justice, seek an answer
>   seek employment, seek re-election

Choose two collocations each for *survey*, *face*, and *seek*, and then use them in your own sentences.

Word Forms Many words have verb and noun forms.

Verb form	Noun form
achieve	achievement
conceptualize	concept
emphasize	emphasis
reject	rejection
rely	reliance

Choose the correct verb or noun forms from the chart above and write them in the following sentences. (Change the verb tenses, if necessary.)

Self-_____ is an important American value. Most Americans
_____ the importance of eventually becoming independent and
standing on your own two feet. They teach this _____ to their children
as they are growing up, expecting them to _____ financial and
emotional independence by the time they are in their early twenties. Americans do
not _____ their adult children; they still love them and believe this is
the best preparation for life in the American culture.

American children often earn spending money by selling lemonade.

Ask Yourself

Do you agree or disagree with each of the following statements? Put a check under the number that indicates how you feel.

+2 = Strongly agree

+1 = Agree

0 = No opinion

−1 = Disagree

−2 = Strongly disagree

	+2	+1	0	−1	−2
1. The welfare of the individual is more important than the welfare of the group.	___	___	___	___	___
2. Our destiny is in our own hands.	___	___	___	___	___
3. People should take care of themselves, solve their own problems, and stand on their own two feet.	___	___	___	___	___
4. If I could have a better life in another country, I would go and live there.	___	___	___	___	___
5. Earning a lot of money is more important than having an interesting job.	___	___	___	___	___
6. The government should take care of the poor and homeless.	___	___	___	___	___
7. Life is basically a competitive race for success.	___	___	___	___	___
8. Money and material possessions are the best indicators of high social status.	___	___	___	___	___
9. People who work hard deserve to have a higher standard of living than others.	___	___	___	___	___
10. If I work hard, I am sure I can be a success and get what I want in life.	___	___	___	___	___

Your teacher will place the numbers +2, +1, 0, −1, −2 on walls around the room. As the teacher reads the above statements, walk to the number that best describes your opinion. Be prepared to explain your choice.

Ask Americans

Interview several Americans of different ages and ask them about their basic beliefs. If this is not possible, try to interview people from several different countries. Ask each one the following questions and record their answers.

1. Some people say that people achieve success by their own hard work; others say that luck and help from other people are more important. Which do you think is more important?

2. Do you agree or disagree with this statement: If you work hard in this country, eventually you will get ahead.

3. On the whole, how satisfied are you with the life you lead? Would you say that you are very satisfied, fairly satisfied, not very satisfied, or not at all satisfied?

4. In the course of the next five years, do you expect your personal situation to improve, to stay about the same, or to get worse?

Compare Polls

In the polls that follow, Americans and Europeans were asked to rate how satisfied they were with their lives today and how optimistic they were about the future (questions 3 and 4 of *Ask Americans*).

Look at the charts that follow. Then, answer the questions on the next page.

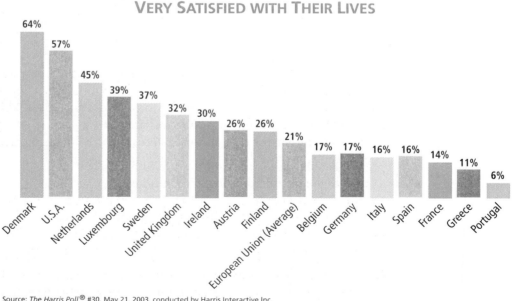

VERY SATISFIED WITH THEIR LIVES

Denmark 64%, U.S.A. 57%, Netherlands 45%, Luxembourg 39%, Sweden 37%, United Kingdom 32%, Ireland 30%, Austria 26%, Finland 26%, European Union (Average) 21%, Belgium 17%, Germany 17%, Italy 16%, Spain 16%, France 14%, Greece 11%, Portugal 6%

Source: *The Harris Poll*® #30, May 21, 2003, conducted by Harris Interactive Inc.

EXPECT PERSONAL SITUATION
WILL IMPROVE IN THE NEXT 5 YEARS

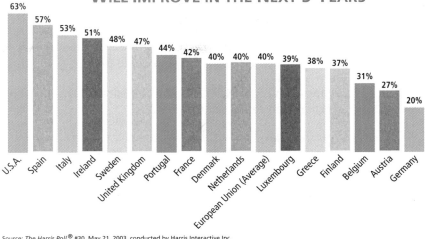

Source: *The Harris Poll* ® #30, May 21, 2003, conducted by Harris Interactive Inc.

1. How do the results you and your classmates obtained compare with the answers the pollsters obtained about how Americans feel about their present and future lives?

2. In general, who are more satisfied with their lives today, Americans or Europeans?

3. In general, who are more optimistic about what their lives will be like in the next five years, Americans or Europeans?

4. In which country are people the most satisfied with their lives today?

5. In which country are people most optimistic about life in the future?

People Watching

Rule: Americans usually stand about two and a half feet apart and at a slight angle (not facing each other directly) for ordinary conversation. They may touch when greeting each other by shaking hands (during a formal introduction) or by placing a hand briefly on the other's arm or shoulder (friends only). Some people kiss on the cheek or hug when greeting a friend. Note that the hug usually is not a full-body hug; only the shoulder and upper part of the bodies touch.

Observation: Observe people who are standing and talking. How far apart are they? Do they touch as they speak? What do you think their relationship is? Observe people greeting each other. What do they do? What is their relationship? Observe formal introductions. Do the people shake hands? Do women usually shake hands? If a man and a woman are introduced, who extends a hand first?

Experiment: Ask someone on the street for directions. When you are standing two or three feet apart and the other person seems comfortable with the distance, take a step closer. What is the person's reaction? Try standing more than two to three feet from the other person. What does the other person do? Try facing the person directly as you talk instead of standing at an angle. What happens?

🌐 Use the Internet

Many Americans interested in tracing their family history can learn when family members immigrated to the United States. Immigrants who came from Europe between 1892 and 1924 first landed on Ellis Island (in the New York harbor). There they went through Immigration. The Statue of Liberty-Ellis Island Foundation has a museum and a website to help people do family research.

Work with a partner. Visit the website www.ellisisland.org and click on *Ellis Island*, then *Immigrant Experience*.

You then have two choices: (1) *Family Histories* will tell you stories about individuals from different countries, or (2) *The Peopling of America* will give you a timeline that traces the history of immigration to the United States.

Choose one of these, read the information, and discuss it with your partner.

WRITE ABOUT IT

A. **Choose one of the following topics. Then write a short composition about it.**

1. Refugees from other countries often get both financial aid and personal support when they first arrive. However, after a few months, Americans expect the refugees to be independent and self-supporting. Write a letter to a refugee who has been in the United States for one year. Explain why Americans now expect him or her to "stand on his or her own two feet" and be self-supporting. Mention the American values that are relevant.

2. Watch advertisements on TV and look at ads in American magazines and newspapers. Some ads suggest that if Americans buy particular products, they will have high status and people will admire and respect them. Bring these ads to class and show them to the members of your small group. Discuss the products, how they are presented, and the messages the ads are sending. Make a collage by pasting all the ads your group has collected on a big piece of paper. Write a report summarizing your conclusions.

B. **Write an essay about the responsibilities people in a community have to each other. Organize your thoughts before you write. Here are a few tips.**

1. Write a short plan, or outline, of your main ideas: an introduction, two or three main ideas, and a conclusion.

2. Begin your essay by defining what you mean by the word *community*.

3. Be sure to introduce each of your main points, using words such as *first*, *second*, *third*.

4. Try to tie your conclusion to the introduction.

C. Off the coast of California is Angel Island, known as the Ellis Island of the West. From 1910 until 1940, many Asian immigrants entered the United States by first going to this island.

Visit the website www.angelisland.org and click on *Immigration Stn*. Write a report about what you learn.

EXPLORE ON YOUR OWN

Books to Read

Sandra Cisneros, *The House on Mango Street*—Esperanza Cordero, a girl coming of age in the Hispanic quarter of Chicago, uses poems and stories to reveal her life in a difficult environment.

Ralph Waldo Emerson, *Self-Reliance*—A classic essay on the American value of self-reliance and Emerson's philosophy of moral idealism.

Richard Rodriguez, *Hunger of Memory: The Education of Richard Rodriguez*—A Mexican American describes his academic success, his assimilation to middle-class America, and his loss of connection to his cultural roots.

Amy Tan, *The Kitchen God's Wife*—A Chinese immigrant mother tells her daughter about growing up in China and her life there before coming to the United States.

John Kenneth White, *The Values Divide: American Politics and Culture in Transition*— A discussion of the split between conservative Republicans and liberal Democrats and the American "culture wars" of the 2000s.

Movies to See

Coming to America—An African prince goes to Queens, New York, to find a wife whom he can respect for her intelligence and independence.

The Immigrants—The story of an immigrant who endures a challenging sea voyage and gets into trouble as soon as he arrives in America.

In America—An Irish immigrant family adjusts to life in the United States.

The Joy Luck Club—The life histories of four Asian women and their relationships with their daughters who were born in the United States.

Trading Places—A rich stockbroker and a street-smart beggar find themselves trading places as part of a bet by two old millionaires.

Religion in the United States: National Cathedral (Episcopal); Islamic mosque; Baha'i temple; Sikh temple; Hawaiian church (Protestant); Mormon temple; Buddhist temple; Jewish synagogue; Spanish chapel (Catholic)

THE AMERICAN RELIGIOUS HERITAGE

CHAPTER 3

The care of every man's soul belongs to himself.

Thomas Jefferson (1743–1826)

BEFORE YOU READ

Preview Vocabulary

A. **Read the following sentences from the chapter and notice the words in italics. Use context clues to help you figure out the meanings. Then choose which definition is best for the italicized word. These key AWL words will help you understand the chapter reading.**

_____ 1. Although the overwhelming majority of Americans are Christians, all religions make important *contributions* to the American culture.

    a. things you give or do in order to help make something successful
    b. official statements made by religious leaders to inspire people

_____ 2. In contrast to Catholic traditions, Protestant leaders had a different *attitude* toward work. They believed that the work of all people was holy.

    a. the opinions, feelings, or beliefs about something
    b. particular practice or customary behavior

_____ 3. The idea of mixing materialism (love of things) and religion may seem *contradictory*. Religion is considered to be concerned with spiritual matters, not material possessions.

    a. different
    b. similar or almost the same

_____ 4. Many businesses encourage their employees to do *volunteer* work, such as helping clean up parks or doing other community projects in their spare time.

    a. without being paid
    b. necessary or required

_____ 5. Perhaps the most *dramatic* example of the idea of self-improvement is the experience of being "born again."

    a. uncertain or undecided
    b. exciting and impressive

_____ 6. America's religious heritage seems to have encouraged certain basic values that members of many diverse faiths find easy to accept. This has helped to unite many different religious groups in the United States without requiring any to *abandon* their faiths.

    a. to leave behind a particular idea or principle
    b. to try to convince others to join your religious faith

B. In this chapter, there are words dealing with religion, such as *priest, soul,* and *church*. Other words have to do with wealth, such as *money, financial,* and *sum*.

Look at the words below and classify them into one of these two groups. Write _R_ next to words dealing with religion and _W_ next to words dealing with wealth.

_____ 1. bless

_____ 2. faith

_____ 3. forgiveness

_____ 4. fortune

_____ 5. holy

_____ 6. material success

_____ 7. missionary

_____ 8. pray

_____ 9. prosperity

_____ 10. Protestant denomination

_____ 11. riches

_____ 12. save and invest

_____ 13. sin

_____ 14. soul

_____ 15. spiritual

_____ 16. tax credit

Preview Content

A. Read the questions below and discuss them with your classmates.

1. Read the quotation by Thomas Jefferson at the beginning of the chapter. What do you think he meant? How could this belief affect religion in the United States?

2. What do you know about religion in the United States? Do you think that the United States has the same religions as your country? Fill in the Venn diagram with the names of religions found only in your country, only in the United States, or in both countries.

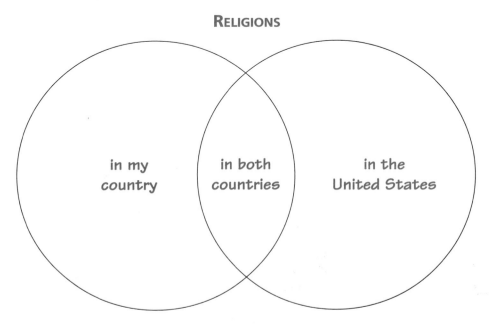

RELIGIONS

in my country

in both countries

in the United States

B. Before you read the chapter, look at the headings for each section. Which sections do you think will have the answers to these questions? Write the heading of the section in the space below each question.

1. Do many Americans believe in God?

_____

2. What is the most popular religion in the United States?

_____

3. Do Americans have an official national religion?

_____

4. How has religion shaped American values?

_____

Freedom of Religion in the United States

1   The fundamental American belief in individual freedom and the right of
individuals to practice their own religion is at the center of religious experience
in the United States. The great diversity of ethnic backgrounds has produced religious
pluralism; most of the religions of the world are now practiced in the United States.
Ninety percent of Americans say that they believe in God, although not all of them
participate in traditional religious organizations. About 80 percent of Americans are
Christians, about 2 percent are Jewish, and another 4 percent belong to other
religious faiths such as Islam, Buddhism, and Hinduism.

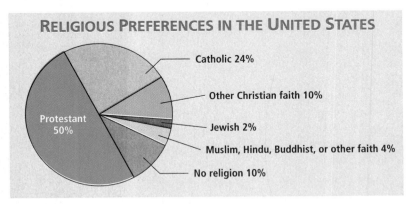

RELIGIOUS PREFERENCES IN THE UNITED STATES

Protestant 50%

Catholic 24%

Other Christian faith 10%

Jewish 2%

Muslim, Hindu, Buddhist, or other faith 4%

No religion 10%

2   Although the overwhelming majority of Americans are Christians, all religions make important contributions to the American
culture. There are now about as many Muslims living in the United States as there are
Jews. People of Hispanic origin now make up about one-half of the Catholic church.
The Asian immigrants have brought with them the traditional religions of East
Asia—Daoism, Confucianism, and Shintoism, as well as Buddhism. And the Native
American religions are still practiced and studied today, particularly for their
teachings about living in harmony with nature.

3   Religion has always played an important role in the history of the United States.
The Catholic faith was first brought to the North American continent by the Spanish
in the 1500s. For the next 300 years, Catholic missionaries and settlers from Spain
and then Latin America came to what is now California and the Southwest. Many of
the cities were named by these missionaries and settlers—San Francisco, Santa Fe,
and San Antonio, for example. French Canadian Catholic missionaries also came
with the explorers and traders from Quebec, down the Mississippi River to New
Orleans. In the 1600s, the European settlers began establishing colonies along the
east coast of North America. Although there were some Catholics, the vast majority
of the European settlers were Protestants, most from England. As the new nation
formed, it was the Protestant branch of the Christian faith that had the strongest
effect on the development of the religious climate in the United States.

The Development of Protestantism

4   The Protestant branch of the Christian faith broke away from the Roman Catholic
church in Europe in the sixteenth century because of important differences in
religious beliefs. (The Eastern Orthodox branch of the Christian faith had separated
from the Roman Catholic Church in 1054.) At the time of the Protestant

Reformation, the Roman Catholic church was the center of religious life in western European countries; the Catholic pope and the priests played the role of parent to the people in spiritual matters. They told people what was right and wrong, and they granted them forgiveness for sins[1] against God and the Christian faith.

5   The Protestants, on the other hand, insisted that all individuals must stand alone before God. If people sinned, they should seek their forgiveness directly from God rather than from a priest speaking in God's name. In place of the power and authority of priests, Protestants substituted what they called the "priesthood of all believers." This meant that every individual was solely responsible for his or her own relationship with God.

6   After the Protestants broke away from the Catholic church, they found that they could not agree among themselves about many beliefs. Therefore, the Protestants began to form separate churches, called *denominations*. (The largest Protestant denominations in the United States now are Baptist, Methodist, Lutheran, Presbyterian, Episcopalian, and the United Church of Christ.) There was much

Children participating in an Easter Sunday service in a Baptist church

bitterness among some of the religious groups in the 1600s, and many Protestant denominations experienced religious persecution.[2] A number of people were even killed because of their beliefs. The result of this persecution was that many Protestants were ready to leave their native countries in order to have freedom to practice their particular religious beliefs. Consequently, among the early settlers who came to America in the 1600s, there were many Protestants seeking religious freedom.

7   In the previous chapter we noted that this desire for religious freedom was one of the strongest reasons why many colonial settlers came to America. Generally speaking, the lack of any established national religion in America appealed strongly to European Protestants, whether or not they were being persecuted. A large number of Protestant denominations were established in America. At first, some denominations hoped to force their views and beliefs on others, but the colonies were simply too large for any one denomination to gain control over the others. The idea of separation of church and state became accepted. When the Constitution was adopted in 1789, the government was forbidden to establish a national church; no denomination was to be favored over the others. The government and the church had to remain separate. Under these conditions, a great variety of different Protestant denominations developed and grew, with each denomination having a "live and let live" attitude toward the others. Diversity was

---

[1] **sins:** things someone does that are against religious laws
[2] **persecution:** cruel or unfair treatment, especially because of religious or political beliefs

accepted and strengthened. Today, the various Protestant denominations have completely separate church organizations, and although there are many similarities, there are also significant differences in their religious teachings and beliefs.

The Protestant Heritage: Self-Improvement

8   Protestantism has been a powerful force in shaping the values and beliefs of Americans. One of the most important values associated with American Protestantism is the value of self-improvement. Christianity often emphasizes the natural sinfulness of human nature. Unlike Catholics, Protestants do not go to priests for forgiveness of their sins; individuals are left alone before God to improve themselves and ask for God's guidance, forgiveness, and grace. For this reason, Protestantism has traditionally encouraged a strong and restless desire for self-improvement.

9   The need for self-improvement, once established, reaches far beyond self-improvement in the purely moral or religious sense. It can be seen in countless books which explain how people can be happier and more successful in life by improving everything from their vocabulary to their tennis game, or even their whole personality. Books of this type are often referred to as "self-help" books, and many are best sellers. They are the natural products of a culture in which people believe that "God helps those who help themselves." In addition, Americans attend thousands of self-help seminars and support group [3] meetings to help them stop smoking or drinking, lose weight, be better parents, have happier relationships, and develop self-confidence.

Material Success, Hard Work, and Self-Discipline

10   The achievement of material success is probably the most widely respected form of self-improvement in the United States. Many scholars believe that the nation's Protestant heritage is also largely responsible for bringing this about. The idea of mixing materialism and religion may seem contradictory; religion is considered to be concerned with spiritual matters, not material possessions. How can the two mix?

11   Some of the early European Protestant leaders believed that people who were blessed by God might be recognized in the world by their material success. Other church leaders, particularly in the United States, made an even stronger connection between gaining material wealth and being blessed by God. In 1900, for example, Bishop William Lawrence proclaimed, [4] "Godliness is in league with [5] riches. . . . Material prosperity is helping to make the national character sweeter, more joyous, more unselfish, more Christlike."

12   American religious leaders, however, never encouraged the idea of gaining wealth without hard work and self-discipline. Many scholars believe that the emphasis on these two values made an important contribution to the industrial growth of the United States. Protestant leaders viewed the work of all people as holy, not just that of priests. They also believed that the capacity for self-discipline was a holy characteristic blessed by God. Self-discipline was often defined as the willingness to save and invest one's money rather than spend it on immediate pleasures. Protestant

---

[3] **support group:** a group of people who meet to help each other with a particular problem
[4] **proclaimed:** said publicly or officially that something is true
[5] **in league with:** working together secretly

tradition, therefore, may have played an important part in creating a good climate for the industrial growth of the United States, which depended on hard work and willingness to save and invest money.

13   The belief in hard work and self-discipline in pursuit of material gain and other goals is often referred to as "the Protestant work ethic" or "the Puritan work ethic." It is important to understand that this work ethic has had an influence far beyond the Protestant church. Many religious groups in the United States share this work ethic, and even Americans who have no attachment to a particular church are influenced by the work ethic in their daily lives. Interestingly, the United States is the only industrialized country that does not have a legal requirement for workers to have a certain number of paid vacation days. Americans take an average of only two weeks of vacation time a year.

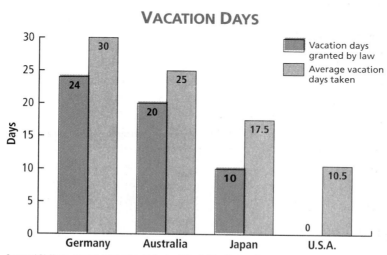

VACATION DAYS

Source: AOL News, June 25, 2003, citing Catherine Valenti, "The No-Vacation Nation," www.ABCNews.com.

Volunteerism and Humanitarianism

14   The idea of self-improvement includes more than achieving material gain through hard work and self-discipline. It also includes the idea of improving oneself by helping others. Individuals, in other words, make themselves into better persons by contributing some of their time or money to charitable, educational, or religious causes that are designed to help others. The philosophy is sometimes called *volunteerism* or *humanitarianism*.

15   Historically, some of the extremely wealthy Americans have made generous contributions to help others. In the early 1900s, for example, Andrew Carnegie, a famous American businessman, gave away more than $300 million to help support schools and universities and to build public libraries in thousands of communities in the United States. John D. Rockefeller, another famous businessman, in explaining why he gave a large sum from his private fortune to establish a university, said, "The good Lord gave me my money, so how could I withhold it from the University of Chicago?" The motive for humanitarianism and volunteerism is strong: Many Americans believe that they should devote part of their time and wealth to religious

or humanitarian causes in order to be acceptable in the eyes of God and in the eyes of other Americans. Many businesses encourage their employees to do volunteer work, and individuals may get tax deductions for money given to charity.

Born-Again Christians and the Religious Right

16 Perhaps the most dramatic example of the idea of self-improvement is the experience of being "born again." Some individuals who have had this experience say that when they truly opened their hearts to God and Jesus Christ, their lives were so completely changed, it was like being born again. Whether they identify themselves as born-again Christians, Evangelicals,[6] mainline Protestants or Catholics, they tend to hold conservative religious beliefs. Estimates are that one-third to one-half of all Americans consider themselves to be religious conservatives, although they do not all have the same beliefs. For example, Democratic President Jimmy Carter and Republican President George W. Bush have both spoken publicly about their born-again experiences.

17 Many of those who are religiously conservative are also politically conservative. Since the 1980s, they have been gaining numbers and political strength in the United States. Under such names as the Religious Right or the Christian Coalition, these individuals have joined together to oppose legalized abortion or to support prayer in the public schools, among other issues.

September 11, 2001, and the National Religion

18 All Americans, and probably most people around the world, can remember exactly what they were doing at the moment they heard that terrorists had attacked the World Trade Center and the Pentagon. People in New York City and Washington, D.C., were especially devastated. As New Yorkers searched for news of missing friends and family members, they held up photos, and then taped thousands of pictures of the missing to building walls. They lit candles and held prayer vigils[7] in parks for their missing loved ones. Strangers united in overwhelming grief held onto each other, praying and crying. A young flight attendant in New York was asked by friends in Europe what it was like in the city. They assumed that New Yorkers must be very angry. They were wrong, she told them. The overwhelming feeling in New York was sadness, a deep, terrible sadness that hung in the air. People spoke quietly and one could feel the heavy sense of loss. Everyone knew someone who was touched by the tragedy.

Photos of missing firefighters a week after September 11. This firehouse lost fifteen men when the Twin Towers collapsed.

---

[6] **Evangelicals**: people who are members of an evangelical Christian church; religious conservatives
[7] **vigils**: periods of time, especially during the night, when you stay awake in order to pray

19   Immediately, there was an outpouring of love, charity, and patriotism around the country. So many people volunteered to help that officials had to limit the numbers. Millions of dollars were raised for the families of the victims, and Americans felt a huge surge of pride and love for their country. Eighty percent of them displayed the American flag—in the windows of their houses, on their cars, even on their clothing. People hung flags and put up signs on highway overpasses and bridges. And over and over, crowds spontaneously sang "God Bless America," a patriotic song that is more popular (and much easier to sing) than the national anthem, along with "America the Beautiful" and "My Country 'Tis of Thee."

20   This mixture of religion and patriotism is what some scholars have called the "national religion" of the United States. The roots of the national religion go back to colonial times. In the countries from which the American colonists emigrated, the dominant values of the nation were often supported by an organized national church. Although Americans made certain that no organized national church would exist in their young country, they have over the years developed a number of informal practices which combine national patriotism with religion. The main function of this national religion is to provide support for the dominant values of the nation, and comfort in times of grief. Thus, it does in an informal and less organized way what nationally organized churches did for European nations in earlier times.

21   Some observers of American society believe that the various practices that are called the national religion can have harmful effects, however. Sometimes these practices can help to create a climate in which disagreement with current national practices is discouraged or not tolerated. There have been times when citizens have disagreed with their government's decision to wage war, for example, and other Americans accused them of being unpatriotic. This happened during the war in Vietnam, when protesters were told, "America—love it, or leave it." A similar division of opinion occurred over the U.S. decision to invade Iraq in 2003.

Firefighters hang a giant American flag over the side of the American Express tower.

Religious Diversity in the United States: A Spiritual Kaleidoscope [8]

22   The belief that the individual, not the organized church, should be the center of religious life has encouraged a tolerance and acceptance of all faiths. This climate of religious freedom has, of course, strengthened the development of cultural

---

[8] **kaleidoscope:** colors or patterns that change quickly

pluralism in the United States. Today there is growing religious diversity. *The World Almanac* now lists over 140 different religious groups that each have at least 5,000 members, and other estimates are that there are at least 2,000 distinct religious groups in the United States.

23   Wade Clark Roof, a professor of religion and society, cites four trends that are creating a spiritual kaleidoscope in the United States. First, there is the change from being a "Protestant-Catholic-Jewish nation" to one with multiple religions. The number of Protestants has declined to a little over 50 percent, and if trends continue, they will probably be in the minority in the next decade. The number of Catholics is increasing due to the large numbers of Latin American Catholic immigrants, who now make up about half the total Catholic community. The number of Jews has stayed the same in recent years, but the number of Americans who choose "Other or None" when asked their religious preference is growing. The number of Muslims, for example, has increased to the point that some estimates are that there are now as many Muslims as there are Jews in the United States.

24   Second, there is religious "expressive individualism," the switching of faiths—from one Protestant denomination to another, or even from one faith to another. Also, within the various faiths, Americans are now picking and choosing among the beliefs, particularly in the mainline faiths. Roof calls this "the privatizing of organized religion," the search for a personal religious identity. For some, this results in a stronger faith; for others, it does not.

25   Third, there are many new religious organizational structures emerging in the United States. Some are ethnic denominations such as the Latvian Evangelical Lutheran Church in America, while others are "special purpose groups"—such as support groups or groups to help the homeless or clean up the environment. Some groups are "liberal, oriented to reforming society; others are conservative, aimed at reforming individual lives," Roof says. He observes the same trend toward fragmentation that Michael J. Weiss noted in his description of American lifestyles, mentioned in Chapter 1. However, Roof says that these new special interest groups are energizing the American religious community.

Muslim men at worship in an Islamic mosque in Florida

26   The fourth trend is toward a new spirituality, especially among young Americans. Many young people prefer to identify themselves as being *spiritual*, rather than *religious*. The majority prefer also to explore the beliefs of several religions, rather than just one. In a survey that Roof conducted, he found that 22 percent of young Americans believe in reincarnation, and many are attracted to Eastern religious teachings. They are looking for a belief

Buddhist women in Los Angeles celebrate the Thai New Year, pouring water on monks' hands.

system that will help them grow and improve as individuals; they are not interested in participating in a religion out of duty.

27   Most Americans believe that religious freedom must be protected; that everyone has the right to practice his or her own religion without interference by the government or anyone else. While the majority of Americans follow the Judeo-Christian tradition, they also believe that freedom of religion should be a basic American right.

28   America's religious heritage seems to have encouraged certain basic values that members of many diverse faiths find easy to accept. This has helped to unite many different religious groups in the United States without requiring any to abandon their faiths. Cultural and religious pluralism has also created a context of tolerance that further strengthens the American reality of many different religions living peacefully within a single nation.

Understand Main Ideas

In Chapters 1 and 2, we discussed the importance of organizing and presenting main ideas for clear writing and formal speaking in English. Academic writing in English looks like a series of capital letter Ts:

Main Idea / Topic Sentence
Supporting Details

Usually, each paragraph has a *topic sentence* that states the main idea of the paragraph. Often, this is the first sentence. The rest of the paragraph contains *supporting details* that develop or explain the main idea. There are many types of supporting details:

- definitions
- facts or opinions
- statistics
- examples or illustrations
- descriptions
- quotations

The first two paragraphs of the reading begin with a topic sentence supported by facts, statistics, examples, and an illustration (chart). (See page 52.) Look back at the reading and find the paragraphs that begin with the following topic sentences. Then find the details that support the main ideas stated in the topic sentence.

1. Topic sentence: *Some of the early European Protestant leaders believed that people who were blessed by God might be recognized in the world by their material success.* (page 54)

   Supporting detail: (quotation) _____

   _____

2. Topic sentence: *American religious leaders, however, never encouraged the idea of gaining wealth without hard work and self-discipline.* (page 54)

   Supporting detail: (definition) _____

   _____

3. Topic sentence: *Historically, some of the extremely wealthy Americans have made generous contributions to help others.* (page 56)

   Supporting details: (example and quotation) _____

   _____

   _____

4. Topic sentences: *All Americans, and probably most people around the world, can remember exactly what they were doing at the moment they heard that terrorists had attacked the World Trade Center and the Pentagon. People in New York City and Washington, D.C., were especially devastated.* (page 56)

Supporting details: (descriptions) _____

_____

_____

5. Topic sentence: *The belief that the individual, not the organized church, should be the center of religious life has encouraged a tolerance and acceptance of all faiths.* (page 58)

Supporting details: (facts and statistics) _____

_____

_____

Understand Details

Write *T* if the statement is true and *F* it is false according to the information in the chapter.

_____ 1. Although there is cultural pluralism in the United States, there is no religious pluralism.

_____ 2. The Protestant denominations (such as Methodist, Baptist, and Presbyterian) are all part of the Roman Catholic church.

_____ 3. No single church has become the center of religious life in the United States because the emphasis is on the individual, not a particular church.

_____ 4. Most of the settlers who came to colonial America to escape religious persecution in Europe were Catholics.

_____ 5. The Constitution of the United States separates church and state and forbids the government from ever establishing a national church.

_____ 6. Protestantism encourages a strong desire for self-improvement.

_____ 7. Some American Protestant leaders have said that people who are rich have been blessed by God.

_____ 8. The Protestant work ethic is the belief that people should share their time and their wealth to help others.

_____ 9. A majority of Americans now consider themselves part of the religious, politically conservative movement.

_____ 10. The national religion of the United States is a mixture of religion and patriotism.

Talk About It

Work in small groups and choose one or more of these questions to discuss.

1. Do the majority of the people in your country belong to one particular church or religious faith? Is there a government-supported church or official religion? What are the advantages and disadvantages of having a government recognize one official religion for a country?

2. The United States does not have a national legal requirement for workers to have a certain number of paid vacation days. Does your country have such a legal requirement? Explain.

3. What is humanitarianism? Do you think that people should volunteer their time to help the poor?

4. What do you think being *religious* means?

Build Your Vocabulary

Use Prefixes Some words use prefixes to create negative or opposite meanings:

encourage—discourage   patriotic—unpatriotic

capable—incapable

Make the following words negative by adding the correct prefix. Scan the chapter to find the words, or use a dictionary.

dis-   un-   in-

1. tolerance   _____ tolerance

2. favorable   _____ favorable

3. respectful   _____ respectful

4. selfish   _____ selfish

5. agreement   _____ agreement

Use the five words with their new prefixes in sentences.

Recognize Word Forms Many adverbs end in *–ly*. Use the following adverbs to fill in the blanks in the sentences from the chapter. (Some have more than one possible answer.)

consequently	immediately	solely	traditionally
historically	particularly	spontaneously	

1. In Protestantism, every individual is _____ responsible for his or her own soul.

2. There was freedom of religion in the new nation. _____, there were many Protestants who came seeking religious freedom.

3. _____, some wealthy Americans, such as Andrew Carnegie in the 1900s, have made generous contributions to help others.

4. Crowds _____ sang "God Bless America" in the weeks after 9/11.

5. The Native American religions are studied today, _____ for their teachings about living in harmony with nature.

6. _____ after 9/11, there was an outpouring of love, charity, and patriotism around the country.

7. Protestantism has _____ encouraged a strong and restless desire for self-improvement.

Collocations This chapter has many adjective + noun collocations. Circle the one word in each of the following groups that will *not* form a collocation with the boldfaced word.

EXAMPLE: European / colonial / national / early / British **settlers**
(You can say European settlers, colonial settlers, early settlers, or British settlers, but not national settlers.)

1. **spiritual** values/beliefs/practices/banks/experiences
2. **religious** freedom/diversity/grief/persecution/climate
3. **overwhelming** grief/examples/fear/frustration/sadness

_____ 1. capacity

_____ 2. cite

_____ 3. consequently

_____ 4. display

_____ 5. function

_____ 6. impose

_____ 7. liberal

_____ 8. persistence

_____ 9. philosophy

_____ 10. primary

_____ 11. sum

_____ 12. trend

a. force people to accept a rule

b. a set of beliefs about how people should live

c. an amount of money

d. ability to do or produce something

e. the way a situation is developing or changing

f. as a result

g. mention something as an example or proof

h. most important

i. the usual purpose of something

j. continuing to do something even though it is difficult

k. put things in a place where people can see them

l. supporting changes in social systems that give people more freedom

```
E  V  A  S  M  P  I  W  I  C  Y  C  C  F  D
Z  S  U  R  B  Y  S  X  D  K  T  O  O  U  I
H  M  O  R  L  Y  S  I  Y  E  I  N  N  N  S
Y  H  M  P  P  V  G  Z  D  J  C  S  F  C  P
O  N  K  D  M  V  H  Q  Y  Q  A  E  X  T  L
Y  S  X  T  E  I  H  M  J  P  P  Q  A  I  A
P  H  I  L  O  S  O  P  H  Y  A  U  S  O  Y
L  A  X  T  J  O  R  K  K  O  C  E  T  N  M
P  H  I  H  D  T  W  E  H  Y  K  N  L  P  O
P  E  R  S  I  S  T  E  N  C  E  T  I  R  N
P  T  C  K  C  B  R  C  B  Y  T  L  B  I  D
A  R  I  I  Q  O  C  U  B  A  V  Y  E  M  E
K  E  T  H  J  A  N  A  A  M  W  A  R  A  C
J  N  E  P  L  W  G  B  C  Z  Z  Y  A  R  T
U  D  O  I  F  O  E  H  H  S  T  L  L  Y  D
```

Ask Americans

Americans have a saying, "Never discuss religion and politics." These are not "safe" topics because they may touch on personal beliefs. Most Americans, however, will be willing to talk to you if you make it clear that this is an assignment for a class you are taking. You could begin by saying: "I wonder if you could help me with an assignment I have. I'm taking a course at _____ (school) and I am supposed to interview Americans about their religious beliefs. Would you be willing to answer some questions? I won't use your name. (Show them the list of questions.) Please tell me if there are any questions you don't feel comfortable answering."

Interview several Americans and ask them the following questions about their religion. If you cannot ask Americans, interview international students or your classmates. Compare your findings with your classmates' findings and with the poll results that follow here and on the next page.

1. How important would you say religion is in your own life: very important, fairly important, or not very important?

2. What is your religion?

3. How often do you attend religious services?

4. Would you say that your religious beliefs are very conservative, somewhat conservative, moderate, somewhat liberal, or very liberal? Do you consider yourself to be *evangelical* or *born again*?

How important is religion in your life?			
Very important	**Fairly important**	**Not very important**	**No opinion**
65%	23%	12%	0%

Source: CNN/USA Today, Sept. 2–4, 2002.

Weekly Attendance of Religious Services*

All men	32%
All women	44%
Catholic men	26%
Catholic women	49%
Protestant men	42%
Protestant women	50%
Jews	23%
Muslim men	35%
Muslim women	26%

*Not counting weddings and funerals, 38 percent of Americans say they go to religious services at least once a week. But there are big differences across demographic groups, with self-reported attendance peaking among older people, women, Southerners, and Baptists, among others.

Source: Polls adapted from ABC NEWS/Beliefnet poll, Feb. 19–20, 2003; the Zogby International Poll for the Georgetown University Center for Muslim-Christian Understanding cited on www.allied-media.com; and a Zogby poll cited in The Jewish Journal of Greater Los Angeles, May 5, 2000.

Self-Identification of "People of Faith"

Poll done by The Gallup Organization for The Interfaith Alliance Foundation in August 2001 on adults who met two criteria:

1. They must have indicated that they attended church or religious service at least once a month, or

2. They must have indicated that religion was "very important" to them

Responses of these "People of Faith"		Religious affiliation	
Very conservative	21%	Evangelicals	31%
Somewhat conservative	25%	Mainline protestants	17%
Moderate	27%	Black protestants	11%
Somewhat liberal	15%	Catholics	22%
Very liberal	8%	Other	19%
No opinion	4%		
Evangelical or born again	51%		

Source: Call for Reform, published by The Interfaith Alliance, August 2001.

Proverbs and Sayings

There are a number of proverbs and sayings about right and wrong. For example, the golden rule, "Do unto others as you would have them do unto you," means that you should treat people the way you want them to treat you. What proverbs do you know that deal with right and wrong?

Ask Americans to explain these sayings to you. Do they know any more sayings about money? Collect as many sayings as you can and share them with your classmates.

1. A penny saved is a penny earned.
2. Early to bed and early to rise makes a man healthy, wealthy, and wise.
3. Save something for a rainy day.
4. Eat, drink, and be merry, for tomorrow you die.
5. Idle hands are the devil's workshop.

Observe the Media

Working with a partner, look at the titles of some popular American self-help books. What aspects of life do they promise to improve? What conclusions about American values can you draw from these titles?

Collect other book titles by visiting an American bookstore, checking best-seller lists or websites, and looking at ads for books in magazines and newspapers. Share your findings with the class.

 Use the Internet

Work with a partner. Search the Internet and find the answers. Discuss your findings.

The Committee for the Study of Religion at Harvard University sponsors a website—www.pluralism.org. The website lists information about their study of religious diversity in the United States. Go to their website and answer the following questions. (Click on *Resources* and then *Statistics*.)

a. Which religions are listed?
b. Are there any that were new to you? Did you know about Baha'i or Sikhism or paganism?
c. Choose one that is interesting to you. Find other websites with information about Americans who practice that religion. What facts and statistics from the website are most interesting to you?

A. **Choose one of the following topics. Then write a short composition about it.**

1. Americans volunteer in many ways: at churches, in libraries or museums, in hospitals, or in schools. Former President Jimmy Carter volunteers with Habitat for Humanity. The goal of this organization is to build houses for poor people. How successful have they been? Go to the Internet and find out. Can you help where you live? How? Write a report about a Habitat for Humanity project that you would like to help with.

Habitat for Humanity volunteers build a house for people in need.

2. Times of crisis often bring out the best in people. When a house burns down and a family is homeless, or when there is a natural disaster such as a flood or earthquake, people often volunteer to help. Think of an event that you have experienced, or one that you have heard about, and write a description of what happened and how people helped.

B. Practice using supporting details such as definitions, facts or opinions, statistics, examples or illustrations, descriptions, or quotations.

Choose one of these topic sentences and write a paragraph with good supporting details. You may use information from the chapter or ideas of your own.

1. September 11, 2001, had a profound effect on the people of the United States.

2. The Protestant work ethic causes many Americans to work very hard.

3. Americans are (or are not) religious.

4. Americans are very interested in self-improvement.

5. Freedom of religion may result in a spiritual kaleidoscope.

C. **The following people are highly regarded for their religious work. Choose one and find out why the person is or was important. Do research on the Internet and then write a report about your findings.**

Dalai Lama   Mother Teresa

Martin Luther King, Jr.   Muhammad

Desmond Tutu

EXPLORE ON YOUR OWN

Books to Read

Diana L. Eck, *A New Religious America: How a "Christian Country" Has Become the World's Most Religiously Diverse Nation*—An explanation of how the immigration of Muslims, Buddhists, Hindus, Sikhs, and other religious groups has brought religious pluralism to the United States.

Richard W. Flory, *GenX Religion*—An examination of the diverse spiritual journeys of young Americans outside traditional churches.

Nathaniel Hawthorne, *The Scarlet Letter*—Set in early colonial times in New England, this classic story reveals the impact of an act of passion in a Puritan society.

Herman Melville, *Billy Budd*—A classic American story of an innocent young man on a ship who is accused of treason by another sailor who dislikes him.

Jacob Neusner, Editor, *World Religions in America: An Introduction*—A discussion of the diverse religions practiced in the United States, including Native American religions, Protestantism, Catholicism, Orthodox Christianity, Judaism, Buddhism, and Hinduism.

Movies to See

Elmer Gantry—Elmer Gantry, a salesman, teams up with Sister Sharon Falconer, an evangelist, to sell religion in America in the 1920s.

Oh, God—God appears to an assistant grocery store manager as a good-natured old man and selects him as His messenger for the modern world.

Saved—A comedy about teenagers in a religious school who have difficulty deciding what is really the right thing to do.

A Simple Plan—Two brothers find a bag of stolen money and must decide what to do with it.

The Spitfire Grill—A girl is released from prison and goes to a small town to start over.

Clint Eastwood as William Munny in Unforgiven

CHAPTER 4

THE FRONTIER HERITAGE

> This ever-retreating frontier of free land is the key to American development.
>
> **Frederick Jackson Turner (1861–1932)**

BEFORE YOU READ

Preview Vocabulary

A. Work with a partner to answer the questions. Make sure you understand the meaning of the AWL words in italics.

1. If "spiritual" has to do with your soul, and "mental" has to do with your mind, what does *physical* have to do with?

2. If people are discussing a *controversial* topic, such as religion or politics, would you expect there to be a lot of agreement or disagreement?

3. If we say that the settlement of the western frontier had an *impact* on American culture, do we mean that it had some influence or that it was not very important?

4. If you wanted to *reinforce* your cowboy *image*, what would you wear?

5. Would someone who had a "can-do" attitude be an *optimist* or a *pessimist*?

6. Is gun control an *issue* in the United States, or do all Americans believe that everyone should have complete *access* to guns? What percentage of American households do you think have guns?

B. Read this paragraph from the chapter. Then use context clues and write the correct word next to its definition

How Americans *reacted* to the terrorist attacks of September 11, 2001, *reveals* another *legacy* of the frontier: Americans' willingness to take the law into their own hands to protect themselves and their families. This tendency usually appears when Americans believe the police cannot *adequately* protect them. For example, when the passengers fought with the terrorists on the 9/11 flight that crashed in Pennsylvania, they were *hailed* as heroes.

_____ 1. well enough for a particular purpose

_____ 2. described someone as being very good

_____ 3. shows something that was hidden

_____ 4. acted in response

_____ 5. a situation that exists as a result of things that happened at an earlier time

Preview Content

A. Read the quotation at the beginning of the chapter. Discuss these questions with your classmates.

1. What is a frontier?

2. Why do you think Turner says that the frontier is the "key" to understanding the development of America?

3. Which of these can be a frontier?

_____ the border between two countries

_____ an unsettled region

_____ space exploration

_____ deep-ocean exploration

_____ understanding how the mind works

_____ new or experimental medical treatments

4. What American movies about the Old West have you seen?

B. Before you read the chapter, look at the headings of each section. Examine the photos and other illustrations. Predict three values that were reinforced by the frontier experience. Write your predictions here.

1. _____

2. _____

3. _____

The Impact of the American Frontier

1 Although the American civilization took over and replaced the frontier more than a century ago, the heritage of the frontier is still evident in the United States today. Many people are still fascinated by the frontier because it has been particularly important in shaping American values. When Ronald Reagan was president in the 1980s, he liked to recall the image of life on the frontier. He was often photographed on his western ranch—chopping wood or riding his horse, and wearing his cowboy hat. President George W. Bush reinforced this cowboy image by inviting members of the press to photograph him on his Texas ranch, wearing his cowboy boots and hat.

2 For many years, the frontier experience was romanticized[1] in popular movies and television shows that featured cowboy heroes fighting Indian villains. Little attention was given to the tragic story of what really happened to the Native Americans, also known as the American Indians. Today, most Americans are more aware of the darker side of the settling of the continent, when thousands of American Indians were killed, their lands taken, and much of their culture destroyed. There is a renewed interest in Indian cultures, and the Smithsonian now has a museum dedicated to Indian culture in Washington, D.C.

3 The frontier experience began when the first colonists settled on the east coast of the continent in the 1600s. It ended about 1890 when the last western lands were settled. The American frontier consisted of the relatively unsettled regions of the United States, usually found in the western part of the country. Here, both land and life were more rugged and primitive than in the more settled eastern part. As one frontier area was settled, people began moving farther west into the next unsettled area, sweeping aside the Native Americans as they went. By settling one frontier area after another, Americans moved across an entire continent that was 2,700 miles wide. They came to believe that it was their destiny to control all the land, and eventually they did. The Native Americans were given small portions of land, called *reservations*, to control, but the United States government broke many promises and created much misery for the Indian nations.

4 While most Americans have a more balanced view of the settling of the West, many Americans still see aspects of the frontier, its people, and their beliefs as inspiring examples of traditional American values in their original and purest form. How did the frontier movement, which lasted more than two centuries, help to shape these basic American values?

5 To be sure, the frontier provided many inspiring examples of hard work as forests were turned into towns, and towns into large cities. The competitive race for success was rarely more colorful or adventurous than on the western frontier. The rush for gold in California, for silver in Montana, and for fertile land in all the western territories provided endless stories of high adventure. When it was announced that almost 2 million acres of good land in Oklahoma would be opened for settlement in

---

1 **romanticized:** talked or thought about things in a way that made them seem more attractive than they really were

April 1889, thousands of settlers gathered on the border waiting for the exact time to be announced. When it was, they literally[2] raced into the territory in wagons and on horseback to claim the best land they could find for themselves.

THE RUN FOR HOMES IN OKLAHOMA.

The 1889 rush to claim land in Oklahoma

6   Although daily life on the frontier was usually less dramatic than the frontier adventure stories would lead one to believe, even the ordinary daily life of frontier men and women exemplified[3] national values in a form which seemed purer to many Americans than the life of those living in the more settled, more cultivated eastern United States.

7   Individualism, self-reliance, and equality of opportunity have perhaps been the values most closely associated with the frontier heritage of America. Throughout their history, Americans have tended to view the frontier settler as the model of the free individual. This is probably because there was less control over the individual on the frontier than anywhere else in the United States. There were few laws and few established social or political institutions to confine people living on the frontier. In the United States, where freedom from outside social controls has traditionally been valued, the frontier has been idealized, and it still serves as a basis for a nostalgic[4] view of the early United States, a simpler time that was lost when the country became urbanized and more complex. Many people living in the West today still hold these beliefs about freedom from government controls.

Self-Reliance and the Rugged Individualist

8   Closely associated with the frontier ideal of the free individual is the ideal of self-reliance. If the people living on the frontier were free of many of society's rules, they were also denied many of society's comforts and conveniences. They had to be self-reliant. Men and women often constructed their own houses, hunted, tended their own gardens, and made their own clothing and household items.

---

[2] **literally:** according to the most basic or original meaning of a word or expression
[3] **exemplified:** was a very typical example of something
[4] **nostalgic:** feeling or expressing a slight sadness when remembering happy events or experiences from the past

9   The self-reliant frontiersman has been idealized by Americans who have made him the model of the classic American male hero with *rugged individualism*. This hero is a man who has been made physically tough and rugged by the conditions of frontier life. He is skilled with guns and other weapons. He needs no help from others. Often, he appears in stories as alone, unmarried, and without children. Standing alone, he can meet all the dangers which life on the frontier brings. He is strong enough to extend his protection beyond himself to others.

10   There are two types of heroic rugged individualists. Each is drawn from a different stage of life on the frontier. In the early frontier, which existed before the Civil War of the 1860s, the main struggle was man against the wilderness. Daniel Boone is probably the best-known hero of this era. Boone explored the wilderness country of Kentucky in the 1760s and 1770s. On one trip, he stayed in the wilderness for two years, successfully matching his strength and skills against the dangers of untamed nature and hostile Native Americans. In 1778, Boone was captured by Native Americans who were so impressed with his physical strength and skills that they made him a member of their tribe. Later, he succeeded in making a daring escape. Boone's heroic strength is seen primarily in his ability to master the harsh challenges of the wilderness. Although he had to fight against Indians from time to time, he is admired mainly as a survivor and conqueror of the wilderness, not as a fighter.

11   The second type of heroic rugged individualist is drawn from the last phase of the western frontier, which lasted from the 1860s until the 1890s. By this time, the wilderness was largely conquered. The struggle now was no longer man against nature, but man against man. Cattlemen and cowboys* fought against farmers, outlaws, Native Americans, and each other for control of the remaining western lands. The traditions of law and order were not yet well established, and physical violence was frequent. The frontier became known as "the Wild West."

12   It is not surprising, then, that the hero drawn from this period is primarily a fighter. He is admired for his ability to beat other men in fistfights,[5] or to win in a gunfight. The principal source of his heroism is his physical prowess[6] and he is strong enough to defeat two or three ordinary men at one time. This rugged individualist is typically a defender of good against evil.

13   The hero of the Wild West is based on memories of a number of gunfighters and lawmen of the time, men such as Jesse James and Wyatt Earp. The Wild West hero had more impact on the American idea of heroism than Daniel Boone, the hero of the earlier wilderness frontier. It is the Wild West hero who has inspired countless western movies; until the 1960s, 25 percent of all American movies made were westerns.

---

*Cattlemen were men who raised large herds of cattle as a business and needed large areas of land on which their cattle could graze before being sent to market. Cowboys usually worked for the cattlemen. They would spend most of the day on horseback rounding up the cattle or taking them on long drives to market.

---

[5] **fistfights:** fights using bare hands with the fingers curled in toward the palm
[6] **prowess:** great skill at doing something

American Macho Heroes

14   Through movies and television programs, this Wild West hero has helped shape the American idea of "macho," or male, strength. For the most part, almost all American male heroes on television and in movies have traditionally had the common ability to demonstrate their strength through physical violence. Once the western macho hero had been created, the model for this hero was used in other settings—for soldiers in battle, and tough detectives and policemen fighting crime. From the cowboy heroes to Rambo and the Terminator, these heroes can fight with their fists or with their guns, or both. Although there are movie and TV heroes who are respected more for their intelligence and sensitivity than their physical prowess, these classic macho male heroes still dominate much of American entertainment and video games. However, there are now female versions of this macho image. Several popular female heroes in TV and movies have also been shown as tough fighters capable of defeating their enemies.

15   The image of the rugged individualist has been criticized for overlooking many factors that played a central part in the development of the frontier. The rugged individualist image overstates the importance of complete self-reliance and understates the importance of cooperation in building a new nation out of the wilderness. Second, because the image has been traditionally masculine, it has overlooked the importance of pioneer women and their strength, hard work, resourcefulness, and civilizing influence on the untamed frontier.

16   Finally, the rugged individualist image is criticized because of its emphasis on violence and the use of guns to solve problems. On the frontier, men did use guns to hunt and protect themselves and their families, but western movies romanticized and glorified gunfights in the Old West. The good guys and the bad guys "shot it out" in classic westerns such as *High Noon*. Incidentally, the classic old western movies always featured the "good guys" wearing white hats, while the "bad guys" wore black hats. Gradually, however, the western hero was largely replaced in the movies by the soldier or the crime fighter—guns still blazing—and the violence in movies, and later on TV, increased.

17   Some Americans worry about the impact of these entertainment heroes on the lives and imaginations of young people. At the very least, many young people have become desensitized[7] to the sight of violence and killings. In the 1990s, guns became a critical issue when there were shootings in several public schools. It is all too easy for teenagers to get guns, and they are much more at risk of being killed by guns than adults are. The problem is particularly bad in the inner cities, where a number of young gang members carry guns. However, several of the most shocking incidents occurred in normally peaceful suburban communities, and now many schools require students to pass through metal detectors as they enter school buildings.

18   Americans have a long history of owning guns, and many people strongly believe having a gun in their house is an important right. In fact, the right to bear arms is even guaranteed in the Constitution, though there is debate about what the founding fathers meant by that. Today, there are over 200 million guns in the United States, enough for every adult to own one. Most guns are owned by Americans who enjoy hunting or gun collecting, and these individuals usually own more than one gun. Some guns are owned by people who want their own gun for protection of their homes and families. After the

---

[7] **desensitized:** made emotionally insensitive

9/11/01 terrorist attacks, the sale of guns rose in the United States. Estimates are that anywhere from 25 percent to 51 percent of U.S. households have at least one gun.

19   How Americans reacted to 9/11 reveals another legacy of the frontier: Americans' willingness to take the law into their own hands to protect themselves and their families. This tendency usually appears when Americans believe the police cannot adequately protect them. For example, when the passengers fought with the terrorists on the 9/11 flight that crashed in Pennsylvania, they were hailed as heroes.

20   The issue of gun control is very controversial in the United States, and people on both sides of the issue have strong opinions. Many Americans favor stricter government controls on the sale of guns, and they would not consider having a gun in their home. Others who oppose gun control feel strongly enough about the issue that they have created powerful political pressure groups, such as the National Rifle Association (NRA), which has worked to prevent most gun control legislation from passing. They argue that limiting gun sales will keep law-abiding citizens, not criminals, from owning guns. On the other side are gun-control organizations such as Handgun Control, Inc., which are especially concerned about the sale of handguns and automatic assault rifles. They argue that American homes, particularly where there are children, are safer without guns.

Inventiveness and the Can-Do Spirit

21   While the frontier idealized the rugged individual as the great American hero, it also respected the inventive individual. The need for self-reliance on the frontier encouraged a spirit of inventiveness. Frontier men and women not only had to provide most of their daily life essentials, but they were also constantly facing new problems and situations which demanded new solutions. Under these circumstances, they soon learned to experiment with new ways of doing things.

22   Observers from other countries were very impressed by the frontiersman's ability to invent useful new farm tools. They were equally impressed by the pioneer woman's ability to make clothing, candles, soap, and many other items needed for the daily life of her family. Lord Bryce, a famous English observer of American life, believed that the inventive skills of American pioneers enabled them to succeed at tasks beyond the abilities of most ordinary men and women in other countries. Although Americans in the more settled eastern regions of the United States created many of the most important inventions in the new nation, the western frontier had the effect of spreading the spirit of inventiveness throughout the population and helping it to become a national character trait.

A nineteenth-century frontier family in front of their sod house

23   The willingness to experiment and invent led to another American trait, a "can-do" spirit, or a sense of optimism that every problem has a solution. Americans like to believe that a difficult problem can be solved

immediately—an impossible one may take a little longer. They take pride in meeting challenges and overcoming difficult obstacles.[8] This can-do spirit has traditionally given Americans a sense of optimism about themselves and their country. Many like to say that if the United States can land a man on the moon, no problem on earth is impossible. In the 1830s, Alexis de Tocqueville said that no other country in the world "more confidently seizes the future" than the United States. Traditionally, when times were hard, political leaders have reminded Americans of their frontier heritage and the tough determination of their pioneer ancestors; the can-do spirit has become a source of pride and inspiration.

Equality of Opportunity

24   The frontier is an expression of individual freedom and self-reliance in its purest (and most extreme) forms, and it is also a pure expression of the ideal of equality of opportunity. On the western frontier there was more of a tendency for people to treat each other as social equals than there was in the more settled eastern regions of the country. On the frontier, the highest importance was placed on what people could do in their own lifetime. Hardly any notice was taken of their ancestors. Frontier people were fond of saying, "What's above the ground is more important than what's beneath the ground."

25   Because so little attention was paid to a person's family background, the frontier offered a new beginning for many Americans who were seeking opportunities to advance themselves. One English visitor to the United States in the early 1800s observed that if Americans experienced disappointment or failure in business, in politics, or even in love, they moved west to make a new beginning. The frontier offered millions of Americans a source of hope for a fresh start in the competitive race for success and for a better life. On the frontier there was a continuing need for new farmers, skilled laborers, merchants, lawyers, and political leaders.

26   There were fewer differences in wealth between rich and poor on the frontier than in the more settled regions of the nation. People lived, dressed, and acted more alike on the frontier than in other parts of the United States. The feeling of equality was shared by hired helpers who refused to be called "servants" or to be treated as such. One European visitor observed, "The clumsy gait[9] and bent body of our peasant is hardly ever seen here. . . . Everyone walks erect[10] and easy." Wealthy travelers to the frontier were warned not to show off their wealth or to act superior to others if they wished to be treated politely.

27   The American frontier may not be *the key* to American development, as Frederick Jackson Turner said, but it is certainly one major factor. The frontier provided the space and conditions which helped to strengthen the American ideals of individual freedom, self-reliance, and equality of opportunity. On the frontier, these ideals were enlarged and made workable. Frontier ideas and customs were continuously passed along to the more settled parts of the United States as newer frontier regions took the place of older ones during a westward march of settlers which lasted more than two centuries. In this way, many of the frontier values became national values.

---

[8] **obstacles:** things that make it difficult for someone to succeed
[9] **clumsy gait:** walking in an awkward way
[10] **erect:** in an upright position

Understand Main Ideas

A. Check the predictions you made on page 72 before you read the chapter. Work with a partner. Answer these questions about the main ideas.

1. What are the three values that are traditionally associated with the frontier heritage?

2. What two new values are introduced in this chapter?

3. What are the two types of rugged individualists?

4. Describe someone with a can-do spirit.

5. What personal characteristics did the frontier settlers share?

B. In academic writing, paragraphs often begin with a topic sentence that contains the main idea. Read and highlight the first sentence of each paragraph of the reading. Then choose one main idea from each of the five main sections that you think is the most important. Write these ideas below. Compare your list with a partner's.

1. _____

2. _____

3. _____

4. _____

5. _____

Understand Details

Write **T** if the statement is true and **F** if it is false according to the information in the chapter.

_____ 1. The frontier experience began in about 1890 and is still continuing in the American West today.

_____ 2. One reason why many Americans are still fascinated by the frontier period is that it represents a time when the traditional basic American values were expressed in their purest form.

_____ 3. The settling of the frontier did little to affect the lives of the American Indians.

_____ 4. Daniel Boone is an example of the earliest type of rugged individualist hero, a man who fights against the wilderness.

_____ 5. The primary qualities of the American macho hero are intelligence, sensitivity, and caring for others.

_____ 6. It is difficult for the average American to buy a gun, so very few people own them.

_____ 7. Members of the NRA (and many gun owners) believe the right to own a gun is guaranteed in the United States Constitution.

_____ 8. The can-do spirit came from the willingness of the pioneers to work together on a cooperative project for the good of all.

_____ 9. On the frontier, family name and ancestry were more important than what a person could do.

_____ 10. On the frontier, the rich and the poor rarely mixed, and social class was more important than in the more settled regions.

Complete a Timeline: Scanning

Scanning is looking for a specific piece of information. Scan the chapter to find these dates. Write what happened next to the date to complete the timline. Some are done for you.

1600s: _Settlers established colonies on the east coast._

1760s and 1770s: _____

1778: _Boone was captured by Native Americans._

1860s: _____

April 1889: _____

1890: _____

until 1960s: _25 percent of all American movies made were westerns._

1980s: _____

1990s: _Gun control became a critical issue after shootings in schools._

2001: _____

Improve Your Reading Skills: Skimming

Skimming is reading quickly to get the general ideas. Skim the ad on the next page and answer these questions.

1. What are the four problems presented in this ad?

2. What solutions are offered by American Indian values?

As you read the morning newspaper, you quickly come to an undeniable conclusion. Our world is in rough shape. Our environment. Our families. Our values.

A SANE, RATIONAL ARGUMENT FOR GIVING THE ENTIRE COUNTRY BACK TO THE INDIANS.

Now, the only way we can change the world we live in, is to change the way we think. And a good place to start is by becoming better acquainted with the traditional American Indian beliefs. For reasons of economy, we'll briefly mention how traditional American Indian thinking applies to just four timely issues: The destruction of the wilderness. The breakdown of the family. Greed. And international turmoil.

The destruction of the wilderness. You can't watch television for fifteen minutes without hearing about another toxic dump or another endangered species. To the American Indian, nature is more than a collection of water and landforms, it's their religion and thus it's treated with the appropriate respect. There is the belief that everything must be kept in balance and to disrupt this balance (pollution, over-hunting, over-developing, etc.) will only result in tragedy.

The breakdown of the American family. It's a sad and widely accepted fact. In traditional American Indian culture, though, the family is not only strong, it spans many generations. The children are also raised by the aunts and uncles and elders for Indians believe it's best for a child to learn from as many people as possible to give them a more well-rounded education. Also, child abuse was unheard-of in the traditional American Indian world. In their journals, Lewis and Clark often commented with amazement how the Indians never struck their children.

Greed. So many modern problems can be directly traced to that emotion. The American Indians, though, believe wealth and success only means that you're able to give more to others, and materialism only removes one further from God.

The international problems. Most often they occur because one culture becomes intolerant of another. The American Indians, on the other hand, believe all cultures are equally important. The Indians often used the analogy of the wagon wheel to explain this belief. The spokes represent all the various cultures, each one unique unto itself. None of the spokes could ever be removed or shortened or lengthened, because they are all absolutely necessary for the wheel (the earth) to turn.

As stated earlier, these are only four examples demonstrating how relevant traditional American Indian beliefs are. But the greater problem is that the American Indian culture is in danger of becoming extinct. 200 years of forced assimilation has done everything possible to dilute and destroy their world. And the greatest hope for survival is through the 26 tribal colleges. The tribal colleges were formed to keep the tribal ways alive and to reintroduce them to a generation of Indians who may know nothing about their heritage. The results have been remarkable. More Indians are becoming educated, tribal pride is increasing, and the old ways are being restored and preserved.

The tribal colleges, though, are struggling financially and to survive this decade, they are going to need your help.

So please call 1-800-776-FUND. And help save a culture that could save ours.

AMERICAN INDIAN COLLEGE FUND

American Indian College Fund, 21 East 65th St., Suite 201 PA, New York, NY 10028. We would like to give a special thanks to US West for all their concern and support.

American Indian College Fund ad

Talk About It

Work in small groups and choose one or more of the following questions to discuss.

1. What effect do you think seeing violence on TV or in movies has on children? What happens when people become desensitized to violence?

2. What qualities should a true hero have? Who are some of your own personal heroes? Why do you admire and respect these people?

3. Would you have a gun in your own home? Why or why not?

4. If you were going to live in the wilderness for a week, what ten things would you take with you? Why?

Build Your Vocabulary

Use Context Clues Review the four kinds of context clues on pages 12–13 of Chapter 1. Use context clues to choose the correct words to fill in the blanks.

desensitized	fascinated	nostalgic	romanticize
exemplified	fists	obstacles	

1. In many action movies, the heroes are expected to be able to fight with their _____ .

2. Some people prefer to _____ life on the frontier; they do not want to look at its negative aspects.

3. If you are reading a book that is so interesting that you can't put it down, you are _____ by the book.

4. Frontier people were good examples of the American national values; these people _____ these values.

5. In order to succeed, people living on the frontier had to overcome many difficulties and _____, such as clearing the land for farming.

6. Americans like to remember the days on the frontier; they feel _____ about the Old West.

7. Some Americans worry that their children are becoming _____ to the violence and killing on television. It doesn't seem to bother them.

More AWL Words: Test your knowledge of these additional AWL words in the chapter by completing the crossword puzzle on the next page.

area	capable	confine	cooperation	evident	phase
automatic	challenge	consist	deny	feature	region
aware	classic	construct	detective	item	survivor

Across

2. someone who is still alive after almost being killed
4. to keep someone in a place that they cannot leave
6. having the skills needed to do something
8. something that tests strength, skill, or ability
9. easily noticed or understood; obvious
10. the act of working with someone to achieve something
14. realizing that a problem exists
16. to build something large

Down

1. designed to operate by itself
3. a fairly large area of a state
5. a single thing in a set, group, or list
6. to be made of a number of things
7. to say that something is not true
8. considered important, with a value that lasts for a long time
11. one of the stages of a process
12. something you notice because it seems interesting
13. someone paid to discover information
15. a particular part of a country or city

Word Partners: Match the word partners to form collocations. Then use the correct collocations in the paragraph.

_____ 1. unsettled   a. fathers

_____ 2. law-abiding   b. spirit

_____ 3. can-do   c. individualism

_____ 4. founding   d. citizens

_____ 5. physical   e. region

_____ 6. rugged   f. prowess

Many Americans believe that when the _____ wrote the
                                                                    1
Constitution, they meant to ensure the right of the people to own guns. They would
argue that _____ should be allowed to keep guns in their homes. The
                            2
frontier strengthened the tradition of owning guns because it was an
_____ and settlers needed guns for hunting and protection. They had to
               3
be tough, and part of the frontier legacy is the _____ and
                                                                        4
_____ of Western movie heroes. Frontier settlers were also known for
               5
their inventiveness and their _____.
                                               6

EXPAND YOUR KNOWLEDGE

Proverbs and Sayings

Ask Americans, if possible, to explain these proverbs and sayings about succeeding on your own or being tough. What similar proverbs and sayings are there in your culture?

1. Pull yourself up by the bootstraps.

2. If at first you don't succeed, try and try again.

3. Actions speak louder than words.

4. Life is what you make it.

5. Every problem has a solution.

6. When the going gets tough, the tough get going.

Ask Yourself

Do you agree or disagree with the statements below? Put a check under the number that indicates how you feel.

+2 = Strongly agree
+1 = Agree
  0 = No opinion
−1 = Disagree
−2 = Strongly disagree

	+2	+1	0	−1	−2
1. I love action movies that have a lot of gunfights.	___	___	___	___	___
2. A real man should be able to defend himself well and even win in a fistfight.	___	___	___	___	___
3. Intelligence and sensitivity in a man are more important than physical strength.	___	___	___	___	___
4. Watching fights in movies and on TV shows probably doesn't hurt children.	___	___	___	___	___
5. Having a gun in your home is a good way to protect yourself against robbers.	___	___	___	___	___
6. I believe people should not own guns and there should be strict laws controlling the sale of them.	___	___	___	___	___
7. Every problem has a solution.	___	___	___	___	___
8. What you do is more important than who your ancestors were.	___	___	___	___	___

Now place the numbers +2, +1, 0, −1, −2 on walls around the room with the zero in the middle. As the teacher reads the above statements, walk to the number that reflects your opinion. Explain your choice.

Ask Americans

Read the statements from the previous exercise to several Americans. If this is not possible, try to interview people from several different countries. Ask them if they agree or disagree with each statement. Write their opinions in your notebook.

Think, Pair, Share

Think about this question, and write your answer. Then share it with a partner and with another pair of students.

In 2003, Arnold Schwarzenegger was elected governor of California in a special election. During his campaign, he frequently referred to his movie role as "the Terminator" and talked about how he was going to clean up the state government. Based on the information in this chapter, why do you think this image appealed to Californian voters?

Arnold Schwarzenegger as "the Terminator"

People Watching

Americans are very conscious of space and have a strong sense of territory—that is, the idea that a particular space belongs to them. Children may have a special place to play with their toys; Mom may have her own desk; Dad may have a workshop. Observe Americans at home, in a public place, or in a social situation to see how they use space. (Watch TV shows, if you are not in the United States.) If someone has been sitting in a particular chair and gets up, does the person tend to come back to the same chair? When someone asks, "Is that seat taken?" what does that person mean?

Conduct the following experiment and record the results in your journal.

Rule: When an American sits down at a table where a stranger is sitting alone, the American will choose a seat across from the other person or at least one chair away. The space is divided in half between them, and personal belongings must be kept on each person's respective side of an imaginary boundary line.

Observation: Observe people sitting in a public place where there are tables, such as a cafeteria or library. What happens when a stranger sits down at a table where a person is sitting alone? If someone sits down next to a stranger, what happens? How do the people acknowledge each other's presence? Does the person who was sitting there first move his or her belongings?

Experiment: Choose a table where a stranger is sitting alone and sit down in the next chair. What happens? Sit across from someone at a table and put some personal belongings (such as books) on the table in front of you. Push them toward the other person so that they are more than halfway across the table. What is the person's reaction?

Observe the Media

Work in small groups. Choose one of the following activities.

1. Cowboys and the Old West are frequently used in advertisements for blue jeans, SUVs, trucks, cars, and other American products. What image do they have? Why does this image help sell this or that product? Collect examples of ads in magazines or newspapers that use cowboys or western themes. Make a collage and share it with your classmates. Explain what the message is to the people who may buy these products.

2. Watch American TV shows or movies that have male heroes. Compare the heroes of several shows. How do they compare with the description of American macho presented in this chapter? What personality traits do they have? Compare the heroes of several shows. Reread the section on page 76 for help with descriptions.

Use the Internet

From May 1804 until September 1806, Meriwether Lewis and William Clark traveled from St. Louis, Missouri, to the Oregon coast, and back again.

Work with a partner to find out more about this historic trip. Do an online search for "Lewis and Clark Expedition." Answer these questions.

1. Who was the U.S. President who ordered the expedition?
2. What territory had the United States purchased from France in 1803?
3. What was the purpose of the expedition?
4. Who was Sacajawea?
5. What route did Lewis and Clark follow?
6. What important discoveries did they make?

WRITE ABOUT IT

A. Choose one of the following topics. Then write a short composition about it.

1. Some Americans are nostalgic for the Old West, and there may be a period of your country's history that is romanticized in a similar way. If you could travel back in time to anywhere in the world, what place and what period in history would you like to visit? Explain why.

2. Americans believe in the importance of teaching their children to be self-reliant. Perhaps this philosophy has something to do with how the frontier was settled. Ellen Goodman, a popular columnist, observes:

   The whole country was settled by one generation of leavers after the next—people who moved to a new frontier or a new neighborhood or a new job, who continually left relationships for opportunities. It was considered unreasonable, almost unpatriotic, for parents to "cling." And it still is.

   The result of this is an emphasis on raising children to live independently and separate from their parents. The goal of parenting in America is to make children competent and confident enough to "leave the nest." What do you think of this philosophy? Compare and contrast this philosophy of raising children with that of your country.

3. Some consider space to be the final frontier. Space exploration is controversial. Although there have been important scientific discoveries, some believe that the cost exceeds the benefits. Write an essay arguing for or against the value of space exploration. You may wish to focus on a particular aspect, such as the support of the international space station, the establishment of a colony on the moon, or whether humans should travel to Mars.

American astronaut David R. Scott salutes the flag on the moon, 1971.

 B. The rush to the West to find gold or silver created a number of very wealthy towns with hotels, opera houses, and beautiful houses. Today, many of these cities are "ghost towns." Some towns have no people living in them; in others, only a few people remain.

Choose one of these ghost towns, and find information about it. Answer the questions and then write a summary of what you learned about the town.

Bodie or Calico, California	Pinos Altos, New Mexico
Gold Hill or Silver City, Utah	Goldfield, Nevada
Shakespeare Ghost Town, New Mexico	

1. Why did people come to the town?

2. What can be seen there today?

3. What did you find most interesting about the town?

Ghost town of Nevada City, Montana

Books to Read

Stephen E. Ambrose, *Undaunted Courage: Meriwether Lewis, Thomas Jefferson and the Opening of the American West*—The best-selling account of the expedition by Lewis and Clark through the American West in the early 1800s, as they traveled from St. Louis, Missouri, to the Pacific Ocean.

Dee Brown, *Bury My Heart at Wounded Knee: An Indian History of the American West*—A best-selling, documented historical account of the systematic destruction of the American Indian during the last half of the 1800s.

Willa Cather, *O Pioneers!*—A classic novel written in 1913 about the physical hardships of the frontier and the enormous changes it brought to the United States.

James Fenimore Cooper, *The Leatherstocking Tales*—A series of five literary novels about the adventures of Natty Bumppo, a scout on the American frontier, from the French and Indian Wars until the early nineteenth century.

Larry McMurtry, *Lonesome Dove*—A best-selling novel about life, love, and adventure on the American frontier.

Movies to See

Bowling for Columbine—In this controversial documentary, filmmaker Michael Moore explores the roots of America's fascination with guns and violence.

Dances with Wolves—A soldier sent to a remote western Civil War outpost makes friends with wolves and Indians, eventually falling in love with a white woman raised by the Indians.

Far and Away—A young Irishman who loses his home after his father's death decides to go to America to begin a new life and eventually goes to live on the frontier.

High Noon—In this classic movie, a sheriff who must face a returning deadly enemy finds that his own town refuses to help him.

Lakota Woman: Siege at Wounded Knee—A movie (made for TV) based on the true story of the life of Mary Crow Dog, the daughter of a poor Indian family, telling how she grew up on a reservation and became involved in the Indian movement.

Indian dancing with rings—Hopi hoop dance

A play structure made from 5,978 plastic containers, 11,203 aluminum cans, and 9,232 soup cans

CHAPTER 5

THE HERITAGE OF ABUNDANCE

For millions of people throughout this world, during the past three centuries, America has symbolized plenty, wealth, and abundance of goods.

David Potter (1910–1971)

BEFORE YOU READ

Preview Vocabulary

A. **Read the following sentences from the chapter and notice the words in italics. These key AWL words will help you understand the reading. Use context clues to help you figure out the meanings. Then choose which definition is best for the italicized word.**

_____ 1. In the aristocratic European nations the settlers left behind, the material wealth and comforts of the ruling classes were *guaranteed* by their birth.

 a. certain to happen
 b. unlikely to happen

_____ 2. Unlike many countries where the love of material things was seen as a vice, a mark of weak moral character, in the United States it was seen as a virtue, a positive *incentive* to work hard, and a reward for successful efforts.

 a. encouragement
 b. discouragement

_____ 3. Mass advertising crosses *media*; there are ads for movies on TV, and ads for TV shows in the movie theaters and at the beginning of movie videos.

    a. TV, radio, and newspapers
    b. interests and viewpoints

_____ 4. Because Americans place such a high value on individual freedom, particularly freedom of speech, they have traditionally been very hesitant to censor, or even *restrict*, the flow of information by any means of communication.

    a. allow
    b. limit

_____ 5. Americans viewed the material wealth and abundance of the United States as an ever-*expanding* pie that would continue to grow so that all people could get a bigger piece of a bigger pie.

    a. becoming larger
    b. becoming smaller

_____ 6. The cost of maintaining a high standard of living has been rising, while the number of high-paying factory jobs has been *declining*.

    a. going up
    b. going down

_____ 7. Many full-time minimum-wage-earners cannot afford to rent an apartment that is not *subsidized* by government funds.

    a. partly paid
    b. guaranteed to be safe

_____ 8. Because of the profound effect abundance has had on the American belief system, a *widespread* perception of its decline could have important consequences.

    a. happening in many situations
    b. happening in only a few situations

B. Read the quotation by David Potter at the beginning of the chapter. Find the words with the following meanings. Write each word next to its meaning.

_____ 1. periods of 100 years

_____ 2. represented an idea or quality

_____ 3. products

_____ 4. enough, or more than enough

_____ 5. a large quantity of something

Preview Content

A. Think about the David Potter quotation and discuss the questions with your classmates.

1. Do you agree with David Potter? Why or why not? What is the source of American abundance?

2. What are the advantages and disadvantages of having abundance? List the positive and negative aspects in the chart.

AMERICAN ABUNDANCE	
Plus +	**Minus –**

3. Think about your daily activities. What do you throw away every day?

4. What are some environmental problems we face today?

5. For these words and phrases, write *P* for the environmental problems, and *S* for the solutions.

_____ endangered species   _____ global warming

_____ trash and garbage   _____ recycling

_____ wastefulness   _____ conserving energy

_____ protecting historical lands   _____ air pollution

B. Read the headings in the chapter and look at the illustrations. Write five topics that you predict will be covered in this chapter.

1. _____

2. _____

3. _____

4. _____

5. _____

A History of Abundance

1   Although the population of the United States accounts for only about 5 percent of the total population of the world, Americans use up about 25 percent of the world's energy per year, generating about seven pounds of trash and garbage per person each day. Only a country that has great abundance could afford to throw so much away. America has sometimes been criticized as a "throw-away" country, a land where there is so much abundance that people are sometimes viewed as wasteful. Scholars like David Potter, an American historian, believe that the abundant material wealth of the United States has been a major factor in the development of the American character.

2   This abundance is the gift of nature. In what is now the continental United States, there are more than 3 million square miles of land. When the European settlers first arrived in the seventeenth and eighteenth centuries, most of this land was rich, fertile farmland, with an abundance of trees and animals. Only about 1 million Native Americans lived on this land, and they had neither the weapons nor the organization necessary to keep the European settlers out. Never again can human beings discover such a large area of rich, unfarmed land, with such a small population and such great undeveloped natural resources.

3   But it would be a mistake to say that the abundant natural resources of North America were the only reason why the United States became a wealthy nation. The beliefs, determination, and hard work of the early settlers were equally important.

4   In the aristocratic European nations the settlers left behind, the material wealth and comforts of the ruling classes were guaranteed by their birth. Therefore, as Tocqueville said, the wealthy took these things for granted and placed little importance on material things. The poor people in those aristocratic nations also did not concern themselves with wealth, since they knew that they had little hope of becoming wealthy or changing their status.

5   In the early years of the United States, however, wealth and social position were not permanently determined at birth. The idea of equality of opportunity in America made the level of material wealth of both the rich and the poor much less certain. At any time, the rich might lose some of their wealth and the poor might increase theirs. Therefore, all classes in American society thought about protecting their material possessions and looked for ways to acquire more. Tocqueville believed that this was not so much a matter of greed; rather, it was a matter of their insecurity. People might be naturally insecure if their material wealth, and that of their children, could change so rapidly either upward or downward during a lifetime, or even a single generation. Tocqueville concluded that it was extremely important both to rich Americans and poor Americans to increase their personal wealth and material comforts. Therefore, the entire population joined in the task of increasing the nation's material abundance as quickly as possible.

6   Tocqueville visited the United States fifty years after the nation had won its independence from England. He was impressed with the great progress made in such a short time. Although the country was still in an early stage of development and there was not much money available for investment, the United States had already made great progress in both trading and manufacturing. It had already become the

world's second leading sea power and had constructed the longest railroads in the world. Tocqueville worried, however, about the effect of all this material success. In such a society, materialism could be made into a moral value in itself rather than a means to an end.

7 Tocqueville's concern, to a large extent, became a reality. In the process of creating a land of abundance, Americans began to judge themselves by materialistic standards. Unlike many countries where the love of material things was seen as a vice, a mark of weak moral character, in the United States it was seen as a virtue, a positive incentive to work hard, and a reward for successful efforts.

8 Traditionally, the people of the United States have been proud of their nation's ability to produce material wealth so that they could maintain a high standard of living. This helps to explain why Americans use materialistic standards not only to judge themselves as individuals, but also to judge themselves as a nation. And the opportunity to share in the good life has attracted immigrants to the United States for generations.

From Producers to Consumers

9 The emphasis on producing wealth and maintaining a high standard of living developed over a period of time. In the 1700s and 1800s, most Americans thought of themselves more as producers than consumers. As farmers they produced food and many of their own household goods, and later as factory workers they produced manufactured goods. It was not until the twentieth century that Americans began to think of themselves more as consumers than as producers. This image change is probably due to the coming of mass advertising, made possible by the invention of the radio in the 1920s and the spread of television programming in the 1950s. In the 1920s, businesses agreed to pay for, or sponsor, radio programs that would run short commercials advertising their products. Companies were able to reach large numbers of Americans at one time to convince them to buy their products. The emphasis was now on consuming.

Mall of America, Bloomington, Minnesota

10 The practice of businesses paying for the cost of producing programs in return for mass advertising continued with television. Television used the same technique that radio had developed: entertainment programs accompanied by short commercials. However, TV soon passed radio as a source of both family entertainment and mass advertising. Today, almost all homes in the United States have at least one television set (the average household has more than two), and the family TV is in use about eight hours a day. The average American sees about 50,000 commercials a year. When popular events such as the Super Bowl are on, mass advertising may reach 50 million or more viewers during a single program.

11   By the end of the 1960s, scholars had began to study the effect of mass advertising on American society. Historian David Potter observed that mass advertising in the United States had become so important in size and influence that it should be viewed as an institution, such as the school or the church. One effect of advertising was that sponsors had some control over the content of television programs. If businesses did not like the content, they could withdraw their sponsorship. A second effect was that advertising techniques were so successful that over time they began to be used to change Americans' attitudes, behavior, and beliefs. For example, politicians paid to advertise their campaigns, the government ran ads to urge teenagers not to use drugs, and charities had ads to ask for donations.

12   Traditionally, however, the purpose of mass advertising has been to persuade people to consume more and more products, and the huge American economy now depends on consumerism. Today, advertising is everywhere. It crosses media: There are ads for movies on TV, and ads for TV shows in the movie theaters and at the beginning of movie videos. And, of course, there are pop-up ads on the Internet.

What American Consumers Like

13   People in the advertising business, and others who study American society, are interested in the question: *What does the American consumer like?* Max Lerner, a well-known scholar who has studied American society, has said that American consumers are particularly fond of three things: comfort, cleanliness, and novelty.

14   Lerner believes that the American love of comfort perhaps goes back to the frontier experience, where life was tough and there were very few comforts. This experience may have created a strong desire in the pioneers and their children for goods that would make life more comfortable. Today, the Americans' love of comfort is seen in the way they furnish their homes, design their cars, and travel. How Americans choose a new mattress for their bed is an example of the American love of comfort. Many Americans will go to a store where beds are set up and lie down on several mattresses to see which is the most comfortable.

15   Cleanliness is also highly valued by Americans. There is a strong emphasis on keeping all parts of the body clean, and Americans see lots of TV commercials for soap, shampoo, deodorants,[1] and mouthwash. Perhaps the Puritan heritage has played some role in the desire for cleanliness. The Puritans, a strict Protestant church group whose members were among the first settlers of America, stressed the need to cleanse[2] the body of dirt and of all evil tendencies, which for them included sexual desire. The saying "Cleanliness is next to godliness" reflects the belief of most Americans that it is

Bathtime for the family dog

---

[1] **deodorants:** substance that you put on the skin under your arms to stop unpleasant odors
[2] **cleanse:** to make something completely clean

important to keep not only their bodies, but also their clothes, their houses, their cars, and even their pets, clean and smelling good. Indeed, many Americans are offended by anyone who does not follow their accepted standards of cleanliness.

16   Along with cleanliness and comfort, Americans love having things that are new and different. Perhaps this love of novelty comes from their pride in their inventiveness. Americans have always been interested in inventing new products and improving old ones. They like to see changes in cars, clothing, and products for the home. Advertisements encourage people to get rid of old products and try new ones, whether the old ones still work or not. And if they cannot afford to buy something now, advertisers encourage consumers to charge it on a credit card—"Buy now—pay later."

17   In addition to the three qualities that Lerner mentions, there is a fourth quality that American consumers like very much—convenience. In the late 1900s, there was a dramatic increase in such labor-saving devices as automatic washing machines, clothes dryers, dishwashers, food processors, microwave ovens, garbage disposals, and power lawn mowers. Today, all of these, and many more, are found in a typical suburban home. These labor-saving devices are designed to reduce the time spent on housework. However, the time that Americans save is quickly spent on other activities.

18   The American desire for convenience also created the concept of *fast-food* restaurants, which are found in every city and almost every small town in the United States, and are now exported all over the world. These fast-food restaurants, such as McDonald's and KFC (Kentucky Fried Chicken), serve sandwiches, salads, fried chicken, seafood, etc., to customers in five minutes or less, often at a drive-up window. There are also many kinds of restaurants that will deliver Chinese food, pizza, and other dishes to people's homes in about a half hour. In many areas, there are "take-out services" that will deliver food from the menus of twenty or thirty different restaurants for a small charge. For those who prefer to prepare their food at home, American grocery stores are full of convenience foods that are packaged and ready to cook, or are even precooked.

19   Like microwaves and dishwashers, fast-food and take-out restaurants are convenient because they save the American consumer time that would otherwise be spent fixing meals or cleaning up. These conveniences, however, do not cause Americans to be less busy. Women now make up about one-half of the American workforce, and the majority of mothers with children under the age of eighteen work outside the home. With both parents employed, children eat a lot of take-out food, a significant contributor to childhood obesity. [3]

20   Thus, the conveniences that Americans desire reflect not so much a leisurely lifestyle as a busy lifestyle in which even minutes of time are too valuable to be wasted. Alexis de Tocqueville was one of the first to see in this a curious paradox in the American character. He observed that Americans were so busy working to acquire comforts and conveniences that they were unable to relax and to enjoy leisure time when they had it. Today, as in Tocqueville's time, many Americans have what one medical doctor has called "the hurry sickness."

---

[3] **obesity:** the condition of being too heavy in a way that is dangerous to your health

An Abundance of Technology

21   New technologies have increased the hectic pace of life in the United States, and they have caused some important changes. First, technology has changed television viewing habits. In the past, broadcast television was dominated by the networks NBC, CBS, ABC, and more recently, Fox. In addition to these commercial networks, there were also public TV stations that offered more educational and cultural programs, supported by contributions from viewers, donations from private companies, and government grants. A viewer could choose from about a dozen different TV shows broadcast at a time.

22   Today, the spread of cable and satellite TV has resulted in a virtually unlimited number of TV programs available. By 2003, the majority of American homes had either cable or satellite TV. For the first time, there were more people watching programs on cable channels (delivered by either cable or satellite systems) than were watching the four original broadcast networks. Many Americans may now view several hundred channels via cable or satellite, in addition to the traditional network shows and public television programs. Some of the cable channels, such as HBO (Home Box Office), are called *premium channels*, and viewers pay an extra monthly fee to receive them. There are no advertisements on these channels or on public television stations.

23   The result is that the viewing audience is more fragmented, with a smaller percentage watching any given program. This means that mass advertisers have to find new ways to reach the buying public. Some companies now pay for product placement in TV shows and movies—the hero drinking a Coke, for example. Also, most companies do extensive market research to find individuals who are most likely to buy their products. They then focus on delivering their ads to these individuals, often using the Internet and other direct-marketing techniques.

The majority of American families have access to the Internet.

24   The technology revolution is changing how Americans get both entertainment and information. By the year 2000, more than one-half of all American households had personal computers (PCs), and the majority of those under age fifty had become users of the Internet. Polls show that today the computer has become the center of entertainment in a number of American households, and many households have more than one. Harris pollster Hal Quinley reports that people look at their computer as "a TV, DVD player, stereo and CD player combined. The increased simplicity in using the computer to acquire, edit, organize and enjoy music, movies and photos is clearly driving this hot trend. . . ." Another important trend is the popularity of computer games played online.

25   The Internet is not only a source of entertainment, it is also a major source of news, information, and goods for sale. Individuals can customize, or personalize, the

news they receive about current events, new products, sales, or special offers. Individuals can set up their own news sites and web logs, or *blogs*. Musicians can record their own CDs and sell them on the web. Indeed, it is now possible to find just about anything or anyone on the Internet.

Challenges of the Technological Revolution

26   There are several issues raised by the technological revolution. The first is the merging of technology providers. A single company can now provide access to television shows, telephone service, cell phone service, and the Internet. On the one hand, as communication media merge, more and more options become available to the home user at lower and lower prices. On the other hand, fewer companies own more of all media (radio, TV, newspapers, magazines). Some worry that this trend will eventually limit the variety of programs and points of view offered. For example, Clear Channel is a company that owns a large number of radio stations throughout the country. The owner has strong political views, and he has on occasion refused to play the music of musicians who publicly criticized the president.

27   Another challenge is the effect of all this technology on children. Some worry that American children and young people are spending too much time watching television, using their computers, and playing video games. Clearly, they are not getting enough exercise, and the lack of physical activity has led to serious problems of childhood obesity and a sharp rise in the number of children with type 2 diabetes.[4]

28   Others worry more about the quality of what children are watching on TV and what they are seeing on the Internet. Americans face a constant dilemma[5]—how to balance the right to free speech with the need to protect children and maintain standards of decency.[6] Because Americans place such a high value on individual freedom, particularly freedom of speech, they have traditionally been very hesitant to censor,[7] or even restrict, the flow of information by any means of communication. True censorship occurs when the government sets the standards; Most Americans would prefer that the entertainment industry regulate itself, and the movie industry does have a rating system for films. Now that many American children have access to the Internet, there is a debate over whether and how to regulate it. For example, there have been arguments over whether public libraries should deny Internet users access to certain websites.

29   Finally, there is concern about the growing "digital divide," the gap between Americans who

"On the Internet, nobody knows you're a dog."

---

[4] **diabetes:** a disease in which there is too much sugar in the blood
[5] **dilemma:** a situation in which you have to make a difficult choice between two or more actions
[6] **decency:** basic accepted behavior, especially moral and sexual behavior
[7] **censor:** to examine books, movies, or letters to remove anything that is offensive

own computers and those who do not. People who have more education and are higher on the socioeconomic scale are likely to spend less time watching television and more time on their computers. Many of those on the other side of the digital divide, those who do not own computers, live in poverty, and some belong to minority populations. As computer literacy[8] becomes increasingly important in American society, the government and concerned individuals look for ways to bridge the digital divide with programs to provide training and free computers. Most public libraries, for example, have computers available that provide Internet access at no cost.

The Ever-Expanding Pie?

30 During the first 200 years of their nation's existence (1776–1976), Americans were never forced to change their great optimism about wealth and abundance. They viewed the material wealth of the United States as an ever-expanding pie. In most other countries, people believe that the rich take a larger piece of the pie and the poor get a smaller piece. Americans, however, have believed that their economic pie would just continue to grow so that all people could get a bigger piece of a bigger pie. This expectation was based on the early experience that as the new nation grew, the pie of wealth and abundance grew at an even faster rate. In the 1800s, the nation grew in size as new western lands were settled and became states. In the 1900s, when the continent had been settled, Americans invented new products and techniques of production, such as Henry Ford's mass production of cars on the assembly line. The expanding economy created new jobs, and the pie continued to grow larger and larger. Under these circumstances, Americans came to believe that their heritage of abundance would last as far as they could see into the future.

31 The belief in an everlasting heritage of abundance had many good effects. It made Americans an optimistic people with confidence that human problems could be solved. It greatly reduced the conflict between the rich and poor that has torn many older nations apart. Perhaps most important, the belief in an always growing abundance gave strong support to such basic national values as freedom, self-reliance, equality of opportunity, competition, and hard work. It seemed to Americans that their high standard of living was a reward for practicing these values.

Or the Decline of American Abundance?

32 Over the last few decades, the American economy has had its ups and downs. In the late 1970s, the energy crisis and the economic recession warned Americans that there might be a limit to their abundant natural resources and the lifestyle that these natural resources had supported. The 1980s and 1990s brought a general turn-around in the economy, but it was often the rich who got richer and the poor who got poorer. The dramatic fall of the stock market in the early 2000s cost many middle-class Americans much of their retirement savings, forcing them to work longer. The response of most Americans to economic downturns is generally to work harder, and their productivity has risen significantly as a result.

33 A high standard of living has been at the heart of the American Dream—a house in the suburbs, one or two cars, a secure job, and enough money to go on vacations

---

[8] **computer literacy:** being able to operate a computer and use the Internet

and to send the children to college. But the cost of all these things has been rising, while the number of high-paying jobs in factories has been declining. Those without a college education are hardest hit. The new jobs are often in the service economy—in stores, restaurants, or hotels—not in the manufacturing economy in factories. Many of the service workers, such as janitors and dishwashers, have relatively low pay and poor benefits. As a result, many Americans must work harder than their parents did to have the same standard of living. Often, young parents believe that it is necessary for both of them to work outside the home in order to maintain their lifestyle. The average number of hours per week that Americans work has risen to well over forty hours, with many professionals (teachers, doctors, lawyers, businesspeople, etc.) working fifty or sixty hours per week.

34   Although Americans are working harder and have less leisure time, many are still having difficulty keeping up with rising costs, particularly for housing. Many people have to spend a larger percent of their income on owning a home or renting an apartment. Today, many families cannot afford to buy a house in the area in which they are living, and so they live in apartments. In some areas, even apartments are too expensive for some full-time minimum-wage-earners to rent unless they are subsidized by government funds. Minority populations are often the hardest hit, especially those with entry-level jobs[9] such as janitors, hotel maids, fast-food cooks, and agricultural workers.

What of the Future?

35   It is difficult to predict the economic future. More and more, Americans find themselves competing in a global economy, and there will continue to be cycles of upturns and downturns. One thing is certain, however. The American tradition of abundance has had a profound effect on the lifestyles and the values of the American people. When Americans experience a decline in abundance, they become more pessimistic. However, even economic downturns may have long-term positive effects.

Children often help their families recycle.

36   On the positive side, a decline in American abundance causes people to become less wasteful and more protective of their environment. Many Americans now recycle aluminum and tin cans, plastic and paper bags, plastic and glass containers, office paper, and newspapers. Children study about environmental issues in school: They learn about care of the local environment and the problems of the earth—air and water pollution, global warming, and the threat to endangered species. Businesses sometimes "adopt" sections of roads, and the company employees volunteer their time to keep the trash picked up. Communities conduct environmental impact studies before developing empty land. Sometimes a

---

[9]**entry-level job:** a first job for a person entering the job market, such as a janitor, a dishwasher in a restaurant, or a day laborer on a construction job

local community chooses to keep its rural lifestyle and protect its historical lands. The people may reject development, even if it means losing potential new jobs. For example, the citizens of a rural community near Washington, D.C., were able to stop the Disney company from building a new theme park in their area, even though Virginia state officials were in favor of the development.

37 ✓   On the negative side, old habits are hard to change. Many Americans are optimistic about their future, but others are pessimistic about the economy of their country and its ability to expand forever. Because of the profound effect abundance has had on the American belief system, a widespread perception of its decline could have important consequences. Whether the traditional American values will remain strong in the coming decades or undergo basic changes is impossible to predict with certainty. Only time will tell.

AFTER YOU READ

Understand Main Ideas

Check the predictions you made on page 93 before reading the chapter. Work with a partner and answer the questions about the main ideas of each section of the chapter. Skim the sections for the main ideas if you do not remember them.

1. *A History of Abundance:* What three values were strengthened by the abundant natural resources of the United States?

2. *From Producers to Consumers:* What caused Americans to change from thinking of themselves mainly as producers to thinking of themselves mainly as consumers?

3. *What American Consumers Like:* What four things do American consumers like?

4. *An Abundance of Technology:* What changes have new technologies brought in American TV-viewing habits and in the way Americans access entertainment and information?

5. *Challenges of the Technological Revolution:* What are the three challenges that the technological revolution has brought?

6. *The Ever-Expanding Pie?* What is the ever-expanding pie, and how did this idea develop?

7. *Or the Decline of American Abundance?* What effects do economic downturns have on Americans?

8. *What of the Future?* What is one possible positive effect of declining abundance?

Understand Details

Write the letter of the best answer according to the information in the chapter.

_____ 1. Which of the following statements is <u>not</u> true?
   a. The European settlers found a North American continent that was rich in undeveloped resources.
   b. The values of the American people inspired them to develop a wilderness continent into a wealthy nation.
   c. The American government discouraged them from developing the natural resources.

_____ 2. Tocqueville believed that in a nation such as the United States, where wealth and social position are not determined by birth,
   a. the rich are not worried about keeping their wealth.
   b. everyone is worried about either acquiring wealth or holding on to it if they have it.
   c. people worry about money so much because they are basically very greedy.

_____ 3. Americans probably think of themselves more as consumers than producers because
   a. few people are still farmers.
   b. they are influenced by mass advertising.
   c. they are concerned about competing on the international market.

_____ 4. The spread of cable and satellite TV means that
   a. there are no longer any public television shows available to watch.
   b. Americans now have to pay for every individual program they choose to watch.
   c. more people are now watching cable programs than network shows on NBC, ABC, CBS, or Fox.

_____ 5. Americans believe that censorship of material on television
   a. should be extremely strict because children must be protected.
   b. is a difficult issue because they believe in the right of free speech.
   c. is the responsibility of the government, not the people who create the programs.

_____ 6. The spread of cable and satellite TV has meant that
   a. more Americans watch the networks ABC, NBC, CBS, and Fox than other channels.
   b. there is a virtually unlimited variety of television programs available.
   c. the number of people watching one program at the same time has increased dramatically.

_____ 7. The "digital divide" means that
   a. people who cannot afford a computer are at a disadvantage.
   b. people are divided between those who have digital television and those who do not.
   c. opinion is divided about the quality of digital cameras and television sets.

_____ 8. Based on information in the *What American Consumers Like* section, which one of these statements is true?
   a. Americans like new products and want to improve old ones.
   b. When buying a chair, most Americans would be more concerned about its beauty than its comfort.
   c. Most Americans don't wear deodorants because they like the natural odors of the body.

_____ 9. Which of these is implied, but not stated directly, in the *What American Consumers Like* section of the chapter?
   a. Fast food is as healthy as home-cooked food.
   b. Most of the cooking is done by women.
   c. Men use credit cards more than women.

_____ 10. The view that a country's economy is an ever-expanding pie
   a. is held by most nations in the world today.
   b. is a belief held by Americans and reinforced by their experiences.
   c. is a belief that a country's food supply will continually expand.

Improve Your Reading Skills: Highlighting

For successful academic reading, use strategies for identifying and remembering the main points. One strategy is to highlight the first sentence in each paragraph as you read. The first sentence is often the topic sentence and states the topic, or main idea, of the paragraph. Practice this strategy. Highlight the first sentence of each paragraph in the *What American Consumers Like* section of the chapter. In your notebook, copy the eight sentences to make a one-paragraph summary of the section.

Talk About It

Work in small groups and choose one of these topics to discuss.

1. Which do you think is more important for economic growth: a good supply of natural resources or the values of the people in the society? Give examples.

2. Should the Internet be regulated? If so, who should do the regulating?

3. Should people be able to download music and movies from the Internet without paying a fee?

4. How do you feel about censorship?

5. What do you think of fast-food restaurants? Are convenience foods (canned goods, frozen foods, TV dinners, etc.) popular in your country?

Build Your Vocabulary

Opposites Match the words with opposite meanings. Then fill in the sentence blanks with the correct words.

——— 1. consumer	a. imports
——— 2. decline	b. pessimistic
——— 3. downturn	c. downward
——— 4. exports	d. vice
——— 5. income	e. upturn
——— 6. optimistic	f. private
——— 7. positive	g. increase
——— 8. public	h. producer
——— 9. upward	i. expenses
——— 10. virtue	j. negative

1. Unlike many countries where the love of material things was seen as a

   _____, a mark of weak moral character, in the United States it

   was seen as a _____, a _____ incentive to work

   hard, and a reward for successful efforts.

2. Tocqueville thought that Americans might be insecure if their material wealth

   could change so rapidly either _____ or _____

   during a lifetime.

3. Mass advertising reinforces the American's self-image as a _____.

4. The goods that a country sends out of the country are called _____.

5. _____ television has no commercials, and programs are paid for

   by donations and government grants.

6. In order to maintain a good standard of living, some couples believe that they

   need two _____.

7. During times of economic _____, Americans become

   _____ about their future lives.

Word Find There are a number of words and phrases in the chapter that deal with technology. Find these technology words in the puzzle. Words may run horizontally, vertically, diagonally, or backwards.

blog	computer	Internet	pop-up ad
cell phone	digital	network	video game
channel	DVD player	online	website

```
A  U  P  O  P  U  P  A  D  I  D  L  L  L  P
N  U  H  M  X  A  V  J  Z  W  V  A  K  E  U
L  I  P  P  B  L  O  G  E  X  D  T  Z  N  O
E  O  F  J  R  R  F  T  P  O  P  I  R  N  E
D  V  I  D  E  O  G  A  M  E  L  G  T  A  X
G  R  F  V  W  V  Y  F  I  B  A  I  W  H  D
V  A  U  W  D  T  X  C  W  O  Y  D  K  C  P
E  X  E  G  U  G  O  O  W  Q  E  Z  R  E  Y
A  W  Q  G  K  M  C  E  Z  G  R  U  O  N  D
P  M  U  F  P  M  B  U  I  N  V  B  W  I  X
V  I  R  U  V  S  B  W  T  A  P  A  T  L  Y
U  Q  T  H  I  J  Z  N  F  X  N  V  E  N  B
N  E  T  T  I  N  T  E  R  N  E  T  N  O  H
R  J  E  E  N  O  H  P  L  L  E  C  Y  R  D
D  U  V  U  A  Q  U  P  X  N  V  V  O  P  R
```

What other technology words do you know? Share your words with a partner.

_____

_____

More AWL Words Test your knowledge of these additional AWL words by filling in the blanks in these sentences from the chapter.

accompanied	emphasis	insecure	period
concluded	generation	institution	task
consumers	image	maintaining	technique

People might be naturally _____ if their material wealth, and that of
                                        1
their children, could change so rapidly either upward or downward during a lifetime,

or even a single _____. Tocqueville _____ that it was
                           2   3
extremely important both to rich Americans and poor Americans to increase their

personal wealth and material comforts. Therefore, the entire population joined in the

_____ of increasing the nation's material abundance as quickly as possible.
           4

The _____ on producing wealth and _____ a high
             5   6
standard of living developed over a _____ of time. It was not until the
                                            7
twentieth century that Americans began to think of themselves more as

_____ than as producers. This _____ change is probably
        8   9
due to the coming of mass advertising, made possible by radio and television.

Television used the same _____ that radio had developed:
                                10
entertainment programs _____ by short commercials. Historian David
                               11
Potter observed that mass advertising in the United States became so important in

size and influence that it should be viewed as an _____, such as the
                                                          12
school or the church.

People Watching

1. Observe what Americans throw away. Visit a fast-food restaurant and count the
   containers that are thrown away from one person's meal. How much food is wasted?
   How does this compare with people eating in fast-food restaurants in your country?

2. Visit a supermarket and note the kinds of convenience or packaged foods available. Be sure to check all the departments. Here are some examples of what you will find: salad in a bag, fruit already cut up and ready to eat, rice and pasta boxed dinners, ready-to-cook meat and poultry dishes, and frozen dinners. Notice what Americans are buying at the grocery store. How does this compare with grocery shoppers in your country? Record your observations in your journal.

A family enjoys fast food at a McDonald's restaurant, Los Angeles, California.

Proverbs and Sayings

Americans have a strong "sense of time." They think of it as a resource—something to be used, saved, spent, shared, etc. How they talk about time is an indication of how they feel about it.

Add to the list of time expressions below by asking Americans for suggestions, by listening to conversations, and by watching TV.

1. A stitch in time saves nine.

2. Time is money.

3. Time and tide wait for no man.

4. I don't have time for that today.

5. Can you give me a few minutes of your time?

6. We lost a lot of time on that.

√ Think, Pair, Share

If you won or inherited $1 million, which of these things, if any, do you think you would do? Check as many as you like.

_____ 1. Put it in a savings account

_____ 2. Buy a new home

_____ 3. Invest for your old age

_____ 4. Start/buy your own business

_____ 5. Invest in stocks

_____ 6. Take a vacation

_____ 7. Buy a new car

_____ 8. Refurnish your house

_____ 9. Quit your job

_____ 10. Buy a boat

_____ 11. Buy a vacation house

_____ 12. Buy a plane

_____ 13. Share it with your family

_____ 14. Contribute to your church or your religious group

_____ 15. Contribute to charities

_____ 16. Other _____
(your choice)

Now arrange the sixteen items in order of their importance to you. Which is the first thing you would spend your money on? Which is the last? Compare your answers with those of your partner, and then share your answers with another pair of students.

Ask Yourself/Ask Americans

What do you think "the good life" is? Roper ASW has been polling Americans for more than thirty years to see what they think the good life is. Americans are asked to choose from a list such as the one below.

Read the list and predict Americans' top three choices.

- four-day work week
- car
- college education for my children
- college education for myself
- good health
- happy marriage
- home computer
- home you own
- job that contributes to the welfare of society

- job that is interesting
- job that pays much more than average
- a lot of money
- one or more children
- nice clothes
- second car
- swimming pool
- travel abroad
- vacation home
- yard and a lawn

1. _____   2. _____   3. _____

Show several Americans the list and ask them these questions. Write down the answers.

1. Which of these are part of the good life for you?

2. How many of these things do you have now?

3. How good are your chances of achieving the good life—very good, fairly good, or not good at all?

The good life in Discovery Bay, California

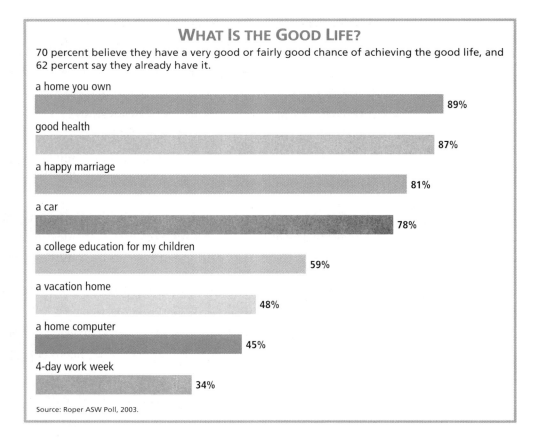

WHAT IS THE GOOD LIFE?

70 percent believe they have a very good or fairly good chance of achieving the good life, and 62 percent say they already have it.

a home you own
89%

good health
87%

a happy marriage
81%

a car
78%

a college education for my children
59%

a vacation home
48%

a home computer
45%

4-day work week
34%

Source: Roper ASW Poll, 2003.

Look at the results of a 2003 poll, above.

What percentage of Americans think the good life means having a happy marriage? What percentage think a vacation home is part of having the good life?

Now conduct a poll in your class. Ask the same questions from before (see page 109). Chart the answers. Compare the results with this poll and with the answers of the Americans you interviewed.

Use the Internet

A. With all the abundance in the United States, a growing number of species are disappearing or are endangered. The U.S. government, through the Fish and Wildlilfe Service, maintains a list of all endangered species (animals, birds, reptiles, amphibians, fish, etc.).

Go to the website http://endangered.fws.gov. Click on *List of Threatened and Endangered Species* and then choose a group to investigate (mammals, birds, reptiles, or amphibians). Answer the following questions and make a report about what you learn.

1. How many species of that group are endangered?

2. How many are endangered in the United States? In other countries?

3. How many were endangered in 1980? In 1990? In 2000?

4. What can you say about the prospects for these animals?

You can also consult www.worldwildlife.org for additional information.

B. The SchoolWorld Endangered Species project attempts to get children involved in helping to save endangered species. School groups do research and then write reports about many endangered species around the world.

Go to their website and look at the various birds or mammals that children in the United States or other countries have chosen to study:

www.schoolworld.asn.au/species/birds.html *or* www.schoolworld.asn.au/species/mammals.html

Then, select one bird or mammal and see what children have found out and written about the following details.

1. The reasons why the bird or mammal is endangered (the problems)

2. The ways that they and other people can help save the bird or mammal (the solutions)

3. Why the children chose this bird or mammal to study

4. Where they found the information for their report

What did you find most interesting about the children's report you selected?

Endangered Sumatran tigers. There may be as few as 400 of them left in the wild.

A. Choose one of the following writing topics. Then write a short composition about it.

1. This chapter lists four things that Americans like: comfort, cleanliness, novelty, and convenience. Find an advertisement in a magazine or newspaper that reveals American tastes. Answer the following questions and then write a description of the ad.

   a. Who are the people in the ad and what do they represent? (Example: A typical housewife struggling to keep her kitchen floor clean.)
   b. What is being sold?
   c. What is the main reason given for buying this product or using this service?
   d. Are any hidden messages in this ad? How are these messages communicated?
   e. Who is likely to use this product or service?
   f. After studying this ad, would you buy this product or service? Do you consider this product or service a luxury or a necessity?

2. Write a report about the Amish, a group of Americans who choose to live without electricity, automobiles, and other modern conveniences.

3. Write about your personal experience doing without electricity or hot and cold running water. Are these necessities?

B. Since 1994, many American families have participated in TV Turn Off, a week in April when they agree to avoid watching any television. Do research on the Internet to find out more about TV Turn Off Week. Write an essay giving reasons why this is a good idea or a bad idea. Use a graphic organizer such as this to help you organize your ideas:

TV TURN OFF WEEK	
Plus +	Minus –

Books to Read

Rachel Carson, *Silent Spring*—This best-selling book published in 1962 was one of the first to warn of environmental problems and the dangers of chemical pollution.

Al Gore, *Earth in the Balance: Ecology and the Human Spirit*—In this best seller, the former vice president calls on Americans to rethink their relationship with the environment or face terrible consequences.

Aldo Leopold, *A Sand County Almanac (Outdoor Essays & Reflections)*—A description of the great diversity and natural beauty of the United States—the mountains, prairies, deserts, and coastlines—and the need to protect our environment.

Eric Schlosser, *Fast Food Nation: The Dark Side of the All-American Meal*—A disturbing look at the fast-food industry in the United States and how it affects American food production, health, and popular culture.

Walt Whitman, *Leaves of Grass* (especially the poem "I Hear America Singing")— First published in 1885, this book of poetry contains classic poems about the United States and its culture.

Movies to See

Erin Brockovitch—An unemployed single mother becomes a legal assistant and almost single-handedly brings down a California power company accused of polluting a city's water supply.

A River Runs through It—The story of two fly-fishing sons of a Presbyterian minister—one educated, one rebellious—growing up in rural Montana.

Silkwood—The story of Karen Silkwood, a nuclear reactor worker who may have been murdered to prevent her exposing wrongdoing at the power plant.

The Truman Show—An insurance salesman discovers that his entire life is a TV show.

Witness—When a young Amish boy is the only witness to a murder, a policeman must go into hiding in Amish country to protect him until the trial.

Jobs on the New York Wall Street Stock Exchange are fast-track and high-pressure.

THE WORLD OF AMERICAN BUSINESS

The business of America is business.
President Calvin Coolidge (1872–1933)

BEFORE YOU READ

Preview Vocabulary

A. **Here are some key AWL words in Chapter 6. Look at their definitions. Put a check next to the words you already know.**

_____ 1. *administrative* relating to activities involved in managing a company or institution

_____ 2. *aid* help or advice given to someone who needs it

_____ 3. *alternative* something you can choose instead of something else

_____ 4. *corporations* big companies

_____ 5. *cycles* events that happen again and again

_____ 6. *flexible* can be changed easily

_____ 7. *innovation* a new idea or invention

_____ 8. *policy* an official way of doing something

_____ 9. *submitting* agreeing to obey

_____ 10. *theoretically* supposed to be true

B. Work with a partner. Read these sentences from the chapter. Fill in the blanks with words from the preceding list.

1. _____, if one business tries to take unfair advantage of its customers, it will lose to a competing business which treats its customers more fairly.

2. Gaining success and status through competition is often seen as the American _____ to systems where social rank is based on family background.

3. Entrepreneurs often began as common people themselves; without the _____ of inherited social title or inherited money, they became "self-made" millionaires.

4. A final characteristic of entrepreneurs which appeals to most Americans is their strong dislike of _____ to higher authority.

5. Small businesses are also an important source of creativity and _____ in the American marketplace, particularly in the field of technology.

6. Arianna Huffington details how CEOs took huge sums of money from the _____ they were managing and spent it on themselves.

7. Americans' respect for their business institutions rises and falls in _____, going back to the Industrial Revolution of the 1800s.

8. Traditionally, Republicans have been in favor of a laissez-faire, or hands-off _____, and Democrats have favored more regulations and safeguards.

9. Today, women hold about one-half of the professional specialty, executive, _____, and managerial occupations in the United States.

10. Some businesses provide _____ working hours and day care centers in the building, but most do not.

Preview Content

A. Read the questions and discuss them with your classmates.

1. Read the quotation by President Calvin Coolidge at the beginning of the chapter. What do you think the quotation means? Do you agree? Why is business so important to Americans?

2. What does it mean to "go from rags to riches"?

3. What is an entrepreneur?

4. What are the advantages and disadvantages of starting and running your own business? Write some ideas in the chart.

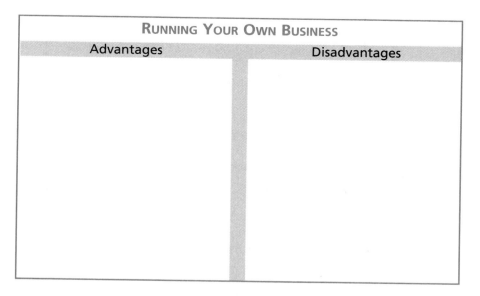

RUNNING YOUR OWN BUSINESS	
Advantages	Disadvantages

B. Preview the chapter by reading the headings and looking at the illustrations. Predict what the chapter is about. Put a check by the ideas you predict will be discussed in the chapter.

_____ the natural resources of the United States

_____ what Alexis de Tocqueville said about business in the 1830s

_____ the role of entrepreneurs in American business

_____ how to start your own business

_____ what Americans think they can do to get rich

_____ what Americans think of corporate CEOs

_____ what products the United States exports to other countries

_____ how the American workforce is different from the way it was fifty years ago

The Characteristics of American Business

1   It is essential to become familiar with two words in order to understand the meaning of *business* to Americans: They are *private* and *profit*. Businesses are directly or indirectly owned and operated by private individuals (or groups of individuals) in order to make a profit. In contrast to these privately owned, for-profit businesses, there are also (1) public, government-owned-and-operated institutions, and (2) nonprofit organizations, such as churches, charities, and educational institutions. These organizations and institutions should not be confused with businesses.

How Business Competition Reinforces Other Values

2   The statement by President Coolidge in the 1920s, "The business of America is business," still points to an important truth today—that business institutions are at the heart of the American way of life. One reason for this is that Americans view business as being more firmly based on the ideal of competition than most other institutions in society. Since competition is seen as the major source of progress and prosperity by most Americans, competitive business institutions have traditionally been respected. Competition is seen not only as a value itself; it is also the means by which other basic American values such as individual freedom, equality of opportunity, and hard work are protected.

3   Competition protects the freedom of the individual by ensuring that there is no monopoly of power. In contrast to one all-powerful government, many businesses compete against each other for profits. Theoretically, if one business tries to take unfair advantage of its customers, it will lose to a competing business which treats its customers more fairly. Where many businesses compete for the customers, they cannot afford to give them inferior products or poor service.

4   A contrast is often made between business, which is competitive, and government, which is a monopoly. Because business is competitive, many Americans believe that it may be even more supportive of freedom than government, even though government leaders are elected by the people and business leaders are not. Many Americans believe that competition is vitally important in preserving freedom. So closely is competitive business associated with freedom in the minds of most Americans that the term *free enterprise*, rather than the term *capitalism*, is most often used to describe the American business system.

5   Competition in business is also believed to strengthen the ideal of equality of opportunity. Americans compare business competition to a race open to all, where success and status go to the swiftest[1] person, regardless of social class. Gaining success and status through competition is often seen as the American alternative to systems where social rank is based on family background. Business is therefore viewed as an expression of the idea of equality of opportunity rather than the aristocratic idea of inherited privilege.

6   Business competition is also seen by most Americans as encouraging hard work. If two businesspeople are competing against each other, the one who works harder is

---

[1] **swiftest:** the quickest and fastest

likely to win. The one who spends less time and effort is likely to lose. Because businesspeople must continually compete against each other, they must develop the habit of hard work in order not to fail.

7   Americans are aware that business institutions often do not live up to the ideals of competition and the support of freedom, equality of opportunity, and hard work. Americans sometimes distrust the motives of businesspeople, believing that they are capable of putting profit before product safety or a cleaner environment. Therefore, most Americans believe businesses need some government regulation, although they may disagree on how much. Even with these flaws,[2] however, most Americans believe that business comes closer than other institutions to encouraging competition and other basic values in daily practice.

The Dream of Getting Rich

8   There is a second reason why business institutions have traditionally received respect in the United States. One aspect of the great American Dream is to rise from poverty or modest wealth to great wealth. In the United States, this has usually been accomplished through successful business careers. All of the great private fortunes in the nation were built by people who were successful in business, many of whom started life with very little. Careers in business still offer the best opportunity for the ambitious individual to become wealthy.

Mar-a-Lago, Trump's palacial residence and club in Palm Beach, Florida

9   Alexis de Tocqueville observed the great attractiveness of business careers for Americans as early as the 1830s. He wrote that Americans strongly preferred business to farming because business offered the opportunity to get rich more quickly. Even those who were farmers were possessed with a strong business spirit. They often ran small businesses to add to the money they made from farming. Tocqueville also noticed that American farmers were often more interested in buying and selling land for a profit than in farming it. Thus, even in Tocqueville's day when most Americans were still farmers, the seeds of a business civilization had already been planted.

10   Not only is business seen as the easiest way for individuals to become rich, it is also seen as benefiting the entire nation. Through competition, more people gain wealth. By contrast, a government-run system of production and distribution of goods is seen as inferior. It is distrusted because of the monopoly of power held by the government, which eliminates competition. However, there is a great deal of debate about the role of the government in providing services such as health care. The United States is one of the few industrialized countries in the world that does not have universal health care guaranteed and managed by the government, but some people believe that should change.

---

[2] **flaws:** mistakes, marks, or defects

The Entrepreneur as Business Hero

11   Because of the many beliefs that connect business to the wealth and the traditional values of the United States, people who are successful in business have sometimes become heroes to the American people. Entrepreneurs provide examples of traditional American values in their purest form for a number of reasons. The first reason is that they succeed in building something great out of nothing. The people who, more than 100 years ago, built up the nation's great industries, such as steel, railroads, and oil refining, were usually entrepreneurs. They started with very little money or power and ended up as the heads of huge companies that earned enormous fortunes.

12   The fact that these early entrepreneurs built great industries out of very little made them seem to millions of Americans like the heroes of the early frontier days, who went into the vast wilderness of the United States and turned forests into farms, villages, and small cities. The entrepreneur, like the earlier hero of the frontier, was seen as a rugged individualist.

13   Entrepreneurs often began as common people themselves; without the aid of inherited social title or inherited money, they became "self-made" millionaires. They were thus perfect examples of the American idea of equality of opportunity in action.

14   The strong influence of the success stories of the early entrepreneurs can be found in the great popularity of the novels of Horatio Alger, which were published in late-nineteenth- and early-twentieth-century America. About 17 million copies of these books were sold to the American public. The central theme of Alger's novels is that in the United States a poor city boy or a poor farm boy can become a wealthy and successful businessman if he works hard and relies on himself rather than others. This is because the United States is a land of equality of opportunity where everyone has a chance to succeed.

15   In Alger's first published novel, *Ragged Dick*, a poor city boy who shines shoes for a living becomes Richard Hunter, a successful and wealthy businessman. The hero rises "from rags to riches" and fulfills the American Dream. Dick succeeds only partly because he lives in a land of equality of opportunity. His success is also due to the fact that he practices the American virtues of self-reliance and hard work. According to Alger, Dick "knew that he had only himself to depend upon, and he determined to make the most of himself . . . which is the secret of success in nine cases out of ten." Dick was also a hardworking shoe-shine boy, "energetic and on the alert for business." This quality marked him for success, explained Alger, because in all professions, "energy and industry are rewarded."

16   Although few Americans today read Horatio Alger's stories, they continue to be inspired by the idea of earning wealth and success as entrepreneurs who "make it on their own." A final characteristic of entrepreneurs which appeals to most Americans is their strong dislike of submitting to higher authority. Throughout their history Americans have admired entrepreneurs who conduct their business and their lives without taking orders from anyone above them. Americans have great respect for those who can say, "I am my own boss." More than half of all American workers dream of one day having their own businesses and being their own boss.

17   In the 1990s, there were thousands of individuals who started companies to do business on the Internet. For a time, some of these "dot-com" start-up businesses were

wildly successful. Millions of dollars of venture capital[3] poured into new technology companies because of their promise, rather than their performance. Stock prices shot up suddenly and young millionaires were created overnight. And then the dot-com bubble burst. Most of these companies were not yet making a profit, and they were heavily in debt. When interest rates rose, they were not able to manage their debt. Investors quickly withdrew their support. Stock prices fell as fast as they had risen, and fortunes made overnight were lost as quickly. Only a relatively few companies, such as Amazon.com and Yahoo.com, survived and became profitable large businesses.

18   Today, many Americans are still willing to take the financial risk that is necessary to start their own small business. Although half of new companies fail within the first

---

[3] **venture capital:** money that is lent to people so that they can start a new business

few years, small businesses still account for the majority of new jobs created in the modern American economy. These companies and their entrepreneur leaders play an important role in the United States. More than half of all American workers are employed in businesses with fewer than 100 employees. Small businesses are also an important source of creativity and innovation in the American marketplace, particularly in the field of technology. Inspired by entrepreneur heroes like Steven Jobs, who started Apple Computer in his garage; Bill Gates, who developed Microsoft into a global giant; and Ross Perot, a self-made billionaire who ran for president as an Independent, risk-taking entrepreneurs still launch[4] their businesses with high hopes of "making it big."

19   Richard Florida, author of *The Rise of the Creative Class*, believes that the role of innovation and creativity is rising in the United States today, and not just in the field of technology. Based on his analysis of census data, Florida estimates that nearly one-third of the American workforce now belong to "the creative class." They either create new ideas, technology, or content in fields such as science, education, design, the arts, and entertainment, or they engage in solving complex problems, in fields such as business, law, finance, and health care. As the map below shows, These creative workers tend to cluster on the east and west coasts, in high-tech centers, and near major research universities and institutions. They will likely have a strong, positive impact on the economic future of these areas.

CREATIVITY AT WORK

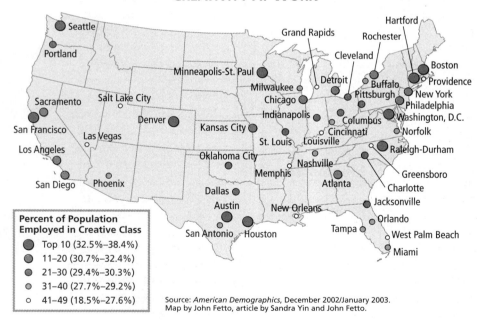

Source: *American Demographics*, December 2002/January 2003.
Map by John Fetto, article by Sandra Yin and John Fetto.

The Corporate CEO

20   The great entrepreneurs of the late nineteenth century built huge business organizations that needed new generations of business leaders to run them in the

---

4 launch: to start something new, such as an activity, plan, or profession

twentieth century. These leaders, sometimes referred to as "organizational men (or women)," are now the CEOs (chief executive officers) of American corporations. They acquire power and wealth, but they do not usually have the hero image of entrepreneurs because they are managing businesses that someone else started. Although most Americans admire the earning power of entrepreneurs and would probably not want to put a limit on their income, they are less generous in their view of CEOs. Indeed, many highly paid CEOs have come under severe attack for their multi-million-dollar-a-year salaries and their self-serving management decisions.

21   In her book *Pigs at the Trough: How Corporate Greed and Political Corruption Are Undermining America*, Arianna Huffington details how CEOs took huge sums of money from the corporations they were managing and spent it on themselves. She describes how John Rigas, the CEO of Adelphia, a large cable company, borrowed $3.1 billion from the company when it was in financial trouble and spent it outrageously:

> He spent $13 million to build a golf course in his backyard,
> $150 million to buy the Buffalo Sabres hockey team, $65 million to fund
> a venture capital group run by his son-in-law, thousands to maintain his
> three private jets, and $700,000 for a country-club membership.

22   Unfortunately, Rigas was not alone. For example, Bernie Ebbers, former WorldCom CEO, managed to get $408 million in loans while he hid more than $7 billion in company losses and destroyed the value of the stock. The early 2000s saw a number of other corporate scandals, when CEOs and other corporate officers received huge sums of money from companies that were failing. One of the worst examples was Enron, which left thousands of employees out of work and destroyed their retirement savings. What angered Americans was not only the outrageous greed of the corporate executives, but also their lies to the stockholders, their criminal mismanagement of the business, and their cruel treatment of their own employees.

23   Americans' respect for their business institutions rises and falls in cycles, going back to the Industrial Revolution of the 1800s. At times, business leaders are seen as greedy and corrupt villains; at other times they are hailed as heroes. In the late 1800s, for example, some business leaders were known as "robber barons" because of their corrupt practices and their disregard for others. This caused the government to pass laws to regulate business practices. When there are business scandals, the government responds with more rules and regulations. Traditionally, Republicans have been in favor of a *laissez-faire*, or hands-off policy, and Democrats have favored more regulation and safeguards. There have also been instances of business leaders saving important corporations. In the 1980s, Lee Iococca led Chrysler from near bankruptcy into profitability, saving thousands of jobs and helping the United States compete in the global market. In the 1990s, Gordon Bethune brought Continental Airlines out of bankruptcy into a position as one of the nation's strongest airlines, rated one of the best American companies to work for.

American Business in the Global Marketplace

24   Until the latter part of the 1900s, the operation of American business took place almost entirely in the United States. For example, in the 1950s, someone who

bought a car from General Motors Corporation knew that the entire car was built in the United States. By the 2000s, this was no longer true. American companies now manufacture or import automobile parts from around the world, and foreign companies manufacture many of their cars in the United States. Today, the money spent to buy a General Motors car might go to a number of other countries: to South Korea for labor; to Japan for advanced parts; to Germany for design and styling; to Taiwan, Singapore, and Japan for small parts; to Britain for advertising; and to Ireland, Barbados, or India for data processing. Some American companies have also started to outsource[5] their customer service and technical support services to countries such as India and Ireland. American business has become a part of a much larger global economy.

25   The United States is the single largest market in the world: a consumer society looking for goods from all over the world. It is also a country with products to sell, and much attention is being given to competing successfully in the global marketplace of the twenty-first century. The World Bank estimates that exports make up about one-quarter of the global economic output. The United States cannot compete with the abundant supply of cheap labor that exists in the countries of the Pacific Rim and Latin America, and therefore many U.S. companies are moving their manufacturing operations to Asia or Latin America. The number of manufacturing jobs in the United States has been declining ever since the late 1990s. Old, giant corporations such as IBM have laid off thousands of workers, downsizing to become more efficient and competitive. Some Americans are alarmed by the loss of these jobs; others see new opportunities. New small businesses provide temporary workers to companies that outsource, and individuals find new ways to do business over the Internet. American business now understands that it must be highly efficient if it is to compete successfully in the global marketplace.

Sallie Krawcheck, CEO of Smith Barney

The Changing American Workforce

26   Traditionally, white males have dominated American business—earning the highest salaries, achieving the greatest successes, and certainly wielding[6] most of the power. They have been the "bosses," setting the standards and the working conditions for the rest of the working population. But times are changing.

27   The percentage of women entering the workforce rose steadily from the 1960s through the 1980s, leveling off in the 1990s. Women now make up about one-half of the workforce. More and more women have reached middle-management positions, but very few (less than 10 or 15 percent) are the chief executives of large corporations. In the past, women were prevented from moving all the way to the top by what some call "the glass ceiling," a subtle[7] form of discrimination.[8] The men above them often did not offer women the opportunities they needed to advance in the company. However, women are now earning more undergraduate college degrees

---

[5] **outsource:** to hire employees in another country instead of using workers where the business is located
[6] **wielding:** having a lot of power or influence and being ready to use it
[7] **subtle:** not easy to notice or understand unless you pay careful attention
[8] **discrimination:** the practice of treating a person or a group differently in an unfair way

than men, and many are receiving MBAs (masters of business administration degrees) as well. Many of the young women now in the workforce feel that the "glass ceiling" no longer keeps them from advancing. Other women would argue that it is still there. Today, women hold about half of the professional specialty, executive, administrative, and managerial occupations in the United States. However, many women still do not receive as high salaries as men do.

Dr. Wang, a National Cancer Institute research scientist, examines a slide.

28   Many jobs in corporate America are "fast-track," requiring that both women and men put their job first and their family second. Studies show that an employee perceived to be on the "mommy track" or the "daddy track" will not earn as much money or be given as much responsibility as the one willing to sacrifice[9] time at home for time at the office. Some families are now beginning to question whether success is really worth the price. Some businesses provide flexible working hours and day care centers in the building, but most do not. A number of women are choosing to drop out of the workforce and stay home with their children. Some find work they can do at home—working on a computer linked to their office (*telecommuting*), for example. Interestingly, more than twice as many women as men now try their hand at starting their own small business, following the dream of the entrepreneur. Many of these small businesses are operated out of their own homes.

29   One of the worst problems facing American women is that overall they earn about seventy-eight cents for every dollar earned by American men. In spite of the ideal of equality of opportunity, women sometimes earn less money than men do for the same work. Minorities often face similar discrimination in the workplace, earning less money than white workers with similar jobs would earn.

30   However, in the future, the white American male may no longer have advantages over other workers. The recent arrival of millions of new immigrants is changing the makeup of the American workforce. Traditionally, within ten or twenty years of their arrival, immigrants (or their children) will earn as much as or more money than people born in the United States who are of similar age, education level, and skills. Some businesses now provide English as a Second Language courses at the workplace, and others conduct *diversity training* to promote understanding among the different racial and ethnic groups who now work together. Many believe that this multicultural workforce will ultimately help the United States compete in the global marketplace, since American workers will represent a microcosm[10] of the world.

31   Although the institution of American business has undergone enormous changes in recent decades, it has remained one of the most important institutions in the United States. In many ways, the business of America is still business.

---

[9] **sacrifice:** to stop having something you like in order to get something more important
[10] **microcosm:** a small group or society that has the same qualities as a much larger one

Understand Main Ideas

Check the predictions you made on page 117 before reading the chapter. Look at the headings in the chapter and work with a partner to complete the outline of the main ideas.

A. The Characteristics of American Business: private, for-profit

B. How Business Competition Reinforces Other Values

    1. Competition protects the freedom of individual _____

    2. Competition strengthens _____

    3. Business competition encourages _____

C. The Dream of Getting Rich

    1. Careers in business offer _____

    2. Americans distrust _____

D. The Entrepreneur as Business Hero

    1. Entrepreneurs are respected because _____

    2. Americans were influenced by Horatio Alger's _____

    3. Americans respect individuals who build businesses from the beginning but not

    _____

    4. Many Americans are still willing to _____

E. The Corporate CEO

    1. CEOs are not self-made entrepreneurs _____

    2. Americans have lost respect for CEOs because _____

F. American Business in _____

    1. In the 1900s _____

    2. In the 2000s _____

G. _____

    1. More and more women are in management positions

    2. Americans are now beginning to question _____

    3. Women still earn _____

Understand Details

Write _T_ if the statement is true and _F_ if it is false according to the information in the chapter.

_____ 1. Most American businesses are directly or indirectly owned by the government.

_____ 2. Most Americans believe that business supports ideals and values which are important to the country.

_____ 3. Americans believe that competition among businesses is good for the economy but it does little to protect the freedom of the individual.

_____ 4. To succeed in American business, Americans believe that family background and social position are more important than anything, including hard work.

_____ 5. Most Americans believe that success in business offers the best chance to fulfill the dream of being wealthy.

_____ 6. The entrepreneur may be admired since he or she started a successful business from practically nothing.

_____ 7. Women now make up about half of the workforce and are CEOs of about half of the large corporations in the United States.

_____ 8. In the global economy, American businesses have become more competitive by hiring many new workers and enlarging their companies.

_____ 9. CEOs have been criticized for spending large amounts of company money on themselves.

_____ 10. Men and women who put their families first may have difficulty getting top managerial jobs in the United States.

Improve Your Reading Skills: Scanning

Scan the chapter to look for these names. Then identify each person with a short phrase.

EXAMPLE: Alexis de Tocqueville <u>observed Americans' attraction to</u>

<u>business in the 1830s</u>

1. Calvin Coolidge _____

2. Arianna Huffington _____

3. Bill Gates _____

4. Lee Iococca _____

5. Bernie Ebbers _____

6. Ross Perot _____

7. John Rigas _____

8. Horatio Alger _____

9. Gordon Bethune _____

10. Steven Jobs _____

11. Richard Hunter _____

12. Sallie Krawcheck _____

Talk About It

Work in small groups and choose one or more of these topics to discuss.

1. What qualities should a good businessperson have in order to be successful? Are these the same personal qualities that you would like your own boss to have?

2. How do you find out about job openings in your country? How important are family and personal connections?

3. Who do you admire more: people who start their own business from nothing, or those who save a big corporation that is in trouble? Why?

4. Would you want to have a fast-track job? What sacrifices would you be willing to make in order to be really successful?

Build Your Vocabulary

Same or Different Read these sentences, which contain AWL words in bold. Look at the list of words after each sentence. Write the letter of the one word that has a different or opposite meaning from the boldfaced word.

_____ 1. A government-run system of production and **distribution** of goods is seen as inferior.
   a. sharing   b. giving   c. supplying   d. collecting

_____ 2. The people who, more than 100 years ago, built up the nation's great industries, such as steel, railroads, and oil **refining**, were usually entrepreneurs.
   a. purifying   b. selling   c. cleaning   d. improving

_____ 3. The strong influence of the success stories of the early entrepreneurs can be found in the great popularity of the novels of Horatio Alger, which were **published** in late-nineteenth and early-twentieth-century America.

   a. produced   b. printed   c. hidden   d. created

_____ 4. There have also been **instances** of business leaders saving important corporations.

   a. strategies   b. examples   c. occasions   d. occurrences

_____ 5. The World Bank estimates that exports make up about one-quarter of the global economic **output**.

   a. production   b. yield   c. goods   d. imports

_____ 6. New small businesses provide **temporary** workers to companies that are outsourcing, and individuals find new ways to do business over the Internet.

   a. permanent   b. passing   c. limited   d. short-term

_____ 7. Today, women make up about one-half of high-paying executive, administrative, and managerial **occupations**.

   a. employers   b. jobs   c. professions   d. employment

_____ 8. A number of women are choosing to drop out of the workforce and stay home with their children or to find work they can do at home—working on a computer **linked** to their office, for example.

   a. connected   b. tied   c. separated   d. coupled

_____ 9. One of the worst problems facing American women is that **overall** they earn about seventy-eight cents for every dollar earned by American men.

   a. on average   b. considering everything   c. generally   d. individually

_____ 10. Many believe that this multicultural workforce will **ultimately** help the United States compete in the global marketplace.

   a. finally   b. firstly   c. lastly   d. eventually

More AWL Words Test your knowledge of these additional AWL words in the reading by doing the crossword puzzle below. (The clues are on the next page.)

acquire	creative	ensure	regulation	status
aware	decline	financial	reinforce	style
benefit	energy	global	rely	team
capable	enormous	guarantee	source	theme
contrast				

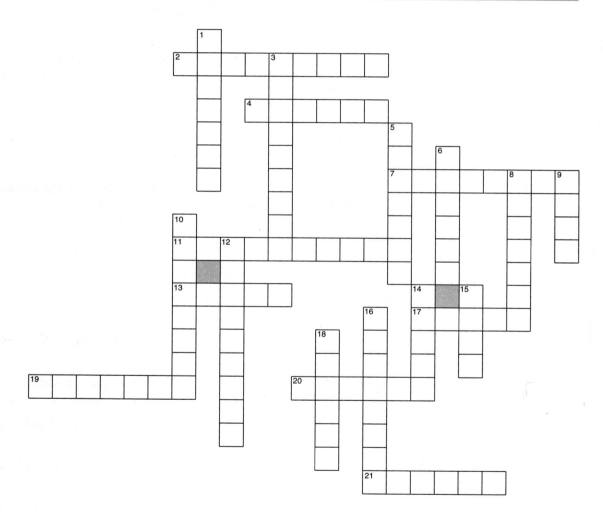

Across

2. to support an idea
4. to make certain that something will happen
7. a difference between things that are compared
11. an official rule or order
13. understanding what is happening
17. a main idea in a piece of writing
19. having the skills needed to do something
20. something that supplies information
21. social or professional position

Down

1. something that improves your life
3. relating to money
5. to decrease in quantity or importance
6. physical and mental strength
8. to buy or obtain something
9. a group of people who play a game or sport together
10. producing or using new ideas
12. a formal written promise that something will be done or will happen
14. a particular way of doing something
15. to depend on
16. extremely large
18. affecting the whole world

EXPAND YOUR KNOWLEDGE

Ask Yourself/Ask Americans

Do you agree or disagree with each of the statements below? Put a check under the number that indicates how you feel.

+**2** = Strongly agree

+**1** = Agree

 0 = No opinion

−**1** = Disagree

−**2** = Strongly disagree

	+2	+1	0	−1	−2
1. I admire a person who is his or her own boss more than someone who must answer to others.	___	___	___	___	___
2. I would like to own my own business.	___	___	___	___	___
3. I think we should work to live, not live to work.	___	___	___	___	___
4. A teacher has more prestige than a businessperson.	___	___	___	___	___
5. Companies should offer loyal employees lifetime employment.	___	___	___	___	___
6. Corporate CEOs deserve as much money as they can get.	___	___	___	___	___

(continued)

| | +2 | +1 | 0 | –1 | –2 |

7. The place where I live is more important to me than where I work.   ___ ___ ___ ___ ___

8. I would take a job I liked for less pay over a job I didn't like for more pay.   ___ ___ ___ ___ ___

9. I would work on an assembly line in a factory if the pay were good.   ___ ___ ___ ___ ___

10. All things considered, a government-run system is better for a country and its people than capitalism.   ___ ___ ___ ___ ___

Ask several Americans these questions, if possible. If there are no Americans available, ask people from other countries.

People Watching

Who works in the United States? What ages? Men, women, teenagers, the elderly? What kind of jobs do they do? To answer these questions, if you are in the United States, look around you in various businesses open to the public: restaurants, banks, stores, drugstores, supermarkets, clubs, dry cleaners, doctors' offices, theaters, and so on. If you are near a university, check to see who is working in the library and the cafeteria. (If you are not in the United States, you may gather information from Americans you know, or you can observe people in your country.)

Observe people working in at least ten different places and record your results in this chart.

Kind of Job	Gender of Worker	Age of Worker	Other Observations
1.			
2.			
3.			
4.			
5.			
6.			
7.			
8.			
9.			
10.			

Proverbs and Sayings

Ask Americans to explain these proverbs and sayings to you. Then ask them for other examples of sayings about competition, winning, or success.

1. When the going gets tough, the tough get going.
2. It's every man for himself.
3. May the best man/woman win.
4. To the winner belong the spoils.
5. It's a dog-eat-dog world.
6. Take care of number one.

Small-Group Discussion

Read the following explanation about how different cultures structure time, and then discuss the questions with members of your small group. When you have finished, report your group's findings to the rest of the class.

Edward T. Hall has described two basic types of cultures, with regard to the ways those cultures deal with time. He calls these "monochronic" and "polychronic" cultures. In monochronic cultures people do one thing at a time. In polychronic cultures people do many things at a time. For example, in a monochronic culture, when someone has a business appointment, that person expects to have the complete attention of the other party until the appointment has ended. On the other hand, in a polychronic culture, a person who has a business appointment expects there to be many others waiting and being dealt with at one time, sometimes both in person and on the phone.

1. How are activities scheduled in your country?
2. Is your culture monochronic or polychronic?
3. Which best describes the United States?
4. Which would best describe the following situations?
   a. You arrive at the airport an hour before your flight to find that there are large crowds pushing their way to the counter. Whoever pushes hardest gets to the front and gets waited on. The ticket agent behind the counter serves several people at once, focusing attention on the one who has made himself or herself most noticed.
   b. The doctor has told you that he will meet you at the hospital at 10:00 A.M. to take care of a minor problem. You have difficulty finding transportation, but finally arrive at 10:45. The doctor is seeing another patient and sends word that he will not be able to see you now until he can "squeeze you in" around his other appointments. You will probably have to wait until late afternoon.
5. What other monochronic or polychronic situations can you think of?

Think, Pair, Share

The *Fortune* magazine website had a quiz, "Could You Make It to CEO?" based on *The Secret Handshake: Mastering the Politics of the Business Inner Circle*, by Kathleen Kelly Reardon, PhD.

Read the two questions, choose your answers, and then share them with a partner. Then read the correct responses, according to *Fortune*, at the bottom of the page.

1. You've come up with a great idea for cutting costs, boosting efficiency, or improving customer satisfaction, but you've described it to your boss, and she just doesn't seem interested in pursuing it. You:

   _____ a. Figure that she must know something you don't about why it isn't practical, so forget about trying to make your idea a reality.

   _____ b. Tell everyone who will listen, especially your boss's boss, about how great your idea is and how shortsighted your boss is for not realizing it.

   _____ c. Reexamine your idea in light of how it could help both the company and your boss achieve their respective goals. Then propose it again, being careful to address any possible doubts or objections she may raise.

2. You're a middle manager now, but you hope someday to be CEO. Your natural inclination is to base your decisions on the consensus of the group. In order to prepare yourself to move up, you:

   _____ a. Take a close look at the leadership styles of the most powerful people in the organization, then try insofar as possible to adapt your style to match theirs.

   _____ b. Go with your true strength and keep leading by consensus and collaboration, doing more listening than talking and rarely giving a direct order to anyone.

   _____ c. Force yourself to adopt a more commanding leadership style, giving orders to the people under you, even though you find this very uncomfortable.

🪐 Use the Internet

Work with a partner. Choose one activity and do research on the Internet.

A. One of the most well-known and colorful businessmen in the United States is Donald Trump. According to the Gallup Organization, 98 percent of Americans have heard of him. In contrast to many other super-rich businesspeople, "The Donald" loves attention, and his personal life is often featured in entertainment magazines. He is a billionaire real estate developer who likes to name his casinos, golf courses, and skyscraper office and apartment buildings after himself, "so people will know that I own them." In 2003, he began hosting a reality TV show called *The Apprentice*. Each week, two teams competed for the ultimate prize: being the CEO of a Trump organization with an annual salary of $250,000.

Working in small groups, imagine that you are reporters for a newspaper or magazine. If you interviewed Donald Trump, what would you ask him about his businesses and his wealthy lifestyle? Write your questions down, and then look on the Internet to find the answers.

B. **Look for information about one of these super-rich business leaders.**

Bill Gates
Ted Turner
Martha Stewart
Liewellyn H. Rockwell
Oprah Winfrey
Roland Hernandez
Linda G. Alvarado
Robert Johnson

Small-Group Project

Work in a group to create a small business.

- Decide on a name and describe what business the company will conduct.
- Choose a slogan for your business.
- List what the qualifications of the employees will be and what benefits the company will offer.
- Make up an advertisement for the business, and if possible, videotape it.
- Present your company to the rest of the class.

A. Choose one of the following topics. Then write a short composition about it.

1. Compare the way American businesses operate with the way businesses operate in your country. For example, compare a typical transaction at a shop. How do the activities differ? Consider these points:
   a. When the employees work
   b. Who the employees are and how long they have worked there
   c. Whether the shopkeeper waits on one person or several people at a time
   d. If the customer bargains or there is a set price
   e. If the employees know the customers
   f. The relationship between the employees and their employer

2. Most businesses in America require those applying for a job to submit a résumé, a summary of their work experience, education, and qualifications. Write a résumé for a job that you would like to have. Describe the position you want, and then write a résumé to convince an employer to hire you. As you write, consider the following advice from Jerrold G. Simon, EdD, a psychologist and career development specialist at Harvard Business School, who advises people to "sell themselves" in their résumé:

   The most qualified people don't always get the job. It goes to the person who presents himself more persuasively in person and on paper. So don't just list where you were and what you did. This is your chance to tell how well you did. Were you the best salesman? Did you cut operating costs? Give numbers, statistics, percentages, and increases in sales or profits.

B. In order to be a contestant on the television show *The Apprentice*, people had to do a ten-minute video and fill out an application. Choose three of the questions they had to answer and write a paragraph answer for each.

1. How would your co-workers describe you?

2. Describe a major event or issue that has affected your life.

3. Tell us an embarrassing story about yourself.

4. Where do you see yourself five years from now?

5. Why are you successful in business?

6. Why do you believe you could ultimately be "The Apprentice"?

Books to Read

Horatio Alger, *Ragged Dick or, Street Life in New York with the Boot Blacks*—The classic story of "rags to riches" about a young boy who works hard and eventually becomes a middle-class gentleman.

F. Scott Fitzgerald, "The Diamond as Big as the Ritz"—A short story set in the 1920s about the corrupting effect of wealth.

Arianna Huffington, *Pigs at the Trough: How Corporate Greed and Political Corruption Are Undermining America*—A best-selling account of how corporate CEOs are mismanaging American businesses and taking huge sums of money for personal use.

Spencer Johnson, *Who Moved My Cheese: An Amazing Way to Deal with Change in Your Work and in Your Life*—A best-seller about how to cope with a changing workplace.

Donald Trump, *Trump: The Art of the Deal*—Trump's best-selling account of his business dealings—his successes and failures.

Movies to See

Class Action—A lawyer who is suing an auto company over a safety defect faces his daughter, who is the attorney representing the company.

Mr. Mom—A comedy about a husband who loses his job and decides to stay home with his children while his wife pursues a career in advertising.

9 to 5—A comedy about three women who are tired of being treated badly by their boss and decide to capture him and make changes at their workplace.

Start-up.com—A documentary look at the American Dream of two college friends who start a promising Internet company in the 1990s.

Wall Street—A young, impatient stockbroker willing to do anything to get to the top discovers that every dream has a price.

Americans gather on the mall to celebrate Earth Day.

GOVERNMENT AND POLITICS IN THE UNITED STATES

A wise and frugal Government shall restrain men from injuring one another, [and] shall leave them otherwise free to regulate their own pursuits of industry and improvements.

Thomas Jefferson (1743–1826)

BEFORE YOU READ

Preview Vocabulary

A. **Read the following sentences from the chapter and notice the words in italics. These key AWL words will help you understand the chapter reading. Use context clues to help you figure out the meanings. Then choose which definition is best for the italicized word.**

_____ 1. The way in which the national government is organized in the U.S. Constitution provides an excellent *illustration* of the American suspicion of governmental power.

    a. example that shows the truth very clearly
    b. argument against an idea

_____ 2. The judicial branch both *interprets* the law and determines whether the law is constitutional—that is, whether the law is permitted under the U.S. Constitution.

    a. explains
    b. rejects

_____ 3. The Senate has certain powers over foreign treaties and *military* actions.

   a. relating to legislative matters
   b. relating to war

_____ 4. This requires the president to have "the advice and *consent* of the Senate" before taking certain action on the international front.

   a. permission to do something
   b. a careful plan for action

_____ 5. The Bill of Rights guarantees the right of a fair criminal *procedure* for those accused of breaking laws.

   a. punishment
   b. method

_____ 6. The recount found an even smaller *margin*, fewer than 1,000 votes separating the two candidates.

   a. difference (in the number of votes)
   b. problem with the voting process

_____ 7. After a *series* of legal challenges, the U.S. Supreme Court decided about a month after the election that the Florida state legislature had a right to stop recounting the ballots and certify the electoral votes.

   a. events that are related and have a particular result
   b. events that break the law and have consequences

_____ 8. The Great *Depression* of the 1930s greatly weakened the businessperson's position as the American ideal of the free individual, and big business lost respect.

   a. a time when there was not much business activity and many people had no jobs
   b. a time when there was much corruption and greed among business leaders

_____ 9. The widespread unemployment and other economic hardships of the Depression gave rise to the *assumption* that individuals could not be expected to rely solely on themselves in providing for their economic security.

   a. promise that something will happen in the future
   b. belief (that you think is true although you have no proof)

_____ 10. Still, it is individuals, their rights, their interests, and their ambitions, not those of the nation as a whole, that are the *focus* of attention.

   a. emphasis
   b. difficulty

B. There are four AWL words in the quotation by Thomas Jefferson at the beginning of the chapter. Read the quotation and find the words with the following meanings. Write each word next to its meaning.

_____ 1. the act of trying to get something

_____ 2. prevent someone from doing something

_____ 3. to control an activity by rules

_____ 4. hurting

Preview Content

A. Before you read, preview the chapter by looking at the illustrations and reading the headings and the captions under the pictures. Work with a partner and answer these questions.

1. Do you agree with the quotation by Thomas Jefferson? Paraphrase (rewrite) the quotation in your own words.

2. In the United States, who has more power, the president or Congress? Why do you think so?

3. What are the two major political parties in the United States? What is the main difference in their beliefs?

B. Make a graphic organizer about government. Write the word _government_ in the center of a piece of paper. Then draw lines out from the center, as you did on page 22. Write all the things you think a government should do for its people.

C. Predict five topics that will be discussed in this chapter. Write your predictions here.

1. _____

2. _____

3. _____

4. _____

5. _____

A Suspicion of Strong Government

1 The ideal of the free individual has had a profound effect on the way Americans view their government. Traditionally, there has been a deep suspicion that government is the natural enemy of freedom, even if it is elected by the people. The bigger and stronger the government becomes, the more dangerous many Americans believe it is to their individual freedom.

2 This suspicion of strong government goes back to the men who led the American Revolution in 1776. These men believed the government of Great Britain wanted to discourage the freedom and economic opportunities of the American colonists by excessive taxes and other measures which would ultimately benefit the British aristocracy and monarchy. Thomas Paine, the famous revolutionary writer, expressed the view of other American revolutionists when he said, "Government even in its best state is but a necessary evil; in its worst state, an intolerable[1] one."

The Organization of the American Government

3 The way in which the national government is organized in the U.S. Constitution provides an excellent illustration of the American suspicion of governmental power. The provisions of the Constitution are more concerned with keeping the government from doing evil than with enabling it to do good. The national government, for example, is divided into three separate branches. This division of governmental power is based on the belief that if any one part or branch of government has all, or even most of the power, it will become a threat to the freedom of individual citizens.

4 The legislative or lawmaking branch of the government is called the *Congress*. Congress has two houses—the *Senate*, with two senators from each state regardless of the size of its population, and the *House of Representatives*, consisting of a total of 435 representatives divided among the fifty states by population. (In the House, states with large populations have more representatives than states with small populations, while in the Senate, each state has equal representation.) The *president*, or chief executive, heads the executive branch, which has responsibility to carry out the laws. The *Supreme Court* and lower national

The Signing of the Declaration of Independence, *a painting by John Trumbull*

---

[1] intolerable: too difficult, bad, or annoying to accept or deal with

courts make up the judicial branch. The judicial branch settles disputes about the exact meaning of the law through court cases. It both interprets the law and determines whether the law is *constitutional*—that is, whether the law is permitted under the U.S. Constitution.

5   If any one of the three branches starts to abuse[2] its power, the other two may join together to stop it, through a system of *checks and balances*. The Constitution is most careful in balancing the powers of the legislative and executive branches of the government because these two (Congress and the president) are the most powerful of the three branches. In almost every important area of governmental activity, such as the power to make laws, to declare war, or to conclude treaties with foreign countries, the Constitution gives each of these two branches enough power to prevent the other from acting on its own.

6   Observers from other countries are often confused by the American system. The national government may seem to speak with two conflicting voices, that of the president and that of Congress. For example, a treaty with a foreign government signed by the president dies if the Senate refuses to *ratify* it—that is, if the Senate doesn't vote to accept it. The Senate has certain powers over foreign treaties and military actions. This requires the president to have "the advice and consent of the Senate" before taking certain action on the international front.

7   On the other hand, the president may prevent a bill passed by Congress from becoming law. When both houses of Congress have agreed on a piece of legislation or a resolution, it is sent to the president. The president has ten days to act, not counting Sundays. At that point, there are four possibilities:
1. The president agrees with the bill, signs it, and it becomes law.
2. The president disagrees with the bill, *vetoes* it, and sends it back to the Congress with his reasons for refusing to sign it. If two-thirds of both the House and the Senate vote to override the president's veto, the bill becomes law.
3. The president may take no action and after ten days (not counting Sundays), the bill becomes law without his signature.
4. If the Congress adjourns[3] before the ten-day period is over, and the president has neither signed nor vetoed the bill, it is defeated. This is called a *pocket veto*. Presidents sometimes do this with bills they do not like but do not want to go on record as having vetoed.

8   Although the American system of divided governmental power strikes many observers as inefficient and even disorganized, most Americans still strongly believe in it for two reasons: (1) It has been able to meet the challenges of the past, and (2) it gives strong protection to individual freedoms.

9   In addition to dividing government powers into three branches, the Constitution includes a *Bill of Rights* which is designed to protect specific individual rights and freedoms from government interference. Some of the guarantees in the Bill of Rights concern the freedom of expression. The government may not interfere with an individual's freedom of speech or freedom of religious worship. The Bill of Rights also guarantees the right of a fair criminal procedure for those accused of breaking laws. Thus, the Bill of Rights is another statement of the American belief in the importance of individual freedom.

---

[2] **abuse:** to deliberately use power or authority for the wrong purpose
[3] **adjourns:** stops meeting for a short time

The Election of the President and the Congress

10   The president and both houses of Congress have almost complete political independence from each other because they are all chosen in separate elections. For example, the election of the Congress does not determine who will be elected president, and the presidential election does not determine who will be elected to either house of Congress. It is quite possible in the American system to have the leader of one political party win the presidency while the other major political party wins most of the seats in Congress. It is also important to remember that the elections of the members of the two houses of Congress are separate from each other. Thus, the Republicans may control one house, while the Democrats may control the other. During the late 1900s, while most of the presidents were Republican, the Democrats often controlled one or both of the houses of Congress. In 1994, the reverse happened: While Bill Clinton, a Democrat, was president, the Republicans won control of both the House of Representatives and the Senate. Then in the early 2000s, for a time the Republican Party controlled the presidency (George W. Bush) and both houses of Congress.

11   In order to understand what is happening in Washington, it is important to know not only the party of the president, but also which parties control the House and the Senate. Because both the House of Representatives and the Senate must agree on all legislation before it goes to the president, legislation may pass one house but be blocked in the other. Furthermore, the party in control of the House or Senate has the potential of changing every two years. Members of the House of Representatives are elected for two-year terms, while senators serve six-year terms. The Senate terms are staggered[4] so that only one-third of the senators run for re-election each time the House elections are held, every two years.

12   Presidential elections are held every four years, on the first Tuesday in November. When the Constitution was written, the founding fathers had a disagreement about how the president should be elected. Some did not want the members of Congress to choose the president, and others were afraid to leave the choice entirely to the voters. The result was a compromise—the electoral college, a system for indirectly electing the president. The system persists today. In presidential elections, people are actually voting for representatives called *electors*, and it is these electors who officially choose the president. With the electoral college system, the winner of the plurality[5] (the highest number) of each state's popular votes gets all of that state's electoral votes. The number of each state's electoral votes is equal to the total number of their representatives in the House and the Senate. Though the number of electoral votes varies according to each state's population, it is still possible for a person to be elected president without getting the highest number of the popular, or individual, votes.

13   Although Americans were aware of the electoral college system, the average voter did not give it much thought until the election of 2000. There had been only three previous instances of presidents ever losing the popular vote but winning the electoral vote, and it seemed a remote possibility. The last time it had happened was in 1888, when Benjamin Harrison won the presidency even though Grover Cleveland had the

---

[4] **staggered:** arranged so that their terms of office (time serving as a senator or representative) do not all begin and end at the same time

[5] **plurality:** the number of votes received by the winning person in an election where there are three or more people trying to be elected

2000 ELECTORAL VOTE DISTRIBUTION

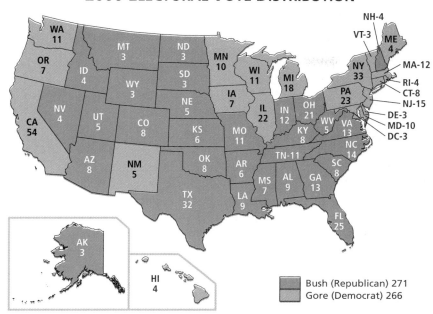

Bush (Republican) 271
Gore (Democrat) 266

majority of popular votes. All through the 1900s, the presidents who were elected had won at least a plurality, the highest number of the popular votes, in addition to winning the electoral votes. However, in the election of 2000, Al Gore, the Democratic candidate, won more popular votes than George W. Bush, the Republican candidate, but Bush won the most electoral votes and became president. In the 2004 election between George W. Bush and John Kerry, the electoral college was not an issue, because Bush won both the popular vote and the electoral vote.

14   The result sent shock waves through the American political system. One reason was that the vote was incredibly close, and several states had to count their votes a second time. The state with the most controversial results was Florida, where the

governor of the state was Jeb Bush, George W. Bush's brother. Although Gore had won the popular vote nationwide, whoever won the twenty-five Florida electoral votes would win the election. The first count of the votes showed a difference of less than one-half of 1 percent, so there was a recount by machine. This found an even smaller margin, fewer than 1,000 votes separating the two candidates.

15   There were many questions about the voting procedures in Florida, especially about certain ballots marked by punching a hole next to the name of the candidate. Some of the holes were not punched all the way through, leaving what's called a "hanging chad." Therefore, a number of the ballots had to be recounted and examined by hand. The results were extremely close. The recount showed Bush winning by 537 votes out of the almost 6 million votes cast. The Florida

Palm Beach County officials examining punched ballots for hanging chads

government declared Bush the winner, but the Gore campaign wanted more ballots recounted because the numbers were so close. After a series of legal challenges, the U.S. Supreme Court decided about a month after the election that the Florida state legislature had the right to stop recounting the ballots and certify the electoral votes. The Supreme Court ruled that a state has the ultimate right to determine how its electors are chosen.

The Ideal of the Free Individual

16   In the late 1700s, most Americans expected the new national government created by the Constitution to leave them alone to pursue their individual goals. They believed the central purpose of government was to create the conditions most favorable to the development of the free individual.

17   Before the Civil War of the 1860s, the American ideal of the free individual was the frontier settler and the small farmer. President Thomas Jefferson expressed this ideal when he said, "Those who labor in the earth are the chosen people of God, if ever he had a chosen people. . . ." Jefferson glorified farmers for being free individuals who relied on no one but themselves for their daily needs. Being dependent on none but themselves, farmers, he believed, were the most honest of citizens. Throughout his life Jefferson favored a small, weak form of government, which he believed would encourage the development of a nation of free, self-reliant farmer citizens.

18   From the end of the Civil War until the Great Depression of the 1930s, the successful businessperson replaced the farmer and the frontier settler as the ideal expression of the free individual. The prevailing view of Americans was that government should not interfere in business. If it were to do so, it would threaten the development of free individuals whose competitive spirit, self-reliance, and hard work were developing the United States into a land of greater and greater material prosperity.

19   Government, therefore, remained small and inactive in relation to the great size of the nation and the amount of power held by business corporations. Some government regulations were in place during this period, but these had only a small impact on business practices. From the 1870s until the 1930s, business organizations and ideas dominated American government and politics. During much of this time, the Republican Party was in power, and it strongly supported these policies.

The Development of Big Government

20   Traditionally, Republicans have favored letting businesses compete with little or no government regulation: Let the free enterprise system regulate itself in the marketplace. On the other hand, Democrats have traditionally favored using government to regulate businesses, protect consumers and workers, and also to solve social problems. Not surprisingly, it was a Democratic president who presided over the creation of "big government."

21   The Great Depression of the 1930s greatly weakened the businessperson's position as the American ideal of the free individual, and big business lost respect. The Depression also created the need for emergency government action to help the needy on a scale never before seen in the United States in peacetime. As a result, the idea that government should be small and inactive was largely abandoned. Moreover, the ideal of the free individual underwent some very important changes.

22   The widespread unemployment and other economic hardships of the Depression gave rise to the new assumption[6] that individuals could not be expected to rely solely on themselves in providing for their economic security. This new assumption, in ✓ turn, led to a large and active role for the national government in helping individuals, meet their daily needs. The Democratic Party, led by President Franklin Roosevelt, brought about a number of changes in the 1930s, which he referred to as a "New Deal" for Americans.

President Lyndon B. Johnson signs the legislation creating "The Great Society," a collection of welfare programs.

23   Even with the return of prosperity after the Depression and World War II (1941–1945), the growth of government's role in helping to provide economic security for individuals did not end. It continued in the prosperous postwar years, and it was greatly expanded during the presidency of another Democrat, Lyndon Johnson, in the 1960s. Roosevelt's New Deal grew into what some saw as a permanent "welfare state" that provided payments for retired persons, government checks for the unemployed, support for families with dependent children and no father to provide income, health care for the poor and the elderly, and other benefits for needy persons.

24   Some Americans fear that economic security provided by the government will weaken self-reliance, an ideal that is closely associated in the minds of Americans with individual freedom. At worst, it presents a danger to individual freedom by making an increasing number of Americans dependent on the government instead of on themselves. In this way, the strong traditions of individualism and self-reliance have made Americans less accepting of welfare programs than the citizens of other democracies such as those in western Europe, which have more extensive welfare programs than those of the United States. Those fears led to the passing of major reforms in the welfare system in 1996, under President Clinton, a Democrat with a Republican-controlled Congress. Limits were set on the number of years a person could receive welfare payments, and the states were given more responsibility for deciding who is eligible for support.

25   On the other hand, most Americans would certainly not consider their government retirement benefits under Social Security or Medicare (health care for the retired) as welfare payments. Americans see these programs as true "entitlements." They have paid a portion of their salaries into the system, and they feel that they are

---

[6] **assumption:** something you think is true although you have no proof

entitled to this government support after they retire. However, the future of Social Security is in question. As the population ages, there are fewer younger workers and their employers paying Social Security taxes into the system, and more retired workers taking money out. Americans are living longer in retirement and their medical expenses are rising. Because older Americans are more likely than young people to vote, politicians pay attention to their needs. They want the older Americans' votes.

The Role of Special Interest Groups

26   Practically all social and economic classes of Americans have seen the need to take advantage of, or to protect themselves from, the actions of government, especially the national government. To accomplish this, Americans with similar interests have formed special interest groups to more effectively influence the actions of government. These special interest groups are often called "lobbying[7] groups" or "pressure groups." Although lobbying groups have existed throughout the nation's history, they have grown significantly in both numbers and power since the late 1900s.

27   The National Rifle Association (mentioned in Chapter 4) is an example of a powerful and effective lobby. Its members are mostly people who own guns for hunting, target practice, and personal protection. The NRA, however, receives a great deal of money from business corporations that manufacture guns. Because of the attitudes and interests of its members, the NRA strongly opposes almost all government restrictions on the sale of both handguns and rifles. Even though most of the general public favors gun control, the NRA is able to block the passage of most gun-control legislation.

28   Although few interest groups have been as successful as the NRA, most well-organized interest groups have achieved a large measure of success. By organizing into groups which put pressure on government officials, people can gain more rewards and avoid more government restrictions than if they tried to do it as individuals.

29   With this principle in mind, business interest groups have multiplied in recent decades so that most major trades, businesses, and even professions have their lobbyists in Washington. There are influential lobbies representing labor unions, farm groups, teachers, doctors, lawyers, and specific industries such as oil and natural gas, pharmaceuticals, and biotechnology. Interest groups representing ethnic groups such as African Americans, Native Americans, Mexican Americans, and Jewish Americans have also expanded. There are also interest groups representing a variety of ideals or causes that want government support. These include groups pressing for a clean environment and those promoting greater protection for consumers. As one congressman exclaimed, "Everybody in America has a lobby!"

30   The political tendency of recent decades is for the size of the government to bring about an increase in the number and size of interest groups, and for the greater demands made on the government by interest groups to increase the size of the government. Groups such as the AARP (American Association of Retired Persons) not only demand new government programs, regulations, and benefits for their members, they also strongly resist any attempts to reduce existing programs that they believe protect their interests. The result of this continuing cycle can be referred to as "interest

---

[7] **lobbying:** trying to influence the government or someone with political power so that they make laws favorable to you

group government." No single interest dominates government and politics as business groups did before the Great Depression. Instead, government and politics are based on reaching compromises with a large number of groups and pleasing as many as possible.

The New Individualism: Interest Group Government

31 Interest group government can be seen as expressing a new form of American individualism. Unlike the old frontier or business individualism, individuals do not claim to succeed on their own, but rather by forming groups to influence the government. Still, it is individuals, their rights, their interests, and their ambitions, not those of the nation as a whole, that are the focus of their attention. The interest group is no more than a tool to achieve the goals of the individual by influencing the government.

32 Although many Americans have benefited in some way from government-sponsored programs, some experts believe that interest group government is harmful to the United States. The effect on politicians is enormous. First, interest groups often focus on one issue that is more important to their members than all others. For example, some people feel very strongly that abortion should not be legal in the United States. They may choose to vote for candidates primarily because of their stand on the abortion issue. Generally, because their members feel so strongly, lobby groups are able to promise that their members will vote for a candidate if he or she promises to support their issue once elected.

33 Second, members of special interest groups contribute large sums of money to election campaigns. Because candidates must rely mostly on private, not public, funding, they are often forced to depend on special interest groups for their campaign funds. Candidates at all levels of government—national, state, and local—must spend enormous amounts of their time raising funds for their re-election. For example, because members of the House of Representatives are elected every two years, they engage in continual fund-raising. Senators and presidential candidates are also pressured. The situation has become so bad that many people are agreeing with the statement, "We have the best government that money can buy!" There are, however, those who are still trying to reform the system. In 2002, the McCain-Feingold Act brought some reforms, but these changes were challenged in court. Many politicians are afraid to reform the system because they are so dependent on it, and there is little support for instituting public funding and doing away with private contributions altogether. Both political parties say they favor campaign reform, but it does not come. Both are probably equally dependent on the current system.

The Political Landscape in the 2000s

34 In order to understand the political landscape of the United States, one should first look at the historical, traditional positions of the two major political parties—the Republicans and the Democrats. The Democratic Party emerged from the New Deal as the supporter of the idea that government should do more for all classes and all kinds of Americans. For this reason, poorer and less-privileged Americans tended to support the Democratic Party. Blacks and other nonwhite minorities (such as Hispanics) tended to vote for Democrats, as did women's rights groups. Therefore, the Democratic Party was traditionally more racially and ethnically diverse than the

Republican Party. This diversity was reflected when Democrat Bill Clinton was elected president in 1992 after twelve years of Republican presidents. In naming his cabinet, the top leaders of the government bureaucracy, President Clinton said that he wanted it to reflect the diversity of America. He then appointed six women, four blacks, and two Hispanics to his cabinet.

35   The Republican Party was not changed by the New Deal as much as the Democratic Party was. The Republicans continued to stress anti-government and pro-business ideas much as they had before the Great Depression. While Democrats tended to see government action as part of the solution to many problems, Republicans tended to see government action as adding to America's problems. The best hope for America, Republicans argued, was to reduce the number of things government does and to give American business more freedom from government taxes, rules, and requirements. Republicans gained most of their political strength from business groups and from the strong anti-government attitudes of millions of Americans. However, with the leadership of President George W. Bush, the Republican Party has made a strong effort to attract more minority voters, particularly Hispanics. And when Bush appointed his cabinet, it

Condoleezza Rice, national security adviser to President George W. Bush

was even more racially and ethnically mixed than Clinton's cabinets had been.

36   In the meantime, the number of Americans who consider themselves neither Republicans nor Democrats has been growing. They consider themselves Independents. From time to time there are attempts to form a third party to capture the independent voters, but the two-party tradition is very strong in the United States. Third parties have succeeded in getting only a small percentage of the votes for president. Sometimes third-party candidates have taken enough votes away from the Republican or Democratic candidates to affect the outcome of a close election. Some believe that Ralph Nader attracted enough Democratic voters to cause Gore to lose to Bush in 2000.

37   In order to get the nomination of their party, Republican and Democratic candidates must both appeal to their traditional, hardcore[8] supporters who control the nominating process. For the Republicans, the process tends to be controlled by conservatives on the right. For the Democrats, the nominating process tends to be controlled by liberals on the left. However, once they have been nominated and the campaign begins, both Democrats and Republicans tend to move toward the center, where the majority of the American voters are. In fact, this has become a necessary strategy. (By 2004, the country was evenly divided—one-third Republican, one-third Democrat, and one-third Independent.) The parties need to appeal to their traditional bases, and also to the independent center, in order to win even a plurality.

---

[8] **hardcore:** having an extremely strong belief or opinion that is unlikely to change

38   Many observers have questioned whether the traditional stances[9] of either party truly serve the needs of the country. It may be that neither the Republican idea of national prosperity through the dominance of business groups, nor the Democratic idea of prosperity through government action to help the many diverse groups of Americans, is adequate to meet the common problems facing Americans in the twenty-first century.

AFTER YOU READ

Understand Main Ideas

Check the predictions you made on page 141 before reading the chapter. Work with a partner and answer these questions about main ideas from each section of the chapter. Skim the sections for the main ideas if you do not remember them.

1. *A Suspicion of Strong Government:* Why are Americans suspicious of a strong government?

2. *The Organization of the American Government:* What are the four possible things that can happen once Congress sends a bill to the president?

3. *The Election of the President and the Congress:* What is the electoral college? How does it work?

4. *The Ideal of the Free Individual:* What effect did the two ideals of the free individual have on the development of the government before the Great Depression of the 1930s? Why?

5. *The Development of Big Government:* What major effect did the Great Depression have on the government?

6. *The Role of Special Interest Groups:* What are special interest groups? Why are they formed and who do they represent?

7. *The New Individualism: Interest Group Government:* How do special interest groups affect how the government operates?

8. *The Political Landscape in the 2000s:* What are the traditional stances of the Republican and the Democratic parties? What role do Independents play in American politics?

---

[9] **stances:** opinions that are stated publicly

Understand Details

Write the letter of the best answer according to the information in the chapter.

_____ 1. Americans do not want to have a strong national government because
  a. they are afraid of their political leaders.
  b. they are afraid it will put limits on their individual freedom.
  c. they are much more concerned with national glory.

_____ 2. The Constitution of the United States
  a. gives by far the most power to Congress.
  b. gives by far the most power to the president.
  c. tries to give each branch enough power to balance the others.

_____ 3. The president of the United States
  a. has the power to make official treaties with foreign governments without the approval of Congress.
  b. can veto a law that has been passed by Congress.
  c. is elected if his political party wins most of the seats in Congress.

_____ 4. The Bill of Rights
  a. explains the rights of Congress and the rights of the president.
  b. guarantees citizens of the United States specific individual rights and freedoms.
  c. is part of the Declaration of Independence.

_____ 5. The American ideal of the free individual
  a. was exemplified by the farmers and the frontier settlers in the late 1700s and early 1800s.
  b. was exemplified by the businessman before the Civil War of the 1860s.
  c. caused the national government to grow in size and strength during the late 1800s.

_____ 6. The number of electoral votes a candidate receives
  a. is determined by who wins the total popular vote nationwide.
  b. is determined by the states the candidate wins.
  c. is equal to the number of seats each state has in the House of Representatives.

_____ 7. Which of these statements is <u>true</u>?
  a. George W. Bush became president in 2000 because he won a plurality of votes nationwide.
  b. The Supreme Court played a major role in the 2000 election.
  c. Most Americans dislike Social Security because they see it as a form of welfare.

_____ 8. Stronger gun-control laws are favored by
  a. the National Rifle Association.
  b. most of the American people.
  c. very few Americans.

_____ 9. Which statement about lobby groups is <u>not</u> true?

    a. They have become less powerful in recent years.

    b. They try to influence the government and public opinion.

    c. They have caused the government to get larger.

_____ 10. Which statement about the traditional stances of the political parties is <u>false</u>?

    a. The Democrats believe that government should play a major role in solving society's problems.

    b. The Republicans believe that business and the free market can solve society's problems.

    c. The Republicans and the Democrats basically agree about the role of government and they have the same political beliefs.

Improve Your Reading Skills: Note Taking

Fill in this graphic organizer with information about how the U.S. government is organized. Take notes about each branch and fill in the boxes with your notes. First write the names of the three branches of government. Then write who the people are in each branch. Finally, write what the responsibilities are for each branch. When you have finished, share your notes with a partner.

Branch	People	Responsibilities
Executive	_____ _Cabinet_	_____ _____ _____ _____ _____
_____	_Congress_ _Senate_ _____ 100 _____ 435 _____	_Enact laws_ _____ _____ _____ _____
_____	_Supreme Court_ _____ _Justices_	_____ _____ _____ _____ _Note: There are many possible responses for responsibilities._

Talk About It

Work in small groups and choose one or more of these topics to discuss.

1. How is the government of your country organized? Which system do you think works better, one that has separate elections for the different branches and divides the power, or a parliamentary system? Why?

2. What personal qualities do you think political leaders should have? Who do you admire?

3. How do lobby groups affect the operation of a government? Who do you think is more trustworthy—business or government leaders?

4. What are the main political issues in your country? What would you like to see your government do in the future?

Build Your Vocabulary

More AWL Words Test your knowledge of these additional AWL words in the reading by completing the word puzzle on the next page. First match the words and definitions. Then find the AWL words in the puzzle.

_____ 1. area	a.	to give someone what they need to be able to do something
_____ 2. challenge	b.	a particular subject or range of activities
_____ 3. conclude	c.	existing or happening in many places or situations
_____ 4. enable	d.	a length of time with a beginning and an end
_____ 5. impact	e.	particular
_____ 6. period	f.	to continue doing something, even though it is difficult
_____ 7. persist	g.	happening before
_____ 8. previous	h.	something that tests strength, skill, or ability
_____ 9. specific	i.	the effect or influence that an event has on something
_____ 10. widespread	j.	to complete

Find and circle each of the AWL words listed on page 154 in the puzzle below. Words may run horizontally, vertically, diagonally, or backwards.

```
C  P  I  C  O  N  C  L  U  D  E  I  A
E  E  W  I  D  E  S  P  R  E  A  D  S
P  S  T  I  E  C  R  L  I  G  I  E  R
C  P  N  I  G  I  M  P  A  C  T  E  I
E  E  E  T  N  D  G  R  S  R  N  I  L
H  C  A  N  L  P  C  L  B  P  S  M  L
C  F  S  S  L  P  S  L  I  E  V  I  D
T  I  B  R  A  P  E  A  S  F  L  E  L
P  C  L  E  H  R  D  D  E  E  R  T  A
R  P  E  P  C  W  O  A  E  F  E  A  D
E  D  T  R  I  I  A  R  E  A  A  A  A
S  P  D  U  R  D  C  I  P  E  W  E  L
P  E  A  E  E  L  R  P  I  N  C  E  R
C  O  P  R  E  V  I  O  U  S  O  L  C
D  D  O  O  L  E  C  E  P  E  O  R  U
```

Which Word Doesn't Belong? This chapter contains a number of words that have to do with government and politics. Look at each group of words, and decide which one does not belong with the boldfaced word. Circle the words which do not belong. Then, use each one in a sentence.

EXAMPLE: **parties:** Republican, Democrat, NRA

1. **executive branch:** president, cabinet, bureaucracy, Congress, policy, veto

2. **legislative branch:** Congress, Supreme Court, Senate, House of Representatives, bill

3. **judicial branch:** national courts, Supreme Court, judges, vice president

4. **elections:** ballot, candidate, vote, veto, plurality, electoral college

5. **politics:** party, campaign, lobby, fund-raisers, strategy, Bill of Rights

Collocations This chapter contains many verb + noun object collocations. Read the sentences below. Fill in the blanks with the missing nouns to complete the collocations.

ballots	bill	candidate	disputes	law	term	treaty

1. The Supreme Court both *interprets* a _____ and determines whether it is constitutional.

2. The president may *veto a* _____ he doesn't like and send it back to Congress.

3. The Senate has to *ratify a* _____ that the president has signed.

4. If an election is very close, a candidate may request that the officials *recount the* _____.

5. The president *serves a* _____ of four years.

6. The judicial branch *settles* _____ about the exact meaning of the law through court cases.

7. The Democratic and Republican parties each *nominate a* _____ for president.

EXPAND YOUR KNOWLEDGE

Group Project

Work in a small group to create the profile of a perfect candidate for public office.

- First decide what office your candidate is running for.
- Then describe what the person would look like (female or male, age, appearance) and what qualifications he or she would have.
- Think about how you would run the campaign.
- What kinds of advertisements would you create? What activities and appearances would you have?
- Make a poster for your candidate, perhaps with a collage of pictures that illustrate the issues your candidate is supporting in the campaign. Look on the Internet or in newspapers and magazines for ideas.
- When you have finished, present your candidate to the rest of the class.

Ask Yourself/Ask Americans

Who do you trust? Look at the list below and put a check next to the people you would trust. Share your list with a group of classmates. Then compare your opinions with the poll results that follow.

_____ Accountants	_____ Members of Congress	_____ Stockbrokers
_____ Bankers	_____ Military officers	_____ Teachers
_____ Civil servants	_____ Police officers	_____ The ordinary man or woman
_____ Doctors	_____ Pollsters	_____ The president
_____ Journalists	_____ Professors	_____ Trade union leaders
_____ Judges	_____ Religious leaders	_____ TV newscasters
_____ Lawyers	_____ Scientists	

WHOM WOULD YOU GENERALLY TRUST?

Would you generally trust each of the following types of people to tell the truth, or not?

	Would Trust	Would Not	Not Sure / Refused
	%	%	%
Teachers	80	12	8
Doctors	77	17	7
Professors	75	16	10
Police officers	69	21	10
Scientists	68	21	12
Military officers	65	26	9
Ordinary man or woman	65	23	12
Civil servants	65	27	8
Judges	65	27	8
The President	65	30	5
Clergymen or priests	64	26	10
Accountants	55	35	9
Bankers	51	41	8
TV Newscasters	46	46	8
Pollsters	44	43	13
Journalists	39	53	8
Members of Congress	35	52	12
Trade union leaders	30	56	14
Lawyers	24	65	11
Stockbrokers	23	66	12

Source: *The Harris Poll*® #63, Nov. 27, 2002. © 2002 by Harris Interactive Inc.

Understand Polls

How should a government spend the people's tax money? When the American economy is growing, most people think health care, education, and defense should be the priorities. A 2003 poll examined this issue. Humphrey Taylor, chairman of the Harris Polls, made the following comments about what the poll revealed:

A Paradox

One of the most striking findings in this survey is that much of health care, most of education, and all of defense are paid for out of taxes, whereas the other items on the list, which only a few people regard as equally high priorities for increased spending and growth—housing, food, automobiles, entertainment, and clothes—are mostly paid for with after-tax dollars by individual consumers.

(continued)

A visitor from outer space who looked at these numbers might conclude that most Americans would be strongly supportive of much higher taxation to spend on health care, education, and defense. This visitor would be puzzled by the popularity of politicians who favor tax cuts and, by implication, less money for the segments of the economy which the public believes should grow the fastest.

Now read the poll yourself. Then answer the questions on the next page.

HIGHEST PRIORITY FOR ECONOMIC GROWTH

Different segments of the economy grow at different rates. This is a list of some of the biggest segments of the whole U.S. economy—how money is spent. As the economy grows, which of these do you think should be the highest priority for future growth? [choose one]

	Total	AGE					
		18–24	25–29	30–39	40–49	50–64	65 +
	%	%	%	%	%	%	%
Health care	34	23	29	32	36	40	36
Education	29	39	36	34	27	21	23
Defense	27	25	24	24	26	31	31
Housing	4	3	5	3	5	4	5
Food	3	5	3	2	3	1	3
Automobiles and transportation	1	1	*	1	1	*	–
Leisure and entertainment	*	*	*	*	*	1	1
Clothes	*	*	*	*	*	*	*
Other	1	1	1	2	1	1	1
Not sure	1	2	2	1	*	*	1

	Total	PARTY I.D.			POLITICAL PHILOSOPHY		
		Republican	Democrat	Independent	Conservative	Moderate	Liberal
	%	%	%	%	%	%	%
Health care	34	22	42	39	23	35	48
Education	29	22	34	29	19	32	35
Defense	27	45	16	22	45	24	10
Housing	4	3	4	5	3	5	3
Food	3	3	2	4	4	2	2
Automobiles and Transportation	1	1	*	*	1	1	1
Leisure and entertainment	*	*	*	*	*	1	*
Clothes	*	*	*	*	*	*	*
Other	1	1	1	1	1	1	1
Not sure	1	2	*	*	2	*	*

* Less than 0.5%.
Note: Percentages may not add up to 100% due to rounding.
Source: *The Harris Poll*® #33, June 11, 2003, conducted by Harris Interactive Inc.

1. Among people ages eighteen to twenty-four, what percentage pick education as the highest priority?

2. Among people aged twenty-five to twenty-nine, what was the highest priority?

3. Which age group picked defense as the highest priority?

4. Which political party ID (identification) chose defense as the highest priority?

5. Which political philosophy chose defense—conservatives, moderates, or liberals?

6. Who favors spending more on health care—Republicans, Democrats, or Independents?

7. Which political party has priorities most similar to those of the Independents?

8. Which groups (age, party, philosophy) thought housing should have top priority?

9. Based on both charts, which group had the highest concerns about food?

10. Based on both charts, which group thought that leisure and entertainment should have the highest priority?

Use the Internet

Work with a partner. Choose one of these topics to research online and then discuss.

1. Look for information about the budget of the United States. A large percentage of the budget is for mandatory programs (those that must be paid). Mandatory expenditures include the interest on the public debt and entitlement programs such as Medicare (medical benefits for the elderly) and Medicaid (medical benefits for the poor). The rest of the budget is discretionary spending. This includes defense and all other expenditures.

2. Look for information about the budget of your country, or choose another country. What has the largest percentage of expenditures? What percentage is spent on defense? How much is spent on social welfare, such as health care and education? What can you tell about the priorities of the people by looking at the budget?

People Watching

As mentioned in Chapter 3, Americans sometimes say that it is dangerous to talk about two topics: religion and politics. It is also often difficult to know what you should say to people when you first meet them. The questions you might ask others from your country may not be appropriate or acceptable in another society or culture.

Ask a number of Americans of different ages, of both sexes, and of different ethnic or racial backgrounds, if possible, to look at the following questions. Ask them whether these are polite, acceptable questions that they would ask someone themselves. Record each person's reaction to each question. If they say certain questions are unacceptable, ask them why. How would it make someone feel if you asked one of these questions? Are there some circumstances when it would be all right to ask a question and other circumstances when it would not be all right? Which questions are acceptable in your country and which are not? Compare your findings with those of your classmates.

1. What is your name?

2. What do you do for a living?

3. Where are you from? or, Where do you live?

4. Do you like your job?

5. How much do you make?

6. Are you a Republican or Democrat? Why?

7. Are you married? Why or why not?

8. Do you have children? Why or why not?

9. How old are you?

10. What is your religion?

WRITE ABOUT IT

A. Choose one of these writing topics.

1. Write a letter to the president of the United States about an issue that interests or concerns you. You might write about health care, global warming, or oil drilling in the Arctic wilderness. Use persuasive techniques:

   a. Begin with a fact or statistic that is an attention-getter.
   b. Order your arguments so that you end with your strongest point.
   c. Anticipate the other side of the argument and deal with those points.
   d. End on a strong, positive note.

2. In 1960, President John F. Kennedy appointed his brother Robert Kennedy to be attorney general of the United States. In 1992, President Bill Clinton announced that he wanted to appoint his wife Hillary to an important government position, perhaps a cabinet-level post. Polls showed, however, that two-thirds of the American public disapproved of Hillary's having a major post, and Clinton was forced to reconsider. Why do you think Americans accepted the appointment of a president's brother but not his wife? What do you think about any president appointing a spouse or family member to government office? Write a "letter to the editor" (of a newspaper) expressing your opinion.

B. Write about what it means to be a political liberal, conservative, or moderate. Visit the website for the Republican Party, www.gop.org, to find information about conservative issues. Look for liberal issues on the site for the Democratic Party, www.democrats.org.

Books to Read

James Agee, *Let Us Now Praise Famous Men: Three Tenant Families*—A book of photographs and stories about the lives of three poor southern farm families in the 1930s.

Lani Guinier, *The Tyranny of the Majority: Fundamental Fairness in Representative Democracy*—Essays written by a distinguished Harvard Law School professor about voting rights issues, race relations, and democracy in America.

Frank Norris, *The Octopus: A Story of California*—A classic American novel based on a true story of the 1880 conflict between farmers and a railroad that was buying up their land.

Kevin Phillips, *American Dynasty: Aristocracy, Fortune, and the Politics of Deceit in the House of Bush*—A controversial book that traces how the Bush family rose to power.

Robert Penn Warren, *All the King's Men*—This classic American novel is about the rise and fall of a fictional southern politician who resembles Huey P. Long, a governor of Lousiana.

Movies to See

All the President's Men—Tells how reporters Woodward and Bernstein uncovered the details of the Watergate scandal that led to President Nixon's resignation.

The American President—A romantic comedy about a widowed U.S. president who falls in love with a lobbyist.

The Candidate—A candidate for the U.S. Senate from California has no hope of winning, so he is able to run his campaign any way he chooses.

Dave—When the president suffers a stroke and is left unconscious, his staff hire a man who looks like the president to take his place.

The Hunting of the President—A controversial movie that shows previously unreleased evidence of a campaign against Bill Clinton's presidency, from his days in Arkansas up to his impeachment trial.

Abraham Lincoln and the Gettysburg Address, Lincoln Memorial, Washington, D.C.

CHAPTER 8

ETHNIC AND RACIAL DIVERSITY IN THE UNITED STATES

So in this continent, the energy of Irish, Germans, Swedes, Poles and all the European tribes, of the Africans, and of the Polynesians—will construct a new race, a new religion, a new state.

Ralph Waldo Emerson (1803–1882)

BEFORE YOU READ

Preview Vocabulary

A. Work with a partner to answer the questions. Make sure you understand the meaning of the AWL words in italics.

1. If a country tries to *accommodate* new immigrants, is it trying to help them succeed or trying to prevent them from entering the country?

2. If there is *discrimination* against a minority group, how might the people be treated differently?

3. Is a *federal* government program one at the state level or at the national level?

4. If you are *inclined* to do something, are you likely or unlikely to do it?

5. Is *instruction* usually given by a teacher or by a student?

6. When public *facilities* were segregated in the South, did blacks and whites go to different schools and sit in separate areas of restaurants and movie theaters?

7. Do most people live in *residential* or commercial (business) areas?

8. If an ethnic minority wants to *retain* its culture, are families more likely to continue speaking their native language at home or to speak English?

9. If smoking is *prohibited* in a public facility, are you allowed to smoke there or not?

10. How many generations back can you *trace* your ancestry?

B. Some words in English have a positive or negative connotation. That is, they give you a good or bad feeling. For example, *hero* has a positive connotation, while *villain* has a negative connotation.

Write a plus sign (+) next to the words that you think have a positive connotation and a minus sign (–) next to words with a negative connotation.

_____ accommodation

_____ civil rights

_____ despair

_____ discrimination

_____ elite

_____ festival

_____ inequality

_____ inferior

_____ inspire

_____ integration

_____ poverty

_____ prejudice

_____ resources

_____ segregation

_____ slavery

Preview Content

A. Before you read, think about what you know about the racial and ethnic diversity of the United States. Discuss the questions with your classmates.

1. Read the quotation by Emerson at the beginning of the chapter. How did people from so many different countries create the American culture in the United States?

2. Skim the first paragraph of the reading. What does *assimilation* mean? What group had the strongest influence on shaping the dominant American culture? Why do you think so?

3. Why do you think some immigrants from some countries might have more success in the United States than others have?

4. What do you know about the history of African Americans in the United States?

B. **Before you read the chapter, read the headings for each section. Which sections do you think will help you answer these questions? Write the heading of each section in the space below each question.**

1. When did slavery end in the United States?

   _____

2. When did legal segregation end?

   _____

3. Why do some people describe American culture as a "salad bowl"?

   _____

4. How will diverse cultures affect the nation in the future?

   _____

5. What group had the strongest influence on the American culture?

   _____

6. What effect did immigrants from southern and eastern Europe have on the American culture?

   _____

7. What contradictions are there in American society today?

   _____

In 1899, an American Indian speaks to a history class at Hampton Institute, Virginia, a historically black college.

Melting Pot or Salad Bowl

1   The population of the United States includes a large variety of ethnic groups coming from many races, nationalities, and religions. The process by which these many groups have been made a part of a common cultural life with commonly shared values is called *assimilation*. Scholars disagree as to the extent to which assimilation has occurred in the United States. As we mentioned in Chapter 1, some have described the United States as a "melting pot" where various racial and ethnic groups have been combined into one culture. Others are inclined to see the United States as a "salad bowl" where the various groups have remained somewhat distinct and different from one another, creating a richly diverse country.

2   The truth probably lies somewhere between these two views. Since 1776, an enormous amount of racial and ethnic assimilation has taken place in the United States, yet some groups continue to feel a strong sense of separateness from the culture as a whole. Many of these groups are really *bicultural*. That is, they consider themselves Americans, but they may also wish to retain the language and sometimes the cultural traditions of their original culture.

3   People of Hispanic origin were on the North American continent before settlers arrived from Europe in the early 1600s. In Florida and the Southwest, Spanish and Latin American settlements were established centuries before the thirteen colonies joined together to form the United States in the late 1700s. Because of their long history and the continued influx of newcomers into the established communities, many Hispanics, or Latinos, have taken a special pride in maintaining their cultural traditions and the use of the Spanish language.

4   Generally speaking, over the years whites from different national and religious backgrounds have been gradually assimilated into the larger American culture, with some exceptions. For example, American Jews are one group who have traditionally retained a strong sense of group identity within the larger culture. This may be a result of the long history of persecution in the Christian countries in Europe, the weaker forms of discrimination and anti-Jewish feeling that have sometimes existed in the United States, and their own strong feeling of ethnic pride. Yet along with their own group identity, American Jews have a strong sense of being a part of the larger American culture.

The Establishment of the Dominant Culture

5   The first census of the new nation, conducted in 1790, counted about 4 million people, most of whom were white. Of the white citizens, more than eight out of ten traced their ancestry back to England. African Americans made up a surprising 20 percent of the population, an all-time high. There were close to 700,000 slaves and about 60,000 "free Negroes." Only a few Native Americans who paid taxes were included in the census count, but the total Native American population was probably about 1 million.

6   It was the white population that had the greater numbers, the money, and the political power in the new nation, and therefore this majority soon defined what the dominant culture would be. At the time of the American Revolution, the white population was largely English in origin, Protestant, and middle-class. Such

Americans are sometimes referred to as "WASPs" (white Anglo-Saxon protestants); however, many people now consider this an insulting term. Their characteristics became the standard for judging other groups. Those having a different religion (such as the Irish Catholics), or those speaking a different language (such as the Germans, Dutch, and Swedes), were in the minority and would be disadvantaged unless they became assimilated. In the late 1700s this assimilation occurred without great difficulty. According to historians Allan Nevins and Henry Steele Commager, "English, Irish, German, . . . Dutch, Swedish—mingled[1] and intermarried with little thought of any difference."

7   The dominant American culture that grew out of the nation's early history, then, was English-speaking, western European, Protestant, and middle-class in character. It was this dominant culture that established what became the traditional values described by Tocqueville in the early 1830s. Immigrants with these characteristics were welcome, in part because Americans believed that these newcomers would probably give strong support to the basic values of the dominant culture, such as freedom, equality of opportunity, and the desire to work hard for a higher material standard of living.

Mulberry Street in the heart of the immigrant area of New York City, early 1900s

The Assimilation of Non-Protestant and Non-Western Europeans

8   As is the case in many cultures, the degree to which a minority group was seen as different from the characteristics of the dominant majority determined the extent of that group's acceptance. Although immigrants who were like the earlier settlers were accepted, those with significantly different characteristics tended to be viewed as a threat to traditional American values and way of life.

9   This was particularly true of the immigrants who arrived by the millions during the late-nineteenth and early-twentieth centuries. Most of them came from poverty-stricken nations of southern and eastern Europe. They spoke languages other than English, and large numbers of them were Catholics or Jews.

10   Americans at the time were very fearful of this new flood of immigrants. They were afraid that these people were so accustomed to lives of poverty and dependence that they would not understand such traditional American values as freedom, self-reliance, and competition. There were so many new immigrants that they might even change the basic values of the nation in undesirable ways.

11   Americans tried to meet what they saw as a threat to their values by offering English instruction for the new immigrants and citizenship classes to teach them basic American beliefs. The immigrants, however, often felt that their American teachers disapproved of the traditions of their homeland. Moreover, learning about American values gave them little help in meeting their most important needs, such as employment, food, and a place to live.

---

1 mingled: met and talked with a lot of different people socially

12   Far more helpful to the new immigrants were the "political bosses" of the larger cities of the northeastern United States, where most of the immigrants first arrived. Those bosses saw to many of the practical needs of the immigrants and were more accepting of the different homeland traditions. In exchange for their help, the bosses expected the immigrants to keep them in power by voting for them in elections.

13   Many Americans strongly disapproved of the political bosses. This was partly because the bosses were frequently corrupt;[2] that is, they often stole money from the city governments they controlled and engaged in other illegal practices. Perhaps more important to disapproving Americans, however, was the fact that the bosses seemed to be destroying such basic American values as self-reliance and competition.

14   The bosses, it seemed, were teaching the immigrants to be dependent on them rather than to rely on themselves. Moreover, the bosses were "buying" the votes of the immigrants in order to give themselves a monopoly of political power in many larger cities. This practice destroyed competition for political office, which Americans viewed as an important tradition in politics just as it was in other facets of American life.

15   Despite these criticisms, many scholars believe that the political bosses performed an important function in the late nineteenth and early twentieth centuries. They helped to assimilate large numbers of new immigrants into the larger American culture by finding them jobs and housing, in return for their political support. Later the bosses also helped the sons and daughters of these immigrants find employment, but the second generation usually had the advantage of growing up speaking English.

16   The fact that the United States had a rapidly expanding economy at the turn of the century made it possible for these new immigrants, often with the help of the bosses, to better their standard of living in the United States. As a result of these new opportunities and new rewards, immigrants came to accept most of the values of the larger American culture and were in turn accepted by the great majority of Americans. For white ethnic groups, therefore, it has generally been true that their feeling of being a part of the larger culture—that is, *American*— has usually been stronger than their feeling of belonging to a separate ethnic group—Irish, Italian, Polish, etc.

The African-American Experience

17   The process of assimilation in the United States has been much more successful for white ethnic groups than for nonwhite ethnic groups. Of the nonwhite ethnic groups, Americans of African descent have had the greatest difficulty in becoming assimilated into the larger culture. African Americans were

Learning skills to make a living: a class for immigrants early in the twentieth century

brought to the United States against their will to be sold as slaves. Except for the American Indian tribes who inhabited the United States before the first white settlers arrived, other ethnic groups came to America voluntarily—most as immigrants who wanted to better their living conditions.

---

[2] **corrupt:** dishonest

18   The enslavement of African Americans in the United States was a complete contradiction of such traditional basic American values as freedom and equality of opportunity. It divided the United States into two increasingly different sections: the southern states, in which black slavery became the basis of the economy, and the northern states, which chose to make slavery against the law.

19   A minority of whites in the North insisted that slavery and freedom could not exist together in a free country and demanded that slavery be abolished,[3] even if this meant war with the South. A much larger number of northern whites believed that freedom and equality of opportunity needed to be protected for white people only, but they were afraid that black slavery would eventually take away their economic freedom. If, for example, the slave system of the South were allowed to spread into the frontier regions of the West, poor and middle-income whites could no longer look to the western frontier as a land of equality and opportunity where people could better their position in life. Rather, whites would have to compete with unpaid slave labor, a situation that they believed would degrade their work and lower their social status.

20   Abraham Lincoln was able to become president of the United States by appealing to both the white idealists who saw slavery as an injustice to African Americans and to the larger numbers of northern whites who saw slavery as a threat to themselves. Lincoln's argument was that if black slavery continued to spread westward, white freedom and equality would be threatened. Lincoln also believed that basic ideals such as freedom and equality of opportunity had to apply to *all* people, black and white, or they would not last as basic American values.

21   When Lincoln won the presidency in 1860, the southern states left the Union and tried to form a new nation of their own based on slavery. A Civil War (1861–1865) between the North and South resulted, which turned out to be the bloodiest and most destructive of all the nation's wars. When the North was finally victorious, black slavery ended in the United States.

22   Back in the 1830s, Tocqueville predicted trouble between blacks and whites in the United States:

> *These two races are fastened to each other without intermingling; and they are unable to separate entirely or to combine. Although the law may abolish slavery, God alone can obliterate[4] the traces of its existence.*

23   Although slavery was abolished in the 1860s, its legacy[5] continued and African Americans were not readily assimilated into the larger American culture. Most remained in the South, where they were not allowed to vote and were legally segregated from whites. Black children were not allowed to attend white public schools, for example, and many received an inferior education that did not give them an equal opportunity to compete in the white-dominated society. Many former slaves and their families became caught in a cycle of poverty that continued for generations. Although conditions were much worse in the segregated South, blacks continued to be the victims[6] of strong racial prejudice in the North as well.

---

[3] **abolish:** officially end a law or system
[4] **obliterate:** to destroy something so that almost nothing remains
[5] **legacy:** a situation that exists as a result of things that happened at an earlier time
[6] **victims:** people who suffer bad treatment even though they have done nothing to deserve it

The Civil Rights Movement of the 1950s and 1960s

24   This state of affairs remained unchanged until the United States Supreme Court declared in 1954 that racially segregated public schools did not provide equal educational opportunities for black Americans and were therefore illegal. Black leaders throughout the United States were greatly encouraged by this decision. They decided to try to end racial segregation in all areas of American life.

25   The most important of these leaders was Martin Luther King Jr., a black Protestant minister with a great gift for inspiring[7] people. From the late 1950s until his assassination[8] by a white gunman in 1968, King led thousands of people in nonviolent marches and demonstrations against segregation and other forms of racial discrimination. King's goal was to bring about greater assimilation of black people into the larger American culture. His

Martin Luther King Jr.'s second visit to Memphis, AFL-CIO Local 1773, 1968

ideals were largely developed from basic American values. He wanted greater equality of opportunity and "freedom now" for his people. He did not wish to separate his people from American society, but rather to gain for them a larger part in it.

26   Some black leaders, such as Malcolm X, urged a rejection of basic American values and complete separation of blacks from the white culture. Malcolm X believed that American values were nothing more than "white men's values" used to keep blacks in an inferior position. Blacks must separate themselves from whites, by force if necessary, and build their own society based on values which they would create for themselves. Because he saw Christianity as a "white" religion, Malcolm turned to a faith based on Islam, and he became a leader of the "black Muslim" faith (founded in 1930). The great majority of American blacks, however, shared Martin Luther King's Protestant religious beliefs and his goal of assimilation rather than separation. Most African Americans continued to look to King as their leader.

27   Largely as a result of King's activities, two major civil rights[9] laws were passed during the 1960s, which brought about great changes in the South. One law made it illegal to segregate public facilities. The other law made it illegal to deny black people the right to vote in elections.

28   The civil rights laws of the 1960s helped to bring about a significant degree of assimilation of blacks into the larger American culture. Most important, the laws eventually helped to reduce the amount of white prejudice toward black people in all parts of the country. A federal program called *affirmative action* required employers to actively seek black workers and universities to recruit black students. As a result of the civil rights laws and affirmative action, the number of African Americans attending the nation's colleges and universities, holding elective public office, and earning higher incomes increased dramatically in the late 1960s and 1970s. In 1984 and

---

[7] **inspiring:** encouraging people to achieve something great
[8] **assassination:** the murder of an important person
[9] **civil rights:** rights that every person should have, such as the right to vote or to be treated fairly by the law, whatever their sex, race, or religion

1988, Jesse Jackson, a black leader who had worked with King in the 1960s, became the first African American to run for president of the United States. Although he did not win, he received significant national attention and greatly influenced the policies of the Democratic Party.

29　　African Americans are now mayors of major cities and members of Congress; they hold offices in all levels of government—local, state, and national. In 1991, Clarence Thomas was the second African American to become a Supreme Court justice. President George W. Bush chose Condoleezza Rice as his national security adviser and Colin Powell as his secretary of state, two very powerful and very visible positions. Today, African Americans are sports and entertainment heroes, university professors, medical doctors, lawyers, entrepreneurs, and reporters. There is now a sizable and growing black middle class and there are a number of wealthy African Americans. Most whites now say they would vote for a black person for president, someone like Colin Powell, for example.

President Bush and Secretary of State Colin Powell

An American Paradox[10]

30　　The civil rights movement benefited not only African Americans, but all minorities in the United States—American Indians, Hispanics, and Asians. Racial discrimination in employment and housing was forbidden by law. The civil rights laws also advanced the rights of women, and these laws have reinforced the ideal of equality of opportunity for all Americans.

31　　However, there is a paradox. Although the amount of diversity in the United States continues to grow with each census, the 2000 census revealed that segregation according to race and ethnicity has persisted to a much larger degree than many Americans had realized. On the one hand, most young Americans say they would have no problem being friends with or even marrying someone of a different race or ethnic background. Polls show that the vast majority of Americans believe that segregation is a bad thing. On the other hand, races and ethnic groups still tend to live in segregated communities. This has been a trend in the cities, and as minority groups have moved into the suburbs the trend has continued. Ethnically diverse neighborhoods do of course exist and are certainly chosen by a number of Americans. However, these neighborhoods are the exception, rather than the rule.

32　　Sociology professor John Logan has studied this phenomenon and reports that the 2000 census found the United States as segregated a nation as it has ever been. "The majority of Americans," Logan found, "are living in neighborhoods that continue to separate whites from blacks, Latinos, and people of Asian descent. In fact, the same color barrier that has dominated urban communities for decades has now spread to our fast-growing suburbs, where people of color tend to congregate in neighborhoods and housing developments apart from whites." Moreover, Logan sees this trend continuing into the future:

---

[10] **paradox:** a situation that seems strange because it involves two ideas or qualities that are opposite or very different

> *We need to be aware that segregation is not going away by itself. And that it hasn't been solved by the growth of the black middle class, the softening of white attitudes on race, or the laws that prohibit racial discrimination in housing. These are all factors that might have had a positive effect on segregation, and the assumption has been that they must have had an effect. But it's very important to realize that they have not.*

33   Is it a bad thing if groups of people choose to live in communities with others of their race or ethnic background? Shouldn't individuals have the freedom to live wherever and near whomever they want? Ethnic communities often provide valuable support to new immigrants, with their native-language newspapers and ethnic restaurants and grocery stores. Most white Americans, particularly those in and near cities, enjoy international food and many participate in cultural festivals from all over the world. They see this diversity as enriching their lives.

34   But there is a negative side to this picture. The bad news is that there is still a gulf[11] between different racial and ethnic groups. Although African Americans represent about 12 percent of the population, they are still grossly under-represented in Congress, and the same is true of Hispanics. The median income of a married black or Hispanic man working full-time is still significantly less than that of a married white man. Segregation and discrimination are against the law, but residential patterns create largely segregated neighborhood schools, particularly in many urban areas. Whites are more likely than blacks and Hispanics to live in the suburbs, where the neighborhood schools are usually in better condition and offer a better education. Many blacks and other ethnic minorities in the inner city are trapped in cycles of poverty, unemployment, violence, and despair. Blacks are the most frequent victims of violent crime, and as many as one in five young males may have a criminal record. More black and Hispanic children than white children live in poverty and may have only one parent at home.

35   On the other hand, Americans continue to believe strongly in the ideal of equality of opportunity and to search for ways to give everyone an equal chance at success. The American Dream still attracts immigrants and inspires people of all races and ethnic backgrounds. In reality, some immigrant groups have more success than others. As one would expect, history shows that immigrants who come with financial resources, a good educational background, and the necessary work skills are likely to do the best. For example, immigrants from the Middle East tend to have a higher socioeconomic level than the average white American. So do Asians, as a group. However, those who come without financial resources and a strong educational background do not do as well. Immigrants from the same country may have a different experience in the United States. For example, the Vietnamese who came in the mid-1970s were the educated elite, and they had better success than the Vietnamese farmers and fishermen who came later. The Cubans who came in the early 1960s had more wealth and education than many of the poorer Cubans who arrived later. Again, the educated elite have had greater success than those who came from poorer backgrounds.

36   Today, immigrants with all kinds of backgrounds and skill levels find their way to the United States. Some of them are highly educated and they may find employment in fields such as technology, medicine, and science. Others may come from poor rural or urban

---

[11] **gulf:** a great difference and lack of understanding between two groups of people

areas and have a limited education. Many of these are young people who risk their lives to come without documentation to do agricultural or construction work. Others find work as janitors, maids, or nannies. Often, they are paid less than a documented worker would be. However, what they are able to earn in dollars and send back to their countries can support many family members there. Many of these individuals do not want to become U.S. citizens; their only wish is to be able to work here. Americans are trying to find ways to accommodate these workers, while still protecting the interests of U.S. citizens.

A Universal Nation

37   It is important to remember that the dominant culture and its value system established by the early settlers had its roots in white, Protestant, western Europe. In the late 1800s and early 1900s, millions of immigrants came from eastern and southern Europe, bringing cultural traditions perceived by the dominant culture as quite different. By the 1920s, Americans had decided that it was time to close the borders to mass immigration, and the number of new immigrants slowed to a trickle.[12] In spite of the worries of those in the dominant culture, the new immigrants did assimilate to life in the United States. They greatly enriched the cultural diversity of the nation, and they ultimately did not cause major changes to its system of government, its free enterprise system, or its traditional values.

38   In 1965, the United States made important changes in its immigration laws, allowing many more immigrants to come and entirely eliminating the older laws' bias in favor of white European immigrants. As a result, the United States now takes in large numbers of new immigrants who are nonwhite and non-European. The majority are from Asia, Latin America, and the Caribbean. In addition to the large numbers of legal immigrants, for the first time the United States has significant numbers of immigrants without legal documentation. Many worry about what the impact will be on American society. Can the American economy offer these new immigrants the same opportunities that others have had? What will be the effect on the traditional value system that has defined the United States for over 200 years?

39   Many Americans see wonderful benefits for their country. Ben Wattenberg, a respected expert on American culture, believes that the new immigration will be of great help to the nation. According to Wattenberg, something very important is happening to the United States: It is becoming the first universal nation in history. Wattenberg believes that the United States will be the first nation where large numbers of people from every region on earth live in freedom under one government. This diversity, he says, will give the nation great influence and appeal to the rest of the world during the twenty-first century.

40   Perhaps the United States will be described not as a "melting pot" or a "salad bowl," but as a "mosaic"—a picture made up of many tiny pieces of different colors. If one looks closely at the nation, the individuals of different colors and ethnic groups are still distinct and recognizable, but together they create a picture that is uniquely *American. E pluribus unum*—the motto of the United States from its beginning—means "one composed of many." *Out of many, one.*

---

[12] **trickle:** a movement of people or things into a place in very small numbers or amounts

Understand Main Ideas

On page 165, you wrote the headings of the sections that you thought would contain the answers to the prereading questions. Working with a partner, write the answer to each question. Then make up seven more questions about other main ideas, one question for each of the seven sections. Answer these questions, then share them with another pair of students.

Understand Details

Write the letter of the best answer according to the information in the chapter.

_____ 1. Scholars who see the United States as a "salad bowl" emphasize

    a. the great extent of racial and ethnic assimilation in the United States.

    b. the many differences between different racial and ethnic groups in the United States.

    c. the rapid growth of the population of the United States.

_____ 2. In American society, there are some members of ethnic groups (such as some Jews and Hispanics) that are bicultural; they feel that

    a. they are fully assimilated into American society.

    b. they do not belong at all to American society.

    c. they belong to American society, but at the same time they also have another separate identity.

_____ 3. Which of the following was not a characteristic of the dominant American culture during the early decades of the nation's history?

    a. Catholic

    b. western European

    c. middle-class

_____ 4. Which of the following was true about the political bosses in northeastern cities during the late nineteenth and early twentieth centuries?

    a. They were more afraid of new immigrants than were other Americans.

    b. They were more cruel to new immigrants than were other Americans.

    c. They were more helpful to new immigrants than were other Americans.

_____ 5. Today ethnic groups in the United States
   a. have no feeling of belonging to an ethnic group (such as Irish, Italian, or Polish) whatsoever.
   b. consider themselves as part of the American culture in varying degrees, often depending on how similar their culture is to the majority.
   c. all feel much more a part of their ethnic group than part of the American culture.

_____ 6. What was the <u>main</u> reason most northern whites disliked slavery?
   a. It went against their religious beliefs.
   b. It went against the U.S. Constitution.
   c. It threatened their own economic opportunities.

_____ 7. After the Civil War, African Americans in the South lived in a social system where
   a. many continued to be slaves.
   b. segregation was legal.
   c. there was racial discrimination, but no laws separated them from whites.

_____ 8. In 1954, the U.S. Supreme Court declared
   a. African Americans could not legally be denied their right to vote for racial reasons.
   b. racially segregated public schools are illegal.
   c. no one may be denied freedom of speech, press, or religion.

_____ 9. On which of the beliefs listed below did Malcolm X <u>disagree</u> with Martin Luther King?
   a. Black people should be assimilated into the larger American society.
   b. Black people were not treated fairly by the larger American society.
   c. Black people should have freedom and equality.

_____ 10. Which of these statements is true?
   a. Most young African Americans today have no interest in learning about the black culture and they identify fully with the white culture.
   b. Racial prejudice, segregation, and discrimination are at an all-time high in the United States today.
   c. Using the word _mosaic_ to describe the American culture suggests a positive image.

Complete a Timeline

Scan the chapter to find these dates. Write what happened next to the date to complete the time line about racial and ethnic diversity in the U.S.

early 1600s: _Mexicans (hispanics latinos)_

1790: _4 m people England_

1860–1865: _Am civil war_

late 1800s and early 1900s: _a big immigration_

1920s: _Borders closed_

1950s and 1960s: _Civil Rights Movement_

1965: _change New immigrant_

1984 and 1988: _Jesse Jackson President_

2000: _segregation still by race ethnicity_

[handwritten margin notes: 1911 WWI, Quota, Quota system]

Talk About It

Work in small groups and choose one or more of these topics to discuss.

1. What are the advantages and disadvantages to having a multicultural society in the twenty-first century?

2. What is your country's policy on immigration? Would you want to be an immigrant in your country? Why or why not?

3. Should a country discourage people from segregating themselves by minorities? What are the advantages and disadvantages to people living in segregated communities?

4. This chapter describes the dominant American culture as being white, English-speaking, Protestant, and middle-class. How would you describe the dominant culture of your country, if there is one?

5. Would you rather live in a country that is described as a "melting pot," a "salad bowl," or a "mosaic"? Why?

Build Your Vocabulary

Definitions Match the word with its definition. Then fill in the sentence blanks with the correct form of the word.

c 1. abolish
f 2. assassination
g 3. civil rights
b 4. corrupt
h 5. gulf
e 6. inspire
j 7. legacy
a 8. mingle
k 9. mosaic
i 10. obliterate
l 11. trickle
d 12. victim

a. to meet and talk together
b. dishonest
c. to officially end a law or system
d. someone who suffers bad treatment
e. to encourage someone to achieve something great
f. the murder of an important person
g. rights that every person should have
h. a great difference between two groups of people
i. to destroy something so that nothing remains
j. a situation that exists as a result of things that happened at an earlier time
k. a picture made by fitting together small pieces of colored stones, glass, or paper
l. a movement of people or things into a place in very small numbers or amounts

1. Although slavery had ended in the North by the late 1700s, it was not _____ in the rest of the country until the 1860s.

2. Black people in the 1950s and early 1960s did not have the same freedom and equality as whites in the South; they had to fight for their _____ _____.

3. Martin Luther King Jr. was able to _____ his followers to demonstrate against segregation.

4. King was the most important black leader in America from the late 1950s until his _____ by a white gunman in 1968.

5. Unfortunately, the _____ of slavery continues in the United States, and there are still problems between the races.

6. Although racial prejudice is at an all-time low, there is still a _____5_____ between the races, particularly in their incomes.

7. People who come to the United States from many different countries have _____8_____ and many have married persons of a different national origin.

8. Often it is the poor minorities who live in the inner cities who are the _____12_____ of crime.

9. Perhaps the United States is really more of a _____9_____ than a melting pot or a salad bowl.

10. Immigration by white Europeans has now slowed to a _____11_____; the majority of the immigrants now come from Asia, Latin America, or the Caribbean.

11. Few people would really want to _____10_____ the rich diversity of cultures living together in the United States.

12. Many of the big city political bosses of the late 1800s and early 1900s were _____4_____; they stole money from the city governments.

More AWL Words **Test your knowledge of these additional AWL words in the reading. Read the sentences below and notice the boldfaced AWL words. Then use context clues and write the correct AWL word next to its definition.**

1. Some are **inclined** to see the United States as a salad bowl where the various groups have remained **somewhat** distinct and different from one another, creating a richly diverse country.

2. The **process** by which these many groups have been made a part of a common cultural life with commonly shared values is called *assimilation*.

3. Many Americans strongly disapproved of the political bosses. **Despite** these criticisms, many scholars believe that the political bosses performed an important **function**.

4. Integrated neighborhoods are the exception, rather than the rule. Sociology professor John Logan has studied this **phenomenon** and reports that the 2000 census found the United States as segregated a nation as it has ever been.

5. Some immigrants risk their lives to come to the United States without **documentation** to do agricultural or **construction** work.

6. In 1965, the United States made important changes in its immigration laws, allowing many more immigrants to come, and entirely **eliminating** the older laws' **bias** in favor of white European immigrants.

7. Segregation and **discrimination** are against the law, but **residential** patterns create largely segregated neighborhood schools, particularly in many urban areas.

_____ 1. have an opinion about whether something is good or bad that influences how you deal with it

_____ 2. working on new buildings

_____ 3. even though something else exists or is true

_____ 4. the practice of treating a person or group differently from another in an unfair way

_____ 5. official papers that are used to prove that something is true

_____ 6. getting rid of something completely

_____ 7. job

_____ 8. influenced toward a particular action or opinion

_____ 9. something that is very unusual

_____ 10. a series of actions

_____ 11. relating to homes

_____ 12. more than a little, but not very

EXPAND YOUR KNOWLEDGE

Think, Pair, Share

Do you agree or disagree with these statements? Draw a circle around your response, then share your answers with a partner and another pair of students.

1. I would emigrate to another country if I could have a better life there for myself and my family.   agree   disagree

2. Foreigners who come from any country in the world are welcomed in my country.   agree   disagree

3. My government should encourage refugees from other countries to settle in my country.   agree   disagree

4. My family would not object if I chose to marry someone of another nationality.   **agree**   **disagree**

5. My family would not object if I chose to marry someone of another race.   **agree**   **disagree**

6. It is important to maintain your own language and cultural traditions even if you have left your country.   **agree**   **disagree**

7. People are really basically the same all over the world.   **agree**   **disagree**

8. People who are very different from the dominant culture (race, religion, or ethnic background) have as high a status as anyone else in my country.   **agree**   **disagree**

9. Every person in the world should learn to speak at least one foreign language.   **agree**   **disagree**

10. I believe that my children will have a higher standard of living than I had growing up.   **agree**   **disagree**

Ask Americans

If possible, ask several Americans to tell you about their ethnic backgrounds. Ask them the following questions. Then report your findings to the class.

1. What nationalities were your ancestors?

2. When did your ancestors immigrate to America?

3. Does anyone in your family still speak the language of the "old (original) country"?

4. Does your family maintain contact with any relatives in the old country?

5. What family customs or traditions from the old country do you observe?

6. Have you or any of your family members done any genealogy research to learn about your family history?

Observe the Media

Work in small groups to discuss these questions.

1. How are ethnic and racial minorities and women represented in the media?

2. If you are in the United States, watch national and local news broadcasts and count the number of women and minorities reporting the news. What percentages do you find?

3. Watch TV commercials and count the racial and ethnic minorities. How do the numbers compare with the news reporters? What conclusions can you draw from these observations?

TOP NON-ENGLISH LANGUAGES SPOKEN IN THE UNITED STATES

LANGUAGE	NUMBER OF SPEAKERS (2000 CENSUS)	PERCENT
Population*	262,375,152	100.0
Speak only English	215,423,557	82.1
Speak a language other than English	46,951,595	17.9
Speak a language other than English	46,951,595	17.9
Spanish of Spanish Creole	28,101,052	10.7
Chinese	2,022,143	0.8
French (incl. Patois, Cajun)	1,643,838	0.6
German	1,383,442	0.5
Tagalog (Philippines)	1,224,241	0.5
Vietnamese	1,009,627	0.4
Italian	1,008,370	0.4
Korean	894,063	0.3
Russian	706,242	0.3
Polish	667,414	0.3
Arabic	614,582	0.2
Portuguese or Portuguese Creole	564,630	0.2
Japanese	477,997	0.2
French Creole	453,368	0.2
African languages	418,505	0.2
Greek	365,436	0.1
Hindi	317,057	0.1
Persian	312,085	0.1
Urdu	262,900	0.1
Gujarati (India)	235,988	0.1
Serbo-Croatian	233,865	0.1
Armenian	202,708	0.1
Hebrew	195,374	0.1
Mon-Khmer, Cambodian (Southeast Asia)	181,889	0.1
Yiddish	178,945	0.1
Navajo	178,014	0.1
Miao, Hmong (Southeast Asia)	168,063	0.1
Scandinavian languages	162,252	0.1
Laotian	149,303	0.1
Thai	120,464	0
Hungarian	117,973	0
All other	2,379,765	0.7

* Data is for persons five years old and over.

Source: U.S. Bureau of the Census.

Have a Debate

Unlike most countries, the United States does not have an official language. While English is widely understood to be the main language of government, commerce, and most education, the people who wrote the Constitution purposely did not declare any one language as the official language.

Organize a debate on whether or not a country should have an official language, or languages. Have one team argue in favor of this and the other team argue against it. When planning your arguments, consider the following questions.

1. Why do you think the founding fathers omitted the designation of an official language?

2. What are the possible consequences of having one official language to speakers of other languages?

3. Do you think that most immigrants recognize the value of knowing the language of their new country?

Immigrant students in an adult education ESL class

Understand Affirmative Action

After the civil rights laws were passed in the mid-1960s, the government began affirmative action programs to deal with racial inequalities. Businesses and universities were expected to take affirmative action and recruit African Americans into jobs and educational programs in proportion to their representation in the population. For example, if 12 percent of the population were black, then 12 percent of the employees or students should be black. Over time, affirmative action was extended to cover other ethnic and racial minorities and also women.

Today, the Equal Employment Opportunity Commission of the federal government enforces laws against discrimination in the workplace. Businesses that employ 15 or more people are required by law to keep records about the race, sex, and certain ethnic categories of their employees. Businesses that have over 100 employees are required by law to report this information to the government each year. If you visit the EEOC website, www.eeoc.gov, you will see that there are nine categories of discrimination that are against the law. They are age, disability, unequal pay, national origin, pregnancy, race, religion, sex, and sexual harassment.

As a result of affirmative action programs, so much progress has been made that many Americans now believe that it has achieved its goals. There is now a debate over the future of affirmative action. Should African Americans and other minorities be given preferential treatment in being hired or promoted on their jobs? Should women be given preferential treatment?

Discuss these questions with Americans and with your classmates.

1. Has affirmative action involving hiring practices for women and minorities been good for society or not good for society?

2. Is affirmative action still necessary to achieve diversity in the American workplace?

3. Have you personally benefited from affirmative action in your career?

4. Have you personally been disadvantaged by affirmative action in your career?

5. What traditional American values are reinforced by affirmative action and laws against discrimination?

Use the Internet

Working in small groups, choose an ethnic group in the United States to research online.

For example, you might choose Turkish Americans, Korean Americans, Ethiopian Americans, Nigerian Americans, Peruvian Americans—any group you wish.

Decide what questions you want answered. These might include the following.

> Where do they live in the United States?
>
> How many of them live here?
>
> What festivals do they have?
>
> What are some typical foods?
>
> Are there native-language newspapers?
>
> Are there special schools?
>
> What kinds of websites are there for this group?

When you have finished your research, make a report to the rest of the class on what you learned.

Begin by giving your classmates clues and having them guess which group you have chosen. You could use the clues for a scavenger hunt and have the last clue direct them to the group's home country on a world map.

WRITE ABOUT IT

A. **Choose one of these writing topics. Then write a short composition about it.**

1. Describe a time when you or a friend or a family member experienced discrimination. Write it as a narrative, following chronological order, with an explanation. You could use either the past or the present tense. Include information such as the following:

   Where this occurred

   What happened

   Who was involved

   What the result was

   How each of the people involved felt

   What can be done to eliminate discrimination and prejudice

2. Write a letter to the president (of the United States, or to the leader of your country) proposing a new immigration policy. Explain how many people should be admitted each year, from what countries, on what basis, and what should be done once they have arrived. Support your opinions carefully. Offer solutions to any problems that might be anticipated.

 B. **A Smithsonian museum in Washington, D.C., is dedicated to the cultures of the American Indian. Visit its website, www.nmai.si.edu, and write a report on what you learn about the museum.**

Books to Read

Julia Alvarez, *How the Garcia Girls Lost Their Accents*—The story of four sisters from the Dominican Republic adjusting to life in the United States and trying to integrate their old culture into their new one.

W.E.B. DuBois, *The Souls of Black Folk*—A classic work by W.E.B. DuBois exploring the culture and "soul" of African-American society around 1900.

Catherine E. McKinley, *The Book of Sarahs: A Family in Parts*—Adopted by whites in the 1960s, the biracial author tells of her struggle to find her birth parents.

Donna Jackson Nakazawa, *Does Anybody Else Look Like Me? A Parent's Guide to Raising Multiracial Children*—A psychological guide to helping multiracial children of all ages develop confidence and a healthy sense of self.

Ronald Takaki, *Strangers from a Different Shore*—The author presents a history of Asian Americans using personal experiences mixed with historical facts.

Movies to See

Cold Mountain—Near the end of the American Civil War, a wounded soldier makes a dangerous journey back home to Cold Mountain, North Carolina, to reunite with his sweetheart.

The Color Purple—The hard life and painful experiences of a young African-American woman living in the South.

Fried Green Tomatoes—A housewife who is unhappy with her life befriends an older woman in a nursing home and is fascinated by her stories of people she used to know.

Real Women Have Curves—The story of a first-generation Mexican-American teenage girl ready to become a woman.

West Side Story—A musical version of the Romeo and Juliet story about the romance of teenagers who belong to different gangs in New York City.

Graduation day at Fairleigh Dickinson University

EDUCATION IN THE UNITED STATES

Americans regard education as the means by which the inequalities among individuals are to be erased and by which every desirable end is to be achieved.

George S. Counts (1889–1974)

BEFORE YOU READ

Preview Vocabulary

A. Read the following sentences from the chapter and notice the words in italics. These key AWL words will help you understand the chapter reading. Use context clues to help you figure out the meanings. Then choose which definition is best for the italicized word.

_____ 1. Parents who live in large cities may send their children to Catholic or other religious schools because they believe that these schools are safer and have higher *academic* standards than the public schools.

    a. relating to education
    b. relating to danger

_____ 2. Although the amount of money spent per child is not always the best *indicator* of the quality of education the child receives, it certainly is an important factor.

    a. increase
    b. sign

_____ 3. Many of the new jobs in the United States either require a college education, even a graduate degree, or are low-paying jobs in the service *sector* of the economy—such as in fast-food restaurants, small stores, and hotels.

    a. information
    b. part, area, or segment

_____ 4. In a test case in 1896, the Supreme Court of the United States stated that racial segregation in public schools and other public facilities in the southern states did not *violate* the Constitution.

    a. protect
    b. disobey or do something against

_____ 5. The Supreme Court of the United States invented what is called the "separate but equal" doctrine to *justify* racial segregation in public schools and other public facilities in the southern states.

    a. explain
    b. prevent something from happening

_____ 6. The public schools in the inner city were composed *predominantly* of African-American students and often shared the neighborhood problems of high crime rates and other forms of social disorder.

    a. mostly or mainly
    b. definitely or exactly

_____ 7. There are some bilingual programs in areas where there is a large *concentration* of one language group, particularly Spanish speakers.

    a. academic achievement
    b. large amount of something in one place

_____ 8. Some have charged that American history has been told from the *perspective* of Anglo-Europeans, rather than by exploring historical events from the various perspectives of those involved.

    a. way of thinking about something
    b. historical event

_____ 9. These attempts to provide multicultural education have ranged from simply adding information and literature to the current textbooks and curricula to more sweeping attempts to *transform* the basic curriculum into one which is more reflective of the diversity of the students who will study it.

    a. to completely change the appearance or form of something
    b. to keep the same appearance or form of something

B. Read these two sentences from the chapter and notice the words in italics. Then use context clues and write the correct word next to its definition.

1. Americans *regard* education as the *means* by which the inequalities among individuals are to be *erased* and by which every desirable end is to be *achieved*.

2. Can a country as diverse as the United States have schools which *reflect* that diversity and still *retain* a *core* national *identity* and culture?

    _____ 1. the most important or central part

    _____ 2. got rid of something so that it did not exist anymore

    _____ 3. show

    _____ 4. think about

    _____ 5. keep

    _____ 6. a method or system

    _____ 7. gotten, reached

    _____ 8. the qualities a group of people have that make them different from other people

Preview Content

A. Think about the George S. Counts quotation at the beginning of the chapter. In small groups, discuss how education can erase inequalities. Make a list of some examples.

B. Discuss these questions with your classmates.

1. What are the differences between public and private schools? Which are better? Why?

2. What qualities do you think American universities are looking for when they decide who will be admitted?

3. What do you know about the system of education in the United States? Work with a partner to fill in the K-W-L chart on the next page with what you *know* about education in the United States and what you *want* to know. Then, as you read the chapter, fill in what you have *learned*.

K	W	L
What We <u>Know</u> About Education in the United States	What We <u>Want</u> to Know About Education in the United States	What We Have <u>Learned</u> About Education in the United States

Education often takes place in an informal setting.

C. **Read the headings in the chapter and look at the illustrations. Write five topics that you predict will be covered in this chapter.**

1. _____

2. _____

3. _____

4. _____

5. _____

The Establishment of Public Schools in America: Tocqueville's Observations

1   As might be expected, educational institutions in the United States reflect the nation's basic values, especially the ideal of equality of opportunity. From elementary school through college, Americans believe that everyone deserves an equal opportunity to get a good education.

2   From the beginning, when Americans established their basic system of public schools in 1825, they reaffirmed[1] the principle of equality by making schools open to all classes of Americans and by financing the schools with tax money collected from all citizens. Those who favored public schools believed that these institutions would help reduce social-class distinctions in the United States by educating children of all social classes in the same "common schools," as they were known at the time.

3   When Alexis de Tocqueville arrived in the United States in 1831, he found a great deal of enthusiasm about the new and growing public elementary schools. The mayor of New York City gave a special dinner for Tocqueville during which a toast[2] was offered in honor of "Education—the extension of our public schools—a national blessing."

4   Because he was a French aristocrat, Tocqueville at first shared the fears of some wealthy Americans who believed that universal education would be a danger rather than a national blessing. He eventually decided, however, that the tendency of public education to encourage people to seek a higher status in life was in harmony, not in conflict, with the customs of American society. The ideal of equal opportunity for all regardless of family background was much stronger in the United States than in France.

5   Tocqueville also noted that American public education had a strong practical content which included the teaching of vocational[3] skills and the duties of citizenship. Thus, public education not only gave Americans the desire to better themselves, but it also gave them the practical tools to do so. Moreover, the material abundance of the United States provided material rewards for those who took full advantage of the opportunity for a public education.

6   During the next century and a half, public schools in the United States were expanded to include secondary or high schools (grades 9–12) and colleges and universities, with both undergraduate and graduate studies.

The Educational Ladder

7   Americans view their public school system as an educational ladder, rising from elementary school to high school and finally college undergraduate and graduate programs. Most children start school at age five by attending kindergarten, or even at age three or four by attending preschool programs. Then usually there are six years of elementary school, two years of middle school (or junior high school), and four years of high school. School systems may divide the

---

[1] **reaffirmed:** formally stated an intention or belief again, especially as an answer to a question or doubt
[2] **toast:** an occasion when you ask everyone who is present to drink something in order to thank or wish someone luck
[3] **vocational:** training or advice relating to the skills needed to do a particular job

twelve years up differently—grouping sixth-, seventh-, and eighth-graders into middle school, for example. Not all school systems have kindergarten, but all do have twelve years of elementary, middle school, and senior high school.

8   After high school, the majority of students go on to college.* Undergraduate studies lead to a bachelor's degree, which is generally what Americans mean when they speak of a "college diploma." Students may also receive an associate degree for two years of study at a community college. Some of these associate degrees are in vocational or technical fields.

Georgetown University, Washington, D.C.

9   The bachelor's degree can be followed by professional studies, which lead to degrees in such professions as law and medicine, or graduate studies, which lead to master's and doctoral degrees. The American public schools are free and open to all at the elementary and secondary (high school) level, but the public universities charge tuition[4] and have competitive entrance requirements.

10   The educational ladder concept is an almost perfect reflection of the American ideal of individual success based on equality of opportunity and on "working your way to the top." In the United States there are no separate public educational systems with a higher level of education for the wealthy and a lower level of education for the masses. Rather, there is one system which is open to all. Individuals may climb as high on the ladder as they can. The abilities of the individuals, rather than their social class, are expected to determine how high each person will go.

11   Although the great majority of children attend the free public elementary and high schools, about 10 percent choose to attend private schools. The majority of these are religious schools that are associated with particular churches and receive financial support from them, though parents must also pay tuition. A major purpose of these schools is to give religious instruction, which cannot be done in public schools, but that is not always the reason that parents send their children to these schools. Parents who live in large cities may send their children to Catholic or other religious schools because they believe that these schools are safer and have higher academic standards than the public schools. The public schools in many of

---

* The word *college* is used in several different ways. It is generally used instead of *university* to refer to the education after high school, as in the expressions "go to college" and "get a college education." It is also used to refer to the school, as in "Where do you go to college?" Often, people use the word *college* to refer to a small school that does not offer graduate degrees or to a two-year community college. *University* is used for large schools that offer both undergraduate and graduate degrees. Universities often call the divisions within them *colleges*, as in the *College of Arts and Sciences* of the University of Maryland, Baltimore County.

---

[4] **tuition:** the money you pay for being taught at a school or college

these cities have encouraged parents and community members to establish charter schools[5] in an attempt to keep these children in the public schools.

12   There are also some elite[6] private schools which serve mainly upper-class children. Students must pay such high tuition costs that only wealthier families can afford them, though scholarships are usually offered to some talented, less affluent children who cannot pay the tuition. Parents often send their children to these schools so that they will associate with other upper-class children and maintain the upper-class position held by their parents, in addition to getting a good education.

13   Unlike private religious schools, elitist private schools do conflict with the American ideal of equality of opportunity. These schools often give an extra educational and social advantage to the young people whose families have the money to allow them to attend. However, because these schools are relatively few in number, they do not displace the public school as the central educational institution in the United States. Nor does the best private school education protect young people from competition with public school graduates for admission to the best universities in the nation.

14   There is another area of inequality in the American education system. Because of the way that schools are funded, the quality of education that American students receive in public schools varies greatly. By far the largest percentage of the money for schools comes from the local level (cities and counties), primarily from property taxes. School districts that have middle-class or wealthy families have more tax money to spend on education. Therefore, wealthier school districts have beautiful school buildings with computers and the latest science equipment, and poorer school districts have older buildings with less modern equipment. Although the amount of money spent per child is not always the best indicator of the quality of education the child receives, it certainly is an important factor. Some believe that all schools, public or private, religious or not, should be eligible for public school funding. They would support a system of vouchers,[7] which parents could use to help pay tuition at any school of their choice. Some states are now experimenting with voucher systems.

Attending an American University

15   Money is also increasingly a factor in a college education. All university students must pay tuition expenses in the United States, and the cost of an education is rising much more rapidly than is the average family income (about five times higher between 1991 and 2001). Because tuition is much lower at public universities than at private ones, wealthy students have more choices. There are a number of financial aid programs in the form of loans and scholarships available at both public and private schools. However, the expenses of buying books and living away from home make it increasingly difficult for many students to attend even the less expensive public universities. Many students must work during their college years to help meet costs.

16   A growing number of students cannot afford to go away to college and pay $15,000–$39,000 each year for a public or private university. They choose instead to attend community college programs for two years in their hometowns, paying as little

---

[5] **charter schools**: schools to which the state government has given money and special permission to operate but that are operated by parents, companies, etc., rather than by the public school system

[6] **elite**: limited to wealthy people with a high social status

[7] **vouchers**: types of tickets that can be used instead of money for a particular purpose

as $2,000 per year in tuition. These two-year colleges offer a wide range of programs. Some offer two-year degrees called *associate degrees*. Students may also take their first two years of college at a community college and then transfer to a state university. Community colleges feed into the state university systems and offer educational opportunities to large numbers of students who ordinarily would not be able to attend a university. More and more students also work while they are in college, reducing the number of courses they can take and increasing the time it takes them to complete a college degree.

17   Despite its costs, the percentage of Americans seeking a college education continues to grow. In 1900, less than 10 percent of college-age Americans entered college. Today, over half of all Americans have taken some college courses, and many have attended for four years or more. There are more than 15 million students attending college now, about six times more than fifty years ago, and there are roughly 3,000 different colleges and universities to choose from. Today, many parents who were not able to attend college when they were young have the satisfaction of seeing their sons and daughters attend.

State schools offer excellent, affordable education.

18   Even the formerly elitist private universities have yielded a great deal to public pressure for greater equality of opportunity in education. Harvard, a private university considered by many to be one of the nation's most prestigious,[8] provides a good example. Before World War II, the majority of Harvard students came from elite private preparatory schools. Now, the majority of them come from public high schools.

The Monetary Value of Education

19   As we have seen in earlier chapters, the American definition of success is largely one of acquiring wealth and a high material standard of living. It is not surprising, therefore, that Americans value education for its monetary[9] value. The belief is widespread in the United States that the more schooling people have, the more money they will earn when they leave school. The belief is strongest regarding the desirability of an undergraduate university degree, or a professional degree, such as medicine or law, following the undergraduate degree. The monetary value of graduate degrees in "nonprofessional" fields such as art, history, or philosophy is not as great.

20   In recent years, there has been a change in the job market in the United States. In the past, it was possible to get a high-paying factory job without a college education. Workers with skills learned in vocational schools or on the job could do work that did not require a college education. These were among the jobs that new immigrants were often able to obtain. Increasingly, however, the advent[10] of new technologies has meant that more and more education is required to do the work. Many of the new jobs in the United States either require a college education, even a graduate degree, or

---

[8] **prestigious:** admired as one of the best and most important
[9] **monetary:** relating to money
[10] **advent:** the time when something first begins to be widely used

they are low-paying jobs in the service sector of the economy—such as in fast-food restaurants, small stores, and hotels. Additionally, many jobs are being outsourced to countries where salaries are much lower. This is true of both higher-paying technical jobs and lower-paying jobs requiring limited skills.

21   Because of the importance of higher education, many adults combine working with taking classes at a college. Many public and private colleges and universities are making it easier for students to take classes through *distance learning*, using the Internet to provide materials and lectures as well as to engage students in discussion. Some students who are living on campus or commuting to classes take at least part of their coursework by distance, but it is also possible for a student to obtain both undergraduate and graduate degrees without ever being on a college campus.

Educating the Individual

22   American schools tend to put more emphasis on developing critical-thinking skills than they do on acquiring quantities of facts. American students are encouraged to ask questions, think for themselves, and express their own opinions in class, a reflection of the American values of individual freedom and self-reliance. The goal of the American education system is to teach children how to learn and to help them reach their maximum potential.

23   The development of social and interpersonal skills may be considered as important as the development of intellectual skills. To help students develop these other important skills, schools have added a large number of extracurricular[11] activities (activities outside classroom studies) to daily life at school. These activities are almost as important as the students' class work. For example, in making their decisions about which students to admit, colleges look for students who are "well-rounded." Grades in high school courses and scores on tests like the SAT are very important, but so are the students' extracurricular activities. It is by participating in these activities that students demonstrate their special talents, their level of maturity and responsibility, their leadership qualities, and their ability to get along with others.

24   Some Americans consider athletics, frequently called *competitive sports*, the most important of all extracurricular activities. This is because many people believe it is important for all young people, young men and young women, to learn how to compete successfully. Team sports such as football, basketball, and baseball are important because they teach students the "winning spirit." At times, this athletic competition may be carried to such an extreme that some students and their parents may place more importance on the high school's sports program than its academic offerings.

25   Student government is another extracurricular activity designed to develop competitive, political, and social skills in students. The students choose a number of student government officers who compete for the votes of their fellow students in school elections. Although these officers have little power over the central decisions of the school, the process of running for office and then taking responsibility for a number of student activities if elected is seen as good experience in developing their leadership and competitive skills, and in helping them to be responsible citizens.

---

[11] **extracurricular:** sports or other activities that you do in addition to your usual classes

26   Athletics and student government are only two of a variety of extracurricular activities found in American schools. There are clubs and activities for almost every student interest—art, music, drama, debate, foreign languages, photography, volunteer work—all aimed at helping the student to become more successful in later life. Many parents watch their children's extracurricular activities with as much interest and concern as they do their children's intellectual achievements in the classroom.

Extracurricular activities such as drama club add to the college experience.

Racial Equality and Education

27   The most significant departure from the ideal of equality of opportunity in education has occurred in the education of African Americans. As we saw in the previous chapter, after the Civil War in the 1860s, the southern states developed a social and legal system which segregated the former black slaves from the white population in all public facilities, including schools. Black people in the southern states were prohibited by law from attending schools with whites. Blacks had separate schools which were inferior to the white schools by almost any measure.

28   In a test case in 1896, the Supreme Court of the United States stated that racial segregation in public schools and other public facilities in the southern states did not violate the Constitution. Equality of opportunity was such an important American value that the Supreme Court had to pretend that the separate black schools and other facilities were equal to those of whites, when everyone knew that they were not. The Supreme Court invented what is called the "separate but equal" doctrine to justify racial segregation in public schools and other public facilities in the southern states. One Supreme Court justice strongly disagreed. Justice John Marshall Harlan believed that the decision violated the nation's highest law and its basic values. "Our Constitution is color-blind," he said, "and neither knows nor tolerates classes among its citizens."

29   Fifty-eight years later a more modern Supreme Court agreed with Justice Harlan. In a historic decision in 1954, it held that laws that forced black students to go to racially segregated schools violated the U.S. Constitution because such schools could never be equal. The opinion of the Court was that "to separate [black school children] from others . . . solely because of their race generates a feeling of inferiority . . . that may affect their hearts and minds in a way unlikely ever to be undone."

30   Although segregated schools were not legal after 1954, they continued to exist in the South until the passage of the Civil Rights Acts of the mid-1960s. In the late 1960s and during the 1970s, a series of court decisions forced the nation to take measures to integrate all of its schools, in both the North and the South. In the North, there had been no legal segregation of schools. However, in both the South and the North, the neighborhood schools reflected the makeup of the races who lived

in the neighborhood. Thus, the residential patterns were often the source of the problem, particularly in urban areas. The public schools in the inner city were composed predominantly of African-American students and often shared the neighborhood problems of high crime rates and other forms of social disorder. These schools were clearly unequal to those in the predominantly white, middle-class neighborhoods in the suburbs.

31   For the next twenty years, the courts required Americans to try to achieve racial balance in the public schools. The most controversial method used to deal with unequal neighborhood schools was the busing of schoolchildren from their home neighborhoods to schools in more distant neighborhoods in order to achieve a greater mixture of black and white children in all schools. Black children from the inner city were bused to schools in predominantly white, middle-class neighborhoods, and students living in the middle-class neighborhoods were bused into the poorer black neighborhood schools. As a result, some children had to ride the bus for an hour each way, going to and from school. Most students did not like it, and neither did their parents. Many school districts have now abandoned mandatory[12] busing and they allow children to attend the school in their own neighborhood, even if it is predominantly black or white. Some school districts have established "magnet" schools in black neighborhoods to attract white children who want to participate in special programs that focus on the arts, science and technology, or foreign languages, which are offered only at the magnet school.

32   Unfortunately, these attempts have met with limited success. The Harvard Project on School Desegregation recently reported that the trend toward ethnic and racial resegregation of the schools is growing, even though the population in the schools is becoming increasingly diverse. Since 1968, white enrollment in the schools has declined by one-sixth, while the African-American population has increased 20 percent and the Hispanic/Latino population has grown by 218 percent. The fastest resegregation is occurring in the South and among Latino communities, usually in low-income communities. Although most would agree that equality of opportunity in education is a goal that should be pursued, it has not been achieved. African-American and Hispanic students continue to have the lowest graduation rates.

33   A new question dealing with racial and ethnic equality in education was brought to the Supreme Court in the late 1970s. The question dealt with the admissions policies of professional schools, such as medical and law schools, which are attached to many of the nation's universities. Some of these schools have attempted to do more than treat all applicants equally. Many have tried in recent years to make up for past discrimination against blacks and other minorities by setting aside a certain number of places specifically for applicants from these groups, a practice known as *affirmative action*. Some schools were so determined to admit minority students that they focused on factors other than high school grades or test scores in their decisions to admit these students, wanting to ensure that the students in their programs reflected the diversity of the eligible student population.

34   This could be seen as special treatment rather than equal opportunity. However, many professional school administrators believed that because of discrimination against these groups in the past, equality now demanded that certain limited numbers of minority students be given some extra advantage in the selection of new

---

12 mandatory: something that must be done, especially because a law or rule says it must be done

professional students. Having a diverse group of students would lead to richer discussions in the classroom and provide a better and more representative academic experience.

35   These minority quotas were challenged by a white student, Allen Bakke, who was denied admission to the medical school at the University of California at Davis, California. He claimed that the medical school had admitted some nonwhite minority students less qualified than he. The U.S. Supreme Court, in the famous *Regents of University of California v. Bakke* case of 1978, agreed that he had been denied an equal opportunity for admission. In a rather complicated decision, the Court held that a professional school could not set aside a certain number of places to be filled only by minority students. Such quotas were a denial of equal educational opportunity. Professional schools, however, could give some extra consideration to nonwhite minority applicants, but the Court was forbidding them to carry this practice too far.

36   After a number of other decisions limiting the use of affirmative action in determining college admissions, in 2003 the Supreme Court seemed to reverse this policy. It decided that the University of Michigan could consider a student's ethnic or racial heritage during its decision making. As Justice Sandra Day O'Connor wrote in the Supreme Court decision, "Effective participation by members of all racial and ethnic groups in the civic life of our Nation is essential if the dream of one Nation, indivisible, is to be realized." Both businesses and the military filed briefs[13] in this case, supporting affirmative action as a means of promoting cross-cultural understanding, helping to break down stereotypes, and fostering better understanding among different groups. As many pointed out at the time, affirmative action does not mean that unqualified students will be accepted; there are many more qualified students than spaces for them in these university programs.

The Increasing Responsibilities of Public Schools

37   Americans place the weight of many of their ideals, hopes, and problems on the nation's public school system. Some observers believe they have placed more responsibilities on the public schools than the schools can possibly handle. For example, public schools are often expected to solve student problems that result from the weakening of family ties in the United States. Rising divorce rates have resulted in an increasing number of children in the public schools who are raised by only one parent. Studies have shown that these children are more likely to have problems at school than are children raised in families with two parents.

38   The education of the new immigrant children provides the public school system with some of its greatest challenges. Many of the children come from countries where they have not had strong educational preparation, and their academic skills are below grade level. Others have come from school systems with standards similar to or more advanced than the American schools, and their academic adjustment is much easier. However, all these children must learn English. This means that they are trying to learn new concepts at the same time that they are struggling to learn a new language. Studies show that it takes five to seven years in order for them to be able to compete with English-speaking American children on an equal basis in classes where English is

---

[13] **filed briefs:** submitted legal documents to be considered by the court

the language of instruction. There are some bilingual programs in areas where there is a large concentration of one language group, particularly Spanish speakers. However, there are more than 400 languages spoken in the United States, and some school districts report that 100 or more different languages are spoken by children in their schools. It is not uncommon for five or six different native languages to be spoken by the students in one classroom.

39   At a time when enormous new burdens[14] are being placed on the public schools, the nation finds itself faced with new limits on its material abundance. These limits have steadily reduced the amount of money available to the public schools as they try to deal with their rapidly growing problems.

American students are encouraged to ask questions.

The Standards Movement

40   Recently, international comparisons of education have revealed that, in general, American students do not perform as well in math, science, and other subjects as do students from many other developed countries. Some believe this is because American standards for education may not be high enough. Traditionally, local community school districts have had responsibility for determining school curricula and selecting textbooks, with only limited state or national supervision. However, since the 1990s, both the states and the federal government have become more involved in determining school *standards*. The federal government has set national goals for education which include standards for early childhood, elementary, secondary, and adult education. Even teacher education programs have to meet federal and state standards. Most major educational associations, such as national associations of teachers of science, math, or language arts, have also evaluated the current curricula and criteria for certification and developed new standards.

41   To ensure that standards are met, the federal government now requires annual testing in reading and mathematics in most elementary and middle grades; states also may require students to pass a series of examinations in such subjects as reading, writing, mathematics, and civics before they can graduate from high school. Preparing for or taking these tests can consume up to 20 percent of the school year. All this testing has caused some concern among educators, since the American belief in local control (and funding) of schools is being challenged by unfunded mandates[15] from the state and federal governments. They also fear that the American tradition of asking questions and thinking for oneself is being replaced by memorization of facts to be tested.

---

[14] **burdens:** difficult or worrisome things that you are responsible for
[15] **unfunded mandates:** things that the U.S. (or state) government demands that school districts do although they do not give the money to meet the demand

Multicultural Education

42 The changing populations of students in American schools has brought some changes in what is taught in the schools as well. One in three students in U.S. schools is a member of a racial or ethnic minority group, and one in five lives with a parent who was born outside the United States. Ethnic and racial minorities have criticized schools and textbooks for focusing too much on the literature and historical events of Anglo-Europeans or white males. They believe that schools have almost ignored the contributions of African Americans, Latinos, or Native Americans. Some have charged that American history has been told from the perspective of Anglo-Europeans, rather than exploring historical events from the various perspectives of those involved. For example, the frontier movement west has been presented more from the perspective of descendants of white settlers than from the perspectives of the descendants of the Native Americans who were moved in the process.

43 During the 1990s, schools began to seriously examine their curricula and to try to incorporate more varied cultural information and perspectives into education. These attempts to provide multicultural education have ranged from simply adding information and literature to the current textbooks and curricula, to more sweeping attempts to transform the basic curriculum into one which is more reflective of the diversity of the students who will study it. At the most basic level, many schools celebrate African-American History Month or Hispanic Heritage Month, or they have international festivals which include dancing, singing, and foods from the native countries of their students. At a deeper level, many schools have adopted history or social studies textbooks which include more information about African Americans, Hispanic Americans, and other minorities, or American literature texts that include poetry and fiction written by Americans of all ethnic backgrounds. In some colleges, the traditional set of Western great books, sometimes called "the canon," has been replaced by a much broader set of literary texts, reflecting the experiences and backgrounds of the students who will be reading them. For example, the University of California at Berkeley requires all students to take a course on American cultures to enable them to better understand the diversity of the United States, which is likely to grow until there is a time when there is no majority population.

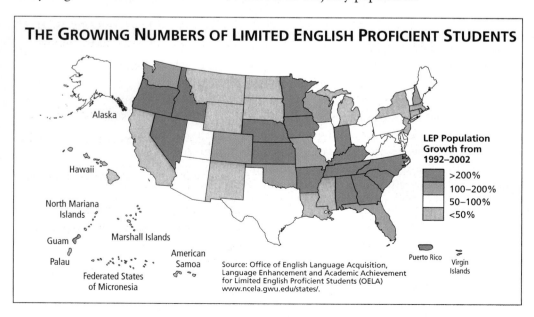

THE GROWING NUMBERS OF LIMITED ENGLISH PROFICIENT STUDENTS

LEP Population Growth from 1992–2002

>200%
100–200%
50–100%
<50%

Source: Office of English Language Acquisition, Language Enhancement and Academic Achievement for Limited English Proficient Students (OELA) www.ncela.gwu.edu/states/.

44   Not all Americans support multicultural education, however. Some fear that replacing the Western civilization and literary traditions which have been the basis of American education with a much broader historical and literary discussion will result in the fragmentation of American society. Schools have traditionally been the place where students of all ethnic, religious, and racial backgrounds have learned *American* history, literature, and values. With so many competing views of history or sets of values in the school, some fear that it will be difficult for the country to remain American. It is a serious question: Can a country as diverse as the United States have schools which reflect that diversity and still retain a core national identity and culture?

AFTER YOU READ

Understand Main Ideas

Read the predictions you made on page 190 before reading the chapter. If you have not already done so, complete the **L** (What We Have Learned) part of the chart you started on page 190 before you read the chapter. With your partner, make up five questions about main points in the chapter and ask another pair of students to answer the questions. Then share your K-W-L chart with the other pair of students.

Understand Details

Write the letter of the best answer according to the information in the chapter.

_____ 1. In the beginning of the chapter it is implied that some wealthier Americans opposed the first public schools in the United States because

a. they cost too much money.
b. they would weaken social-class barriers.
c. people who did not pay for their education would not value it.

_____ 2. Tocqueville finally concluded that public education in the United States would

a. give Americans not only the desire but also the means to better their position in life.
b. not provide any practical training in vocational skills.
c. not work because people would be prevented from rising to a higher class by the aristocracy.

_____ 3. Which of these statements is <u>false</u>?

    a. American high school students have the choice of going to a free public school or a private one where they must pay tuition.

    b. The American education system is based on strong principles of equality of opportunity—all students should have an equal opportunity to get a good education.

    c. After twelve years of school, American students receive a bachelor's degree diploma at graduation.

_____ 4. Which of these statements is <u>true</u>?

    a. Most of the money to pay for American public schools comes from local taxes.

    b. Religious schools that serve middle-class students receive money from the national government, but elite private schools do not.

    c. The national Department of Education determines the curriculum for all schools and sets the standards for high school graduation and college admission.

_____ 5. From 1900 to 2000, the percentage of young Americans who take at least some college courses

    a. increased enormously, from less than 10 percent to over 50 percent.

    b. increased slightly, from about 10 percent to about 20 percent.

    c. stayed about the same, at around 20 percent.

_____ 6. What most Americans probably value most about higher education is

    a. its cultural value.

    b. its monetary value.

    c. its moral value.

_____ 7. Which of the following would <u>not</u> be considered an extracurricular activity?

    a. a school baseball team

    b. the student government of a school

    c. a classroom research project

_____ 8. In 1896, the U.S. Supreme Court said that racially segregated schools and other public facilities

    a. violated the principle of equality.

    b. violated the U.S. Constitution.

    c. did not violate the principle of equality or the U.S. Constitution.

_____ 9. Which of these statements is <u>false</u>?

    a. Public schools that are mainly black or mainly white today usually are the result of the racial makeup of neighborhoods.

    b. African-Americans are the fastest growing minority in the schools today.

    c. In some school districts, 100 different languages may be spoken.

_____ 10. Which of these statements is <u>true</u>?

    a. In the United States, all immigrant children attend bilingual programs until they learn English very well and are allowed to attend regular classes with native speakers.

    b. In the United States there are almost no uniform standards for any schools.

    c. Multicultural education discusses history from the perspectives of all the ethnic groups involved, not just the Anglo-American.

Improve Your Reading Skills: Scanning

Scan the chapter to find the answers to these questions.

1. When were public schools first established in the United States?

2. What did the mayor of New York City say in his toast at the dinner for Tocqueville?

3. What is a charter school?

4. How much does a college education in the United States cost per year?

5. What did the Supreme Court rule in 1954 about segregated schools?

6. Who was Allen Bakke?

7. What segment of the population in the public schools has increased by 218 percent since 1968?

8. Who said, "Effective participation by members of all racial and ethnic groups in the civic life of our Nation is essential if the dream of one Nation, indivisible, is to be realized"?

9. What is the "canon"?

10. What is the SAT?

Talk About It

Work in small groups and choose one or more of these topics to discuss.

1. Should universities be free or have very low tuition? Why or why not?

2. Are most schools in your country coeducational? What are the advantages and disadvantages of having boys and girls in the same classroom?

3. Is it possible for college teachers and students to be friends? What do you think the role of a teacher should be?

4. Are students _vessels to be filled_ or _lamps to be lit_? Which do you think is more important—learning a large quantity of facts or learning to think creatively? Why?

5. What should the requirements for entering a university be? Should extracurricular activities in high school or personal characteristics be considered? Why, or why not?

Build Your Vocabulary

Vocabulary Check Use the words in the box to complete the sentences.

burdens	extracurricular	mandatory	tuition
diplomas	facilities	perspective	violated
elite	fragmentation	transform	vocational

1. In 1954, the Supreme Court ruled that segregation denied black children an equal opportunity to an education; it _____ the Constitution.

2. In the past, many students who went to competitive schools such as Harvard received their high school education at _____ private schools for the rich.

3. Sports, clubs, and other _____ activities held after school help students get a well-rounded education.

4. Maintaining discipline and trying to teach children who come from broken homes and have severe problems are two of the numerous _____ the public schools are now expected to carry.

5. At school graduation ceremonies, students receive _____.

6. Some Americans worry that if students do not study a core body of knowledge, they will not learn enough about American culture, and this could lead to the _____ of American society.

7. At the university level, there is no free system of public education; even universities supported by public funds charge students _____.

8. In order to integrate public schools, the courts ordered _____ busing; parents and children had no choice.

9. Some Americans would like to see major changes in their public education system; they want to _____ it.

10. Before the civil rights laws were passed, segregation of public _____ was legal in the South.

11. Those who are in favor of multicultural education believe that it is important to study history from the _____ of a number of cultures.

12. Some American high schools offer _____ education to prepare

students for jobs right after school; these students do not attend college.

More AWL Words Test your knowledge of these additional AWL words in the reading by doing the word puzzle below. First match the words and definitions. Then find and circle the AWL words in the puzzle. Words may run horizontally, vertically, diagonally, or backwards.

_____ 1. annual   a. relating to practical knowledge or skills

_____ 2. criteria   b. to get something that you want

_____ 3. evaluate   c. fully grown and sensible

_____ 4. grade   d. a planned way of doing something

_____ 5. ignore   e. to choose carefully

_____ 6. mature   f. to consider something carefully

_____ 7. method   g. happening once a year

_____ 8. obtain   h. to deliberately pay no attention to

_____ 9. select   i. established standards used to judge something

_____ 10. technical   j. one of the twelve years of school in the United States

```
Q  S  D  C  E  L  F  U  O  B  L  G  X  D  F
E  N  D  R  B  V  A  Q  T  A  S  I  E  F  Y
X  N  Q  I  Q  B  A  C  R  P  W  M  F  I  N
B  C  I  T  D  V  H  L  I  L  T  C  F  S  J
Q  X  W  E  F  C  V  E  U  N  U  U  Q  P  N
S  A  H  R  Y  Y  R  U  T  A  H  T  N  P  D
N  G  A  I  B  O  A  A  V  Q  T  C  J  D  M
J  O  U  A  N  M  A  T  U  R  E  E  E  E  Z
G  K  I  G  O  C  Q  C  E  E  K  K  T  T  V
B  B  I  T  F  N  W  B  D  Z  E  H  G  Z  A
B  Q  I  W  C  L  N  A  Q  H  O  O  Q  L  N
S  U  I  E  I  E  R  X  K  D  A  T  B  B  N
A  E  P  C  E  G  L  Y  O  B  T  A  I  N  U
T  P  Z  Y  V  N  B  E  Q  L  U  B  F  D  A
Q  A  Y  E  Z  T  U  S  S  G  M  J  B  K  L
```

Which Word Doesn't Belong? There are many words in this chapter that have to do with education. Work with a partner. Circle the word or phrase which does not belong in each group.

1. kindergarten, elementary school, middle school, high school, medical school

2. financial aid, tuition, scholarships, grades, vouchers

3. private, public, textbook, vocational, charter

4. test scores, grades, extracurricular activities, athletics, monetary value

5. associate degree, bachelor's, magnet school, master's, doctoral

6. coursework, lectures, busing, examinations, curricula

EXPAND YOUR KNOWLEDGE

Ask Americans

Find out how Americans feel about education. Ask several Americans the following questions and record their answers.

1. Should there be prayer in public schools?

2. Should public school systems provide vouchers that could be used to pay tuition in private schools?

3. Should there be sex education in the schools? If so, what should be taught?

4. Are drugs and violence problems in the schools in your neighborhood? What is being done to protect children in public schools?

5. How important is a college education? What difference does it make in a person's life?

Think, Pair, Share

What should be taught in public schools? What should be the priorities? Read the following list of areas which are covered in American schools and decide which are the most important.

Arrange the items in order from most important to least important by renumbering the sentences. Then share your list with a partner and with another pair of students.

_____ 1. Developing students' moral and ethical character

_____ 2. Teaching students how to think

_____ 3. Preparing students who do not go to college for a job or career after graduation

_____ 4. Helping students to become informed citizens so that they will be adequately prepared to vote at age eighteen

_____ 5. Preparing students for college

_____ 6. Developing students' appreciation of art, music, and other cultural pursuits

_____ 7. Other (your opinion) _____

Small-Group Project

Some American parents are so dissatisfied with the public schools that they are educating their children at home. _Homeschooling_ now provides education for an increasing number of American children, and the trend is growing rapidly. Some public school educators agree that the current model for public schools needs to be changed, and they themselves have begun to create alternative or _charter_ schools, experimenting with class size, grouping, schedules, and curriculum. Perhaps most dramatic, these alternatives to traditional public or private schools are transforming the roles of the teachers and the students, giving students much more power to decide what they want to learn.

Plan an ideal school. With your group, decide whether it would be homeschooling or an alternative school. Name your school, and then describe it in detail. Decide on school colors and a motto for your school. You may include these points in your description:

- Who would the students be (age, social class, ethnicity)?
- What kind of a building would you use?
- Would the school have a special emphasis (science, music)?
- What would the teachers be like (age, experience, roles)?
- How many students would be in a class?
- Who would determine the curriculum?
- What about tests and homework?
- How would discipline be maintained?
- What would be the role of the parents?
- What special activities would the students have?
- What would a typical day be like?
- What do you think others would say about this school?

When your description is complete, share your new school with the rest of the class.

People Watching

Find the answers to the following questions. Then compare your answers with those of your classmates.

1. When is the right time to ask a question in an American classroom? Watch others and notice the following. (If you have difficulty finding the answers to these questions, ask a fellow student or ask the teacher to explain when it is the right time for questions.)

   a. Is the teacher talking when students ask questions?

   b. How do students indicate that they have a question to ask?

   c. How does the teacher indicate that he or she is ready for questions? Does the teacher ask, "Are there any questions?" Does the teacher pause and look up from notes or from the chalkboard?

   d. What other signals does a teacher send to indicate that questions are invited?

2. One of the most difficult things for students to understand is when an interview or an appointment with a teacher or professor is over. How do you know when you should leave? Watch a teacher and student in an interview or appointment, if possible, and see which of these are used to indicate the appointment is over. If you cannot observe a teacher and student, perhaps you can watch another similar situation, such as a job interview, a meeting with a counselor, or an appointment with a doctor. Look for the following:

   a. The teacher moves noticeably in the chair—maybe closer to the desk or toward the door.

   b. The teacher says, "Well . . ." or "It has been nice talking to you" or "I think you understand now. . . ."

   c. The teacher turns his or her attention to other business such as papers on the desk or a schedule of appointments.

   d. The teacher moves the chair back from the desk.

American students often have discussions with their professors after class.

Ask Yourself/Ask Americans

Schools around the world differ in their expectations of students. In some schools, students are expected only to listen and remember what their teachers say; in others, they are expected to ask questions. It's important to know these differences if you are going to be successful in a school in another country.

Respond to the following statements. Write _T_ (True) or _F_ (False) in the first column to indicate how you think students should behave in your country. Then ask an American (preferably a student) for his or her opinion and record those answers in the second column.

	You	American Student
1. Students should not ask questions; they should only answer them.	_____	_____
2. Students should rise when the teacher enters the classroom.	_____	_____
3. Asking a teacher questions challenges his or her authority.	_____	_____
4. Students should never address teachers by their first names.	_____	_____
5. Students should memorize everything their teachers assign; education is primarily memorizing books and teachers' lectures.	_____	_____
6. Male and female students should attend the same classes.	_____	_____

What differences do you notice in the responses? Compare your answers with others in the class.

Use the Internet

Work with a partner and do one of these activities.

1. Some people predict that of the 6,000 languages currently spoken in the world, about half will not be spoken by the next century.

   Use the Internet to find information about languages in danger of becoming extinct. Then discuss these questions in small groups.

   a. Why should anyone care if a language is "dying"?

   b. What can be done to help maintain or revitalize a language that is in danger of being lost?

   c. How important do you think it is to preserve languages?

   d. What can individuals like you do to help preserve languages?

2. American Indian languages are among the most endangered in the world. Many of the 155 languages have not been written. Even those which have been written may have very few people who still speak the language.

Use the Internet to find information about Native American languages spoken in the United States and the number of their speakers. Then work with a partner and answer these questions.

    a. How many speakers are there of the most widely spoken languages, Navajo and Ojibwa?

    b. In what states do most of these people live? (What are the five most common?)

    c. How many languages have twenty speakers or fewer?

WRITE ABOUT IT

A. **Choose one of the following writing topics. Then write a short composition about it.**

    1. What are the advantages and disadvantages of working while attending college?

    2. What do you think the real value of a college education is? Is it monetary? Is it intellectual? Is it social? Write an essay explaining your views.

B. The English language has always been friendly to *borrowing* from other languages. Given the closeness of so many Spanish-speaking countries to the United States, and the presence of Spanish-speaking peoples in the Southwest before the colonists moved there from the East Coast, it is not surprising that a number of Spanish words have entered English, especially the English spoken in the United States. Look at this list of words borrowed from Spanish.

alcove	broncos	chaps	patio	siesta	tango
alfalfa	burrito	desperado	poncho	stampede	tornado
alligator	cafeteria	lasso	rodeo	taco	vanilla
avocado	canyon	macho			

What do you notice about these words? How many words relate to food? How many words relate to the life of the cowboy or to the West? (Note: The word for the fair that brings horseback riding, cow roping, and other cowboy feats to many western towns each year is *rodeo*.) Were there any words that surprised you?

Compare borrowings in English with those in other languages that you know. What similarities or differences do you see? Write a report about your findings.

Books to Read

Latoya Hunter, *The Diary of Latoya Hunter: My First Year in Junior High*—A young black girl writes about her family and her experiences in school.

Jonathan Kozol, *Savage Inequalities: Children in America's Schools*—A disturbing look at the differences in public schools attended by rich children versus those attended by poor children and the consequences of the inequalities.

Mike Rose, *Lives on the Boundary*—A teacher in the inner city describes his innovative methods for reaching children and adults who are educationally disadvantaged.

Leonard Q. Ross, *The Education of Hyman Kaplan*—The humorous story of an immigrant's attempt to learn English and become an American.

Beverly Daniel Tatum, *Why Are All the Black Kids Sitting Together in the Cafeteria? And Other Conversations About Race: A Psychologist Explains the Development of Racial Identity*—A discussion of whether self-segregation is a behavior to be discouraged or supported.

Movies to See

Lean on Me—Based on the true story of Joe Clark, a dedicated, but extremely tough, principal of a terrible inner-city school that he is determined to improve.

Music of the Heart—The story of a schoolteacher's struggle to teach violin to inner-city children in New York City's Harlem.

October Sky—The true story of Homer Hickam, a coal miner's son who, against his father's wishes, was inspired by the first *Sputnik* launch to build rockets.

Rudy—A boy who has always been told that he is too small to play college football is determined to overcome the odds and fulfill his dream of playing for Notre Dame.

Stand and Deliver—A dedicated teacher inspires his disadvantaged students to learn calculus to build up their self-esteem and pass an advanced placement exam.

Houston Rockets star Yao Ming

CHAPTER 10

HOW AMERICANS SPEND THEIR LEISURE TIME

> *The form and type of play and sports life which evolve in any group or nation mirror the development in other segments of the culture.*
> **American Academy of Physical Education**

BEFORE YOU READ

Preview Vocabulary

A. Read these sentences from the chapter. Then use context clues to figure out the meanings of the AWL words in italics.

1. The form and type of play and sports life which *evolve* in any group or nation mirror the development in other segments of the culture.

2. The competitive ethic in organized sports contains *elements* of hard work and physical courage. Hard work is often called "hustle," "persistence," or "never quitting" in the sports world, while physical courage is referred to as "being tough" or "having guts."

3. "The Bible says leisure and lying around are morally dangerous . . . sports keep us busy. . . . There are probably more really *committed* Christians in sports, both collegiate and professional, than in any other occupation in America."

4. Some people are particularly concerned about the injuries that high school players get in football games. The pressure to "hit hard" and win high school games is *intense*.

5. In the past, teams and most players stayed in one city and *bonded* with the fans. Now professional sports are more about money and less about team loyalty.

6. The people who enjoy these physical activities often say that they find them very relaxing *mentally* because the activity is so different from the kind of activity they must do in the world of work, often indoor office work *involving* mind rather than body.

7. Children are also *exposed* to sexual situations on TV that are much more *explicit* than they were a generation ago. Some of the most popular TV programs feature their characters in stories about having sex outside of marriage or choosing to have a baby without getting married.

8. Computers are also extremely popular with children and teenagers, and this of course raises questions of where they are traveling on the Internet and what are they seeing. Now parents have to worry about *monitoring* the computer, in addition to monitoring the TV.

Now write the correct AWL word next to its definition.

_____ 1. willing to work very hard at something

_____ 2. parts or features of a whole system

_____ 3. develop by gradually changing

_____ 4. clear, direct

_____ 5. shown, faced with

_____ 6. very strong

_____ 7. including something as a necessary part

_____ 8. affecting the mind

_____ 9. watching carefully

_____ 10. developed a special relationship

B. Classification: Recreational activities are usually not competitive and are done for fun, relaxation, and sometimes self-improvement. Sports are more organized and usually involve competition and rules of how to play.

Write *S* if the word or phrase concerns sports and *R* if it has to do with recreation.

_____ 1. team

_____ 2. hobby

_____ 3. handicrafts

_____ 4. hustle

_____ 5. gold medal

_____ 6. do-it-yourself projects

_____ 7. professional tennis

_____ 8. going to the theater

_____ 9. video games

_____10. helicopter skiing*

Preview Content

A. Think about the quotation by the American Academy of Physical Education at the beginning of the chapter. Then discuss these questions with your classmates.

1. How do you think Americans like to spend their leisure time?

2. What are the advantages and disadvantages of playing competitive sports?

3. What do you know about Americans' eating habits? What is "junk food"?

4. What is the impact of television on children?

5. How has technology impacted leisure time?

B. Read the headings in the chapter and look at the illustrations. Write five topics that you predict will be covered in this chapter.

1. _____

2. _____

3. _____

4. _____

5. _____

---

* A helicopter takes people to the top of a mountain that has no established ski trails and drops them off to ski down by themselves. (It is a dangerous adventure sport.)

Sports and American Values

1   Most social scientists believe that the sports that are organized by a society generally reflect the basic values of that society and attempt to strengthen them in the minds and emotions of its people. Therefore, organized sports may have a more serious social purpose than spontaneous, unorganized play by individuals. This is certainly true in the United States, where the three most popular organized sports are football, basketball, and baseball, with soccer gaining in popularity. Among young people, soccer is the game of choice. Boys and girls can play on the same team, and not much equipment is required. Nowhere are the ways and words of democracy better illustrated than in sports.

2   Organized sports are seen by Americans as an inspiring example of equality of opportunity in action. In sports, people of different races and economic backgrounds get an equal chance to excel. For this reason, notes sociologist Harry Edwards, Americans view organized sports as "a laboratory in which young men, regardless of social class, can learn the advantages and rewards of a competitive system." Although Edwards specifically mentions young men, young women also compete in organized sports without regard to their race or economic background. The majority of American football and basketball players, both college and professional, are African-American, and about one-quarter of baseball players are Hispanics or Latinos. Women's sports have grown in popularity in the United States, and they now have more funding and stronger support at the college level than in the past. The Olympics provide evidence of the increased interest in women's organized sports. American women have won gold medals for several team sports—softball, basketball, and soccer.

3   The American ideal of competition is also at the very heart of organized sports in the United States. Many Americans believe that learning how to win in sports helps develop the habits necessary to compete successfully in later life. This training, in turn, strengthens American society as a whole. "It is commonly held," says one sports writer, "that the competitive ethic taught in sports must be learned and ingrained[1] in youth for the future success of American business and military efforts."

4   The competitive ethic in organized sports contains elements of hard work and physical courage. Hard work is often called "hustle," "persistence," or "never quitting" in the sports world, while physical courage is referred to as "being tough" or "having guts."

Mia Hamm, star of the American women's soccer team that has won two Olympic gold medals

---

1 ingrained: attitudes or behavior that are firmly established and therefore difficult to change

Slogans are sometimes used to drive home the competitive virtues for the young participants:

Hustle—you can't survive without it.

A quitter never wins; a winner never quits.

It's easy to be ordinary, but it takes guts to excel.

5   Amateur athletics, associated with schools and colleges, are valued for teaching young people traditional American values. Professional sports, in addition to their profit and entertainment purposes, are seen as providing an example to inspire the young to take part in organized sports. In the process of serving as an inspiration for traditional basic American values, organized sports have become part of what was referred to in Chapter 3 as "the national religion," a mixture of patriotism and national pride on the one hand with religious ideas and symbols on the other. Billy Graham, a famous American Protestant religious leader, once observed: "The Bible says leisure and lying around are morally dangerous . . . sports keep us busy. . . . There are probably more really committed Christians in sports, both collegiate and professional, than in any other occupation in America."

Competition Carried to an Extreme?

6   Although sports in the United States are glorified by many, there are others who are especially critical of the power of sports to corrupt when certain things are carried to excess. An excessive desire to win in sports, for example, can weaken rather than strengthen traditional American values.

7   Critics have pointed out that there is a long tradition of coaches and players who have done just this. Vince Lombardi, a famous professional football coach, was often criticized for stating that winning is the "only thing" that matters in sports. Woody Hayes, another famous football coach, once said: "Anyone who tells me, 'Don't worry that you lost; you played a good game anyway,' I just hate." Critics believe that such statements by coaches weaken the idea that other things, such as fair play, following the rules, and behaving with dignity when one is defeated, are also important. Unfortunately, many coaches still share the "winning is the only thing" philosophy.

8   There is, however, also a tradition of honorable defeat in American sports. Sociologist Harry Edwards, for example, has pointed out that "The all-important significance of winning is known, but likewise, there is the consoling[2] 'reward' of the 'honorable defeat.' Indeed, the 'sweetness' of winning is derived . . . from the knowledge of having defeated a courageous opponent who performed honorably."

9   When the idea of winning in sports is carried to excess, however, honorable competition can turn into disorder and violence. In one game the players of two professional baseball teams became so angry at each other that the game turned into a large-scale fight between the two teams. The coach of one of the teams was happy about the fight because, in the games that followed, his team consistently won. He thought that the fight had helped to bring the men on his team closer together. Similarly, a professional football coach stated, "If we didn't go out there and fight, I'd be worried. You go out there and protect your teammates. The guys who sit on the

---

[2] **consoling:** making someone feel better when they are feeling sad or disappointed

bench, they're the losers." Both coaches seemed to share the view that if occasional fights with opposing teams helped to increase the winning spirit of their players, so much the better. Hockey coaches would probably agree. Professional hockey teams are notorious[3] for the fights among players during games. Some hockey fans seem to expect this fighting as part of the entertainment.

10   There are some who criticize this violence in American sports, particularly in football, which is probably America's favorite spectator sport. From time to time articles appear in newspapers or magazines such as *Sports Illustrated*, one of the nation's leading sports magazines, criticizing the number of injuries that have resulted from the extreme roughness of the game, increased by a burning desire to defeat one's opponent. Some people are particularly concerned about the injuries that high school players get in football games. The pressure to "hit hard" and win high school games is intense. In some parts of the country,

Tennessee Titans quarterback Steve McNair is tackled by Indianapolis Colts tackle Montae Reagor.

especially in the South, boys start playing tackle football in elementary school, bringing the risks of competitive pressure to nine- and ten-year-olds.

11   Most Americans would probably say that competition in organized sports does more to strengthen the national character than to corrupt it. They believe that eliminating competition in sports and in society as a whole would lead to laziness and vice rather than hard work and accomplishment. One high school principal, for example, described the criticism of competitive sports as "the revolutionaries' attempt to break down the basic foundations upon which society is founded." Comments of this sort illustrate how strong the idea of competition is in the United States and how important organized sports are as a means of maintaining this value in the larger society.

12   Another criticism of professional sports is that the players and the team owners get too much money, while fans have to pay more and more for tickets to the games. Basketball, baseball, and football stars get multi-million-dollar contracts similar to rock singers and movie stars. Some have asked whether these players are really athletes or entertainers. Furthermore, players are traded to other teams, or choose to go as "free agents," and a whole team may move to another city because of money. In the past, teams and most players stayed in one city and bonded with the fans. Now professional sports are more about money and less about team loyalty. College football and basketball programs are also affected by big money. The teams of large universities generate millions of dollars, and there is enormous pressure on these sports programs to recruit top athletes and have winning seasons.

---

3 notorious: famous or well-known for something bad

13   Another problem facing organized sports is the use of performance-enhancing drugs.[4] With the pressure to win so strong, a number of athletes have turned to these drugs. Although the use of most performance-enhancing drugs is illegal, it has now spread from professional sports down to universities and even high schools and middle schools. The use of these drugs puts the health of the athletes in danger and it is ethically wrong. It goes against the American values of equality of opportunity and fair competition. By 2004, the problem had become so significant that President George W. Bush mentioned it in his State of the Union address. He said, "Athletics play such an important role in our society, but, unfortunately, some in professional sports are not setting much of an example. The use of performance-enhancing drugs like steroids in baseball, football, and other sports is dangerous, and it sends the wrong message—that there are shortcuts to accomplishment, and that performance is more important than character."

Recreation: A Time for Self-Improvement

14   Unlike organized sports, what is generally called recreation in the United States is not expected to encourage competition. For this reason, it is much more spontaneous and serves the individual's needs beyond the competitive world of work. Nevertheless, much can be learned about the values of Americans from an examination of the kinds of recreation in which they engage.

15   Some Americans prefer recreation that requires a high level of physical activity. This is true of the most popular adult recreational sports: jogging or running, tennis, and skiing. It would seem that some Americans carry over their belief in hard work into their world of play and recreation. The well-known expression "We like to work hard and play hard" is an example of this philosophy.

16   Physical fitness has become a way of life for many. A number of people regularly work out at sports clubs—lifting weights, swimming, playing squash or racquetball, participating in aerobic exercise classes, or using exercise bikes, treadmills, rowing machines, or stair-steppers. Long-distance marathon races are so popular that the organizers often have to limit the number of people who can participate. In addition to the famous Boston and New York marathons, there are races in many other cities and even in small towns, drawing from several hundred to as many as 80,000 participants. Few of the people expect to win—most just want to finish the race. Most races are open to all, young and old alike, even those in wheelchairs.

2004 Women's Olympic marathon trials

---

[4] **performance-enhancing drugs:** drugs such as steroids that some athletes use illegally to improve their strength or endurance

17   The high level of physical activity enjoyed by many Americans at play has led to the observation that Americans have difficulty relaxing, even in their leisure time. Yet the people who enjoy these physical activities often say that they find them very relaxing mentally because the activity is so different from the kind of activity they must do in the world of work, often indoor office work involving mind rather than body.

18   The interest that Americans have in self-improvement, traceable in large measure to the nation's Protestant heritage (see Chapter 3), is also carried over into their recreation habits. It is evident in the joggers who are determined to improve the distance they can run, or the people who spend their vacation time learning a new sport such as sailing or scuba diving. The self-improvement motive, however, can also be seen in many other popular forms of recreation which involve little or no physical activity.

19   Interest and participation in cultural activities, which improve people's minds or skills, are also popular. Millions of Americans go to symphony concerts, attend live theater performances, visit museums, hear lectures, and participate in artistic activities such as painting, performing music, or dancing. Many Americans also enjoy hobbies such as weaving, needlework, candle making, wood carving, quilting, and other handicrafts.[5] Community education programs offer a wide range of classes for those interested in anything from using computers to gourmet cooking, learning a foreign language, writing, art, self-defense, and bird-watching.

20   The recreational interests of Americans also show a continuing respect for the self-reliance, and sometimes the adventure and danger, of frontier life. While some choose safe pastimes such as handicrafts, gardening, or "do-it-yourself" projects like building bookcases in their den, others are ready to leave home and take some risks. Adventure travel has grown to be a multi-billion-dollar business, perhaps as much as a fifth of the U.S. leisure travel market. Millions of Americans have bought mountain bikes to explore the wilderness on their own. Many others are choosing to go white-water rafting, mountain climbing, rock climbing, skydiving, helicopter skiing, and bungee jumping. U.S. park officials complain about the number of people who take life-threatening risks in national parks and have to be rescued.

Many Americans enjoy rock climbing, white-water rafting, and motorcycling.

"It is as if they are looking for hardship," one park official stated. "They seem to enjoy the danger and the physical challenge."

---

[5] **handicrafts:** skills needing careful use of your hands, such as sewing or making baskets

21   Not all Americans want to "rough it" while they are on their adventure holidays, however. There are a number of travelers in their forties or fifties who want "soft adventure." Judi Wineland, who operates Overseas Adventure Travel, says, "Frankly, it's amazing to us to see baby boomers seeking creature comforts." On her safari trips to Africa she has to provide hot showers, real beds, and night tables. The Americans' love of comfort, mentioned in Chapter 5, seems to be competing with their desire to feel self-reliant and adventurous.

Health and Fitness

22   Not all Americans are physically fit, or even try to be. The overall population is becoming overweight, due to poor eating habits and a sedentary[6] lifestyle. Government studies estimate that less than half of Americans exercise in their leisure time. Experts say that it is not because Americans "don't know what's good for them"—they just don't do it. By mid-2000, the Centers for Disease Control sounded the alarm—almost two-thirds of Americans were overweight, and more than one in five were obese. The CDC reported that obesity had become a national epidemic.

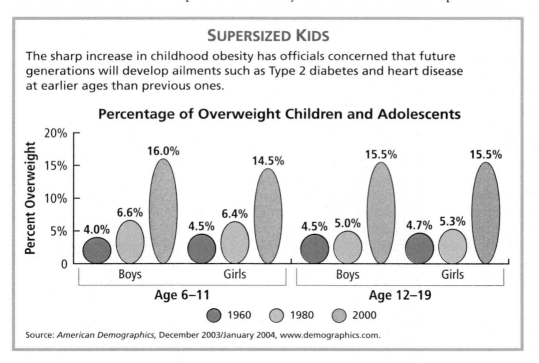

SUPERSIZED KIDS

The sharp increase in childhood obesity has officials concerned that future generations will develop ailments such as Type 2 diabetes and heart disease at earlier ages than previous ones.

Percentage of Overweight Children and Adolescents

Source: *American Demographics*, December 2003/January 2004, www.demographics.com.

After smoking, obesity was the number-two preventable cause of death in the United States. The government began a campaign to urge people to lose weight and get more exercise.

23   It's not that Americans lack information on eating well. Newspapers and magazines are full of advice on nutrition, and diet books are best-sellers. Indeed, part of the problem may be that there is too much information in the media, and much of it is contradictory. For thirty years the government encouraged people to eat a diet high in

---

[6] **sedentary:** doing or requiring much sitting

carbohydrates and low in fat, to avoid health risks such as heart disease and certain types of cancer. Many Americans ate low-fat, high-carbohydrate foods and gained weight. Then in the early 2000s, high-protein, low-carbohydrate diets became popular.

24   Many Americans have tried a number of diets, searching for the magic right one for them. Some overweight people say the diet advice is so confusing that they have just given up and eat whatever they want. Since 1994, the government has required uniform labeling so that consumers can compare the calories, fat, and carbohydrates in the food they buy. More than half of Americans say they pay attention to the nutritional content of the food they eat, but they also say they eat what they really want when they feel like it. For example, they have switched to skim milk but still buy fancy, fat-rich ice cream. As one American put it, "Let's face it—if you're having chips and dip as a snack, fat-free potato chips and fat-free sour cream just don't taste as good as the real thing."

25   Experts say that it is a combination of social, cultural, and psychological factors that determine how people eat. A *Newsweek* article on America's weight problems refers to "the culture of over-indulgence"[7] seemingly ingrained in American life. "The land of plenty seems destined to include plenty of pounds as well," they conclude. Part of the problem is that Americans eat larger portions[8] and often go back for second helpings, in contrast to how much people eat in many other countries.

26   Another factor is Americans' love of fast food. Although the fast-food industry is offering salads on its menus, most Americans still prefer "junk food." They consume huge quantities of pizza, hamburgers, French fries, and soft drinks at restaurants, not only because they like them, but also because these foods are often the cheapest items on the menu. Another significant factor is Americans' busy lifestyle. Since so many women are working, families are eating a lot of fast food, frozen dinners, and restaurant takeout. Some experts believe that Americans have really lost control of their eating; it is not possible to limit calories when they eat so much restaurant and packaged food. It takes time to prepare fresh vegetables and fish; stopping at a fast-food chain for fried chicken on the way home from work is a much faster alternative. Often, American families eat "on the run" instead of sitting down at the table together.

Nutrition Facts
Serving Size 1 Bag (21 g)

Amount Per Serving	
Calories 110	Calories from Fat 50

	% Daily Value*
Total Fat 6g	9%
Saturated Fat 1.5g	8%
Cholesterol 0 mg	0%
Sodium 270mg	11%
Total Carbohydrate 13g	4%
Dietary Fiber 0g	0%
Sugars 1g	
Protein 1g	

Vitamin A 0%	•	Vitamin C	0%
Calcium 0%	•	Iron	0%

* Percent Daily Values are based on a 2,000 calorie diet. Your daily values may be higher or lower depending on your calorie needs:

		Calories:	2,000	2,500
Total Fat	Less than		65g	80g
Sat Fat	Less than		20g	25g
Cholesterol	Less than		300mg	300mg
Sodium	Less than		2,400mg	2,400mg
Total Carbohydrate			300g	375g
Dietary Fiber			25g	30g

Calories per gram:
Fat 9 • Carbohydrate 4 • Protein 4

Label from a small bag of chips

The Impact of Television

27 Ironically, as Americans have gotten heavier as a population, the image of a beautiful woman has gotten much slimmer. Marilyn Monroe, a movie star of the 1950s and 1960s, would be overweight by today's media standards. Television shows, movies, and TV commercials feature actresses who are very slender.[9] Beer and soft drink commercials, for example, often feature very thin girls in bikinis. As a result, many teenage girls have become insecure about their bodies and so obsessed[10] with losing weight that some develop eating disorders such as anorexia or bulimia.

---

[7] **overindulgence:** the habit of eating or drinking too much
[8] **portions:** the amount of food for one person, especially when served in a restaurant
[9] **slender:** thin, graceful, and attractive
[10] **obsessed:** thinking about a person or a thing all the time and being unable to think of anything else

FAVORITE PASTTIMES AND EXERCISE		
The proportion of favorite pasttimes involving exercise has declined significantly since 1995.		
	1995	**2003**
Favorite Activities	%	%
involve exercise*	38	29
involve little or no exercise	62	71

*Includes fishing, gardening, playing team sports, swimming, golf, walking, exercise, hunting, bicycling, hiking, camping, running, bowling, dancing, tennis, horseback riding, skiing, or housework/yard work.

Source: *The Harris Poll* ® #72, December 1, 2003, conducted by Harris Interactive Inc.

28   Another irony is that although television seems to promote images of slender, physically fit people, the more people watch TV, the less likely they are to exercise. Television has a strong effect on the activity level of many Americans. Some people spend much of their free time lying on the couch watching TV and eating junk food. They are called "couch potatoes," because they are nothing but "eyes." (The small marks on potatoes are called *eyes*.) Couch potatoes would rather watch a baseball game on TV than go play softball in the park with friends, or even go to a movie. Cable and satellite TV bring hundreds of stations into American homes, so there is an almost limitless choice of programs.

29   With so many programs to choose from, it is not surprising that the average family TV set is on about six hours a day. Estimates are that some children spend twenty hours or more a week watching TV programs and DVDs. Many adults are worried about the impact of so much television on the nation's children. They are not getting as much exercise as they should, and the level of childhood obesity is alarming. But the effect on their minds may be as serious as the effect on their bodies. Many children do not spend enough time reading, educators say. And some studies have shown that excessive watching of television by millions of American children has lowered their ability to achieve in school.

30   One effect of watching so much TV seems to be a shortening of children's attention span.[11] Since the advent of the remote control device and the proliferation[12] of channels, many watchers like to "graze" from one program to the next, or "channel surf"—constantly clicking the remote control to change from channel to channel, stopping for only a few seconds to see if something catches their attention.

31   And what do children see? Too much sex and violence, most Americans would say. The American Psychological Association estimates that the average child will witness 8,000 made-for-TV murders before finishing elementary school. Children are also exposed to sexual situations on TV that are much more explicit than they were a generation ago.

---

[11] **attention span:** the amount of time that you are able to carefully listen to or watch something that is happening

[12] **proliferation:** a rapid increase in the amount or number of something

32   Some of the most popular TV programs feature their characters in stories about having sex outside of marriage or choosing to have a baby without getting married. Many Americans worry about the effect of explicit sex and violence on the moral values of the young.

33   As an alternative, there are many educational channels such as The History Channel, Discovery, The Science Channel, and the Public Broadcast System. But most people, including children, spend the majority of their viewing time watching entertainment programming such as dramas, situation comedies, reality shows, movies, MTV, and sports events. In 1990, Congress passed a law requiring the entertainment industry to improve the quality of programs directed at children on commercial television. Unfortunately, most experts would probably say that the 1990s brought few positive changes in children's programming. Indeed, some studies have discovered that there are even more violent acts committed on children's shows, many of them by cartoon characters, than there are on adult shows. Some groups want Congress to provide even stricter controls over sex and violence on television.

34   Others argue that parents are responsible for supervising their children's TV viewing. But how? Children are often watching television when their parents are not in the room, or even at home. Many parents think they can use help in monitoring what their children see. The reality is that one in four families is headed by a single parent, and in two-thirds of the two-parent families, both parents are working. Furthermore, about half of the children between the ages of six and seventeen have their own TV sets in their bedrooms. The possession of their own TV is an indication of both the material wealth and the individual freedom that many children have in the United States. We will explore these issues more in the next chapter.

The Impact of the Internet

35   The popularity of home computers and "surfing the Net" has brought a whole new world of leisure-time activities to Americans. Estimates are that more than a third of adults spend some of their leisure time on the Internet. Some value the enormous educational opportunities it brings, while others prefer spending their time in *chat rooms*, having discussions with others online, communicating with friends or family via e-mail and instant messaging, or playing the latest computer games. Computers are also extremely popular with children and teenagers, and this of course raises questions of where they are traveling on the Internet and what are they seeing. Now parents have to worry about monitoring the computer, in addition to monitoring the TV.

36   There is a debate about whether the Internet should be regulated by the federal government. On the one hand, there have been instances where adults have met children or teenagers over the Internet and have persuaded them to meet in person. In several instances teenagers have been kidnapped. Parents have great fear about their children meeting strangers on the Internet and about their possible exposure to pornography. It is against the law to send pornography through the U.S. mail, and many believe it should be outlawed on the Internet as well.

37   On the other hand, many Internet users believe that government regulation could threaten the growth and vitality of the Internet. Some would argue that the lack of regulation has permitted the Internet's explosive growth and the development of new technologies to deliver it. Wireless technology now allows Americans to access the

Internet just about anywhere. For example, they can use their laptop computers to connect to a wireless network and access the Internet while having coffee in a Starbucks. But this access is not limited to laptops. Technological convergence has brought the Internet to Personal Communication Systems (PCS). Now many Americans have cell phones and handheld devices that have multiple functions: talking on the phone, taking and exchanging pictures, instant messaging, sending and receiving e-mail, surfing the Internet, playing games, voice recording, paging, and communicating by coast-to-coast walkie-talkies. [13]

38   Many people are happy that technology has made it possible for them to communicate with just about anyone anywhere. However, this 24/7 access (24 hours a day, 7 days a week) has a huge impact on leisure time and Americans' ability to relax. Joe Robinson, in his book *Work to Live: Reclaim Your Life, Health, Family, and Sanity*, states, "The line between work and home has become so blurred that the only way you can tell them apart is that one has a bed." Robinson and others are trying to get American companies to offer more vacation time. The majority of Americans work more than forty hours a week, and many only get one or two weeks a year of paid vacation time. When the economy has a downturn, many are afraid to take the short amount of vacation time they have. The Travel Industry of America reports that half of all U.S. travel is two- or three-day trips.

39   Robinson has organized the Work to Live campaign, with the goal of changing the national labor laws so that everyone would be entitled to at least three weeks of vacation per year. He says that our founding fathers Thomas Jefferson and John Adams "believed that democracy was at risk if all attention in society was focused only on making money. It's hard to be an engaged citizen, not to mention a parent or actual human, when the overwork culture abducts you from all other responsibilities in life." He argues that Americans would be even more productive if they could have a month of vacation like most Europeans do.

40   Vacation time renews the spirit and gives people the energy and vitality to lead productive lives. Leisure time in the United States offers something for everyone; the only complaint that most Americans have is that they do not have enough of it. Americans, like people everywhere, sometimes choose recreation that just provides rest and relaxation. Watching television, going out for dinner, and visiting friends are simply enjoyable ways to pass the time. However, as we have seen, millions of Americans seek new challenges involving new forms of effort even in their leisure time. "Their reward," states *U.S. News & World Report*, "is a renewed sense of vitality," [14] a sense of a goal conquered and confidence regained in dealing with life's "ups and downs."

---

[13] **walkie-talkie:** battery-operated, two-way-radio telephone
[14] **vitality:** great energy and cheerfulness, and the ability to continue working effectively

Understand Main Ideas

Review the predictions you made on page 215 before you read the chapter. Work with a partner and find examples of how Americans' traditional values affect organized sports and how Americans spend their leisure time.

First match the examples with the values they illustrate, and then look for additional examples in the chapter. Answers may be used more than once.

_e, h_ 1. individual freedom   _____ 4. competition

_____ 2. self-reliance   _____ 5. material wealth

_____ 3. equality of opportunity   _____ 6. hard work

   a. both boys and girls play organized sports

   b. hustle and persistence, never quitting

   c. great emphasis on winning in sports

   d. many blacks on professional basketball teams

   e. Americans free to pursue a great variety of individual interests in their leisure time

   f. love of adventure travel in the wilderness, roughing it

   g. TVs in bedrooms of many American children

   h. professional sports team members free to change teams as free agents

   i. emphasis on children playing competitive sports

   j. popularity of do-it-yourself projects

   k. buying teenagers cell phones and computers

   l. having very little vacation time

Understand Details

Write the letter of the best answer according to the information in the chapter.

   _____ 1. Organized sports in a society
      a. are a poor reflection of the values of that society.
      b. are a good reflection of the values of that society.
      c. are leisure activities and games which tell us very little about the social values of a country.

_____ 2. Which of the following ideals is at the very heart of organized sports in the United States and is therefore the most important ideal expressed in organized sports?

    a. self-reliance
    b. self-denial
    c. competition

_____ 3. Which of these statements is <u>not</u> true?

    a. Billy Graham, a Protestant religious leader, has criticized sports for having a negative effect on the morals of young Americans.
    b. Most Americans would probably agree that organized sports are an important way for young people to learn to compete.
    c. Organized sports are an example of the "national religion," the mixing of national pride and religious values.

_____ 4. Vince Lombardi, a famous professional football coach, expressed the view that

    a. sports help boys grow into men.
    b. a good football player makes a good soldier.
    c. winning is the only thing that matters.

_____ 5. Leading sports publications such as _Sports Illustrated_ have stated that

    a. sports are good in general, but excessive violence in sports should be stopped.
    b. sports corrupt the American spirit and should be replaced with noncompetitive activities.
    c. many aspects of American culture, such as music and art, have been replaced by the love of sports.

_____ 6. Some of the most popular forms of recreation in the United States, such as jogging, reflect the attitude that

    a. Americans like the challenge of adventure sports.
    b. contact with nature is good for the soul of man.
    c. it is good to work hard and to play hard.

_____ 7. Which of these statements is <u>not</u> true?

    a. Many Americans like to spend their leisure time learning new skills in order to improve themselves.
    b. The American respect for self-reliance can be seen in the popularity of adventure travel, where people often have to rough it.
    c. Because of their active lifestyles, the number of people who weigh more than they should is decreasing.

_____ 8. According to the chapter, why do so many Americans have poor eating habits?

    a. They are unaware of the dangers of high-fat diets.
    b. The foods that they buy in the stores have no labels that give nutritional information.
    c. They are too busy to cook and they eat a lot of fast food.

_____ 9. Which of these statements is <u>not</u> true?

  a. The majority of American homes have TV systems that can get fifty channels or more.
  b. Most Americans have such a busy lifestyle that they watch very little TV.
  c. American children watch a lot of television, and many even have their own TV in their room.

_____ 10. Which of these statements <u>is</u> true?

  a. Most Americans are not concerned about the level of violence on television.
  b. Channel surfing may lower a child's attention span.
  c. Children's television programs are educational and have much less violence than adult programs.

Improve Your Reading Skills: Scanning

Scan the chapter for these names and terms. Then identify each with a short phrase.

1. junk food: _____

2. couch potato: _____

3. Vince Lombardi: _____

4. channel surf: _____

5. Joe Robinson: _____

6. PCS: _____

7. Harry Edwards: _____

8. Judi Wineland: _____

9. CDC: _____

10. Woody Hayes: _____

Talk About It

Work in small groups and choose one or more of these topics to discuss.

1. What is your favorite sport, and why? Have you ever played on a team? Explain.

2. What are popular forms of recreation in your country? What do you like to do in your leisure time?

3. How would you compare the day-to-day level of physical activity of people in your country with that of Americans?

4. Do you think college sports teams are really like professional teams? Should the players be paid? Why or why not?

5. What is the most violent sport? Have you ever been at a sports event where there was fighting? Explain.

Build Your Vocabulary

Opposites Read the sentences below that contain pairs of opposites in parentheses. Choose the correct words and write them in the sentence blanks.

1. Baseball, football, basketball, and soccer are popular (**individual/team**) _____ sports.

2. Slogans are sometimes used to drive home the competitive (**vices/virtues**) _____ for the young participants: A quitter never wins; a (**winner/loser**) _____ never quits.

3. When the idea of winning in sports is carried to excess, honorable competition can turn into (**order/disorder**) _____ and violence.

4. There are some who (**criticize/praise**) _____ this violence in American sports, particularly in football, which is probably America's favorite (**participant/spectator**) _____ sport.

5. (**Amateur/Professional**) _____ athletics, associated with schools and colleges, are valued for teaching young people traditional American values.

6. Most Americans would probably say that competition in organized sports does more to (**corrupt/strengthen**) _____ the national character than to (**corrupt/strengthen**) _____ it.

7. Some Americans prefer recreation that requires a high level of (**physical/mental**) _____ activity such as jogging, tennis, and skiing.

8. The overall population is becoming overweight due to poor eating habits and a (**sedentary/active**) _____ lifestyle.

9. Another irony is that although television seems to promote images of

(**obese/slender**) _____, physically fit people, the more people watch

TV, the less likely they are to exercise.

10. Unfortunately, most experts would probably say that the 1990s brought few

(**positive/negative**) _____ changes in children's programming.

More AWL Words Test your knowledge of these additional AWL words in the reading by completing the crossword puzzle below. The clues are on the next page.

comment	illustrate	label	principal	relax
contract	image	lecture	project	symbol
derive	injury	likewise	psychological	uniform
equipment	item	overseas	range	via

4. most important
6. a piece of paper with information about the thing attached to it
8. a carefully planned work
9. a single thing in a group
11. the way a person or product is presented to the public
13. different things of the same general type
14. in the same way
15. to make the meaning of something clearer by giving examples
16. a legal written agreement
17. using a person or machine to send something
18. in a foreign country across the ocean

1. something that represents an idea
2. a wound to your body caused by accident or attack
3. being the same in all its parts
5. relating to the way that people's minds work
6. a long talk given to a group
7. special things needed for a sport
10. an opinion that you express
12. to get or produce from something
13. to feel calm and comfortable

Play a Vocabulary Game Work in small groups, and think of words and phrases that would fit into categories. Challenge another group to a competition—you tell them the words and phrases, and they guess the category. You can use information in this chapter or choose other vocabulary having to do with sports, recreation, health and fitness, diet, television, or computer technology. Here are some suggestions for categories:

things that have to do with soccer

(names of) basketball players

(names of) popular diets

things relating to culture or the arts

things you can do on the Internet

things teenagers like to do

food that is good for you

junk food

things that might happen to a couch potato

things a couch potato might use

dangerous leisure activities

equipment you need for football

Olympic sports

Classify Words Work with a partner. Circle the words or phrases that do not belong in each category.

EXAMPLE: **team sports:** football, baseball, hockey, (tennis)

Tennis does not belong because it is an individual sport, not a team sport.

1. **adventure sports:** helicopter skiing, African safaris, white-water rafting, gardening, rock climbing, bungee jumping, skydiving, mountain climbing

2. **things parents worry about:** pornography, explicit sex on TV, strangers on the Internet, gourmet cooking, childhood obesity, shortening of child's attention span, violence

3. **reasons why many Americans are overweight:** fast-food restaurants, larger portions, second helpings, sedentary lifestyle, overseas travel, poor eating habits, lack of exercise

4. **hobbies:** weaving, playing professional football, painting, performing music, bird-watching, making candles, Chinese cooking, learning a foreign language, traveling

5. **things made possible by technology:** wireless networks, handicrafts, laptop computers, accessing the Internet in a Starbucks, cell phones, e-mail, instant messaging, paging, Internet games, walkie-talkies, exchanging digital photos

EXPAND YOUR KNOWLEDGE

Think, Pair, Share

How do you prefer to spend your leisure time? Read this list of leisure-time activities and decide which you enjoy most. Number them in order of importance, with number 1 as your favorite choice. Share your list with a partner and then with another pair of students.

____ Go on a walk or hike

____ Read a good book

____ See a movie

____ Play a sport

____ Work out at a gym

____ Have dinner at a restaurant

____ Watch TV

____ Go swimming

____ Listen to music

____ Attend a concert

____ Have a family picnic

____ See a play

____ Visit a museum

____ Go shopping

_____ Go to a friend's house   _____ Watch a game

_____ Have a friend visit you   _____ Other: _____

Ask Americans/Ask Yourself

If possible, ask several Americans the following questions. Then do a poll among your friends or classmates. Compare their responses with the poll that follows. (For the latest poll information, check the Harris Poll® website.)

1. First, we would like to know approximately how many hours a week you spend at your job or occupation, and that includes keeping house or going to school, as well as working for pay or profit. How many hours would you estimate you spend at work, housekeeping, or studies, including any travel time to and from the job or school?

2. About how many hours each week do you estimate you have available to relax, watch TV, take part in group sports or hobbies, go swimming or skiing, go to the movies, theater, concerts, or other forms of entertainment, get together with friends, and so forth?

3. What are your two or three most favorite leisure-time activities?

LEISURE-TIME ACTIVITIES*				
What are your two or three most favorite leisure-time activities? (Unprompted replies)				
	Top Mentions			
	2003	**2002**	**2001**	**2000**
	%	%	%	%
Reading	24	26	28	31
Spending time with family, kids	17	11	12	14
TV watching	17	15	20	23
Fishing	9	8	12	9
Going to movies	7	6	7	6
Socializing with friends, neighbors	7	5	4	6
Playing team sports	6	7	5	5
Exercise (aerobics, weights)	6	4	5	6
Gardening	6	8	10	13
Church/Church activities	5	2	3	4
Watching sporting events	5	2	3	4
Computer activities	5	4	7	6
Eating out/Dining out	5	2	1	1

* Most Americans estimate that they spend 49–50 hours per week working, keeping house, studying, etc., and have 19–20 hours per week for leisure activities.

Source: _The Harris Poll_® #72, December 1, 2003, conducted by Harris Interactive Inc. N=1,017 adults nationwide. Margin of error ± 3.

People Watching

In many countries, lunch is a leisurely meal that may take two or three hours. Some people eat at a nice restaurant with friends or co-workers, while others return home to eat with their families. For many, lunch is the main meal of the day. In contrast, many Americans eat lunch "on the run."

If possible, observe Americans eating lunch. Compare their lunch habits with those of your culture. Record your observations in the chart. Compare your observations with those of your classmates.

Observation Questions	Americans at Lunch	_____ at Lunch
1. Where are they eating?		
2. What are they eating?		
3. What size are the portions?		
4. How long do they stay?		
5. Do they take any food with them when they leave?		

Use the Internet

Work with a partner to learn about popular American diets. Use the Internet and find information on several diets. Decide which one you think is best and why. Then share your diet choice with your classmates. These are some popular diets:

Vegetarian, or vegan

Dean Ornish, or low-fat

Atkins, or low-carbohydrate

South Beach

The Zone

Weight Watchers

Jenny Craig

Dr. Phil's Weight Loss Program

Small-Group Projects

A. Some people say that Americans don't have any culture. By that they probably mean that the United States has not been a country long enough to have developed its own art forms—music, dance, or theater—usually referred to as the *fine arts*.

Work in small groups to test that theory or hypothesis. If you are living in the United States, find out about your local community. Are there libraries? Museums? Theaters where concerts and plays are performed? Check the entertainment section of your local newspaper (or a website) and see if any of the following are scheduled:

1. Ballets or other dance performances

2. Art or other exhibitions

3. Symphony concerts

4. Other concerts or musical performances

5. Poetry readings

6. Operas

7. Plays

American Ballet Theater

Make a list of these performances or exhibitions and indicate the nationality of both the artist who is performing the work and the artist who created it. Share your findings with your classmates.

B. Work in small groups and design an adventure travel brochure. Decide all the details of the trip.

1. What kind of adventure is it?

2. Where will it take place?

3. What are the dates?

4. How much will it cost and what is included?

5. What experiences will the travelers have?

You may wish to include an itinerary and some pictures, if possible. When you have finished, share your brochure with your classmates.

WRITE ABOUT IT

A. **Choose one of the following writing topics. Then write a short composition about it.**

1. Some would say that American homeowners have an obsession with having a beautiful lawn. In the United States, lawns occupy more land than any single crop, including wheat and corn, and in western cities as much as 60 percent of water is used for lawns. Do you think green spaces are important? Write about the use of land for private lawns or public parks, and describe differences between the United States and your country.

2. Write about the problem of protecting children from sex and violence in television programs and movies, and on the Internet. Use a graphic organizer to plan your essay.

3. Two of the fastest growing sports are NASCAR racing and golf. Write a report about why you think they are so popular, or choose another sport to write about.

4. Many American children are very impressed with sports stars like Michael Jordan. Do you think sports super stars have a responsibility to be positive role models for young people? Write an essay explaining why or why not, and give examples.

B. Reality TV shows have become very popular in the United States and in other countries. Use the Internet to find out how to become a contestant on these shows.

Choose one program and write a report about how to apply to appear on the show.

Books to Read

Arthur Ashe and Frank Deford, *Arthur Ashe: Portrait in Motion*—Arthur Ashe's diary of his life on and off the court between his Wimbledon matches in 1973 and 1974.

Jim Bouton, *Ball Four*—This funny, controversial account by Bouton gives readers an insider's look at baseball life in the early 1970s.

Jerry Kramer and Dick Schaap, *Instant Replay*—A diary with humorous and informative stories about pro-football featuring the Green Bay Packers in the 1960s.

Michael Mandelbaum, *The Meaning of Sports: Why Americans Watch Baseball, Football, and Basketball and What They See When They Do*—The author, a well-respected foreign policy analyst, explores Americans' fascination with team sports and how they satisfy deep human needs.

George Plimpton, *Paper Lion*—Plimpton recounts his story of being a 36-year-old rookie playing for the Detroit Lions.

Movies to See

A League of Their Own—Two sisters join the first female professional baseball league and struggle to help it succeed amidst their own growing competitiveness.

Miracle—The true story of Herb Brooks, the player-turned-coach who led the 1980 U.S. Olympic hockey team to victory over the seemingly unbeatable Russian team.

Radio—The story of a high school coach and the developmentally challenged young man who he "took under his wing."

Remember the Titans—The true story of a newly appointed African-American coach and his high school team in their first season as a racially integrated unit.

Supersize Me—A documentary of what happened to a man who ate nothing but fast food for a month.

Rhoda M. Sommer, her husband, Donald Friedman, and their children, Aaron and Whitney

THE AMERICAN FAMILY

The American has fashioned anew the features of his family institutions, as he does everything else about him.

Max Lerner (1902–1992)

BEFORE YOU READ

Preview Vocabulary

A. Read the following questions and notice the words in italics. These key AWL words will help you understand the reading. Use context clues to help you figure out the meanings. Then work with a partner and answer the questions.

1. If a *nuclear* family consists of a husband, wife, and their children, what is an extended family?

2. If you had a problem to solve, would you want your family to offer their *insight* into ways to solve it?

3. If you had children, would sending them to private schools be a *priority* for you, or would something else be more important?

4. How does the *location* of your house or apartment affect your lifestyle? Does it matter where you live?

5. Do you think husbands and wives should be equal *partners* in a marriage?

6. If we say that *approximately* one out of every two marriages now ends in divorce, what does that mean? Does it mean "more or less" or "exactly"?

7. Do you think that men and women should be *compensated* equally for doing the same work, or should they be paid different salaries?

8. What might happen if conscientious parents keep their eyes *exclusively focused* on their children, thinking about what they need instead of what responsibilities and obligations their children have?

9. If we say that by the end of the 1970s *considerably* less than half of the women in the United States still believed that they should put their husbands and children ahead of their own careers, does that mean a little less than half or a lot less than half?

10. Do you think American families are more or less *stable* than families in your country, or is divorce common in your country also?

B. Read the following paragraph from the chapter and notice the words in italics. Then use context clues and write the correct word next to its definition.

Juggling career and family responsibilities can be as difficult for men as it is for women, especially if there is truly an equal division of duties. American fathers are often seen dropping the kids off at the babysitter's or taking a sick child to the doctor. Some businesses are recognizing the need to *accommodate* families where both parents work. They may open a day care center in the office building, offer fathers *paternity leave* to stay home with their new babies, or have *flexible* working hours. Unfortunately, these *benefits* are available to only a few. While young *couples* strive to achieve equality in their careers, their marriages, and their parenting, society at large still lacks many of the *structures* that are needed to support them.

_____ 1. advantages that you get from your job

_____ 2. accept someone's needs and try to do what they want

_____ 3. trying to fit two or more jobs or activities into your life

_____ 4. things arranged in a definite pattern of organization

_____ 5. a period of time away from work that a father of a new baby is allowed

_____ 6. pairs of people who are together

_____ 7. can be changed easily to suit any new situation

Preview Content

A. Discuss these questions with your classmates.

1. Read the quotation by Max Lerner at the beginning of the chapter. What changes do you think Americans have made in the institution of marriage?

2. Look at the photo on page 238. Why do you think the authors chose this family photo to begin the chapter? How do you think this family relates to the basic traditional values presented in this book?

3. Who do you think lives in a typical American household?

4. Compare what you know about American families with typical families in your country. Use a Venn diagram to list how they are the same and how they are different.

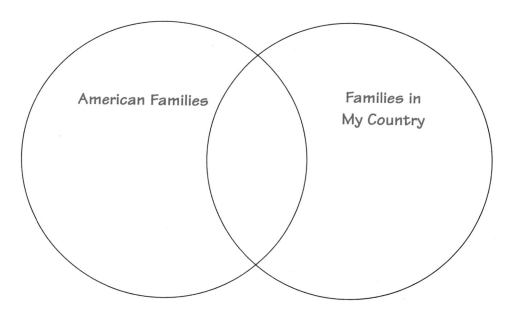

5. Americans often talk about "family values." What do you think they mean?

B. Read the headings in the chapter and look at the illustrations. Write five topics that you predict will be covered in this chapter.

1. _____
2. _____
3. _____
4. _____
5. _____

Family Structures

What is the typical American family like? If Americans are asked to name the members of their families, family structure becomes clear. Married American adults will name their husband or wife and their children, if they have any, as their *immediate family*. If they mention their father, mother, sisters, or brothers, they will define them as separate units, usually living in separate households. Aunts, uncles, cousins, and grandparents are considered *extended family*.

Traditionally, the American family has been a nuclear family, consisting of a husband, wife, and their children, living in a house or apartment. Grandparents rarely live in the same home with their married sons and daughters, and uncles and aunts almost never do. In the 1950s, the majority of the American households were the *classic* traditional American family—a husband, wife, and two children. The father was the "breadwinner" (the one who earned the money to support the family), the mother was a "homemaker" (the one who took care of the children, managed the household, and did not work outside the home), and they had two children under the age of eighteen. If you said the word *family* to Americans a generation ago, this is the traditional picture that probably came to their minds.

Today, however, the reality is much different. A very small percentage of American households consist of a working father, a stay-at-home mother, and children under eighteen. Only about one-quarter of American households now consist of two parents and their children, and the majority of these mothers hold jobs outside the home. The majority of American households today consist of married couples without children, single parents and their children, or unrelated people living together. Perhaps most surprising, 25 percent of Americans live alone.

What has happened to the traditional American family of the 1950s, and why? Some of the explanation is demographic.[1] In the 1950s, men who had fought in World War II had returned home, married, and were starting their families. There was a substantial increase (or *boom*) in the birthrate, producing the "baby boomers." A second demographic factor is that today young people are marrying and having children later in life. Some couples now choose not to have children at all. A third factor is that people are living longer after their children are grown, and they often end up alone. And, of course, there is a fourth factor—the high rate of divorce. But numbers alone cannot account for the dramatic changes in the family. Understanding the values at work in the family will provide some important insights.

Only 25 percent of American families are "traditional"—made up of two parents and their children.

---

[1] **demographic:** related to a part of the population that is considered as a group

The Emphasis on Individual Freedom

5   Americans view the family as a group whose primary purpose is to advance the happiness of individual members. The result is that the needs of each individual take priority in the life of the family. This means that in contrast to many other cultures, the primary responsibility of the American family member is not to advance the family as a group, either socially or economically. Neither is it to bring honor to the family name. This is partly because the United States is not an aristocratic society.

6   Family name and honor are less important than in aristocratic societies, since equality of opportunity is considered a basic traditional American value. Moreover, there is less emphasis on the family as an economic unit because relatively few families maintain self-supporting family farms or businesses for more than one generation. A farmer's son, for example, is very likely to go on to college, leave the family farm, and take an entirely different job in a different location.

7   The American desire for freedom from outside control clearly extends to the family. Americans do not like to have controls placed on them by other family members. They want to make independent decisions and not be told what to do by grandparents or uncles or aunts. For example, both American men and women expect to decide what job is best for them as individuals. Indeed, young Americans are encouraged by their families to make such independent career decisions. What would be best for the family is not usually considered to be as important as what would be best for the individual.

Marriage and Divorce

8   Very few marriages are "arranged" in the United States. Traditionally, young people are expected to find a husband or wife on their own; their parents do not usually help them. In fact, parents are frequently not told of marriage plans until the couple has decided to marry. This means that most parents have little control, and generally not much influence, over who their children marry. Most Americans believe that young people should fall in love and then decide to marry someone they can live happily with, again evidence of the importance of an individual's happiness. Of course, in reality this does not always happen, but it remains the traditional ideal and it shapes the views of courtship[2] and marriage among young Americans.

9   Over the years the value placed on marriage itself is determined largely by how happy the husband and wife make each other. Happiness is based primarily on companionship. The majority of American women value companionship as the most important part of marriage. Other values, such as having economic support and the opportunity to have children, although important, are seen by many as less important.

10   If the couple is not happy, the individuals may choose to get a divorce. A divorce is relatively easy to obtain in most parts of the United States. Most states have "no-fault" divorce. To obtain a no-fault divorce, a couple states that they can no longer live happily together, that they have irreconcilable differences,[3] and that it is neither partner's fault.

---

[2] **courtship:** the period of time during which a man and a woman have a romantic relationship before getting married
[3] **irreconcilable differences:** strong disagreements between two people who are married, given as a legal reason for getting a divorce

11   The divorce rate rose rapidly in the United States from the 1960s through the 1980s, and then leveled off. Approximately one out of every two marriages now ends in divorce. Often children are involved. The majority of adult Americans believe that unhappy couples should not stay married just because they have children at home, a significant change in attitude since the 1950s. Many people do not believe in sacrificing individual happiness for the sake of the children. They say that children actually may be better off living with one parent than with two who are constantly arguing. Divorce is now so common that it is no longer socially unacceptable, and children are not embarrassed to say that their parents are divorced. However, psychologists and sociologists are still studying the long-term consequences of divorce.

12   Judith Wallerstein has studied the effect of divorce on children as they grow up. In her book *The Unexpected Legacy of Divorce: A 25 Year Landmark Study*, she notes that by the year 2000, almost half of the American adults under the age of forty were children of divorced parents. For twenty-five years she followed a group of children whose parents were divorced and compared their experiences with others whose parents stayed together "for the sake of the children." She found that the key factor was whether or not the parents could set aside their differences enough to focus on the needs of their children, regardless of whether the parents divorced or stayed together. However, even in the best cases, divorce had a lasting effect on children as they grew into adulthood and formed their own relationships. In fact, over half of them said they did not want to have children of their own because they were afraid of causing their children the pain that they had experienced growing up.

The Role of the Child

13   The American emphasis on the individual, rather than the group, affects children in a contradictory way. On the one hand, it may cause them to get more attention and even have more power than they should. On the other hand, because most children have mothers who are working outside the home, they may not get enough attention from either parent. Worse yet, parents who feel guilty for not having enough time with their children may give them more material things to compensate for the lack of attention. Working parents constantly struggle to find enough time to spend with their children.

Ready to go trick-or-treating on Halloween

14   Some American families tend to place more emphasis on the needs and desires of the child than on the child's social and family responsibilities. In the years after World War II, much stress was placed on the psychological needs of children and the number of experts in this field increased enormously. Child psychologists, counselors,[4] and social workers were

---

[4] **counselors:** people whose job is to help and support people with personal problems

employed to help children with problems at school or in the family. Many books on how to raise children became best-sellers. Sometimes these books offered conflicting advice, but almost all of them shared the American emphasis on the development of the individual as their primary goal.

15   Some Americans believe that the emphasis on the psychological needs of the individual child was carried too far by parents and experts alike. Dr. Benjamin Spock, one of the most famous of the child-rearing experts, eventually came to this conclusion. He said, "What is making the parent's job most difficult is today's child-centered viewpoint." Many conscientious[5] parents, said Spock, tend to "keep their eyes exclusively focused on their child, thinking about what he needs from them and from the community, instead of thinking about what the world, the neighborhood, the family will be needing from the child and then making sure that he will grow up to meet such obligations."

16   The current generation of parents seem more concerned about teaching their children responsibility. Although Americans may not agree on how best to nurture[6] and discipline their children, most still hold the basic belief that the major purpose of the family is the development and welfare of each of its members as individuals.

Equality in the Family

17   Along with the American emphasis on individual freedom, the belief in equality has had a strong effect on the family. Alexis de Tocqueville saw the connection clearly in the 1830s. He said that in aristocratic societies inequality extends into the family, particularly to the father's relationship to his children. The father is accepted as ruler and master. The children's relations with him are very formal, and love for him is always combined with fear. In the United States, however, the democratic idea of equality destroys much of the father's status as ruler of the family and lessens the emotional distance between father and children. There is less formal respect for, and fear of, the father. But there is more affection expressed toward him. "The master and constituted [legal] ruler have vanished,"[7] said Tocqueville; "the father remains."

18   What Tocqueville said of American fathers and children almost two centuries ago applies to relations between parents and children in the United States today. There is much more social equality between parents and children than in most aristocratic societies or societies ruled by centuries of tradition. In fact, some Americans worry that there is too much democracy in the home. They would argue that there has been a significant decline in parental authority and children's respect for their parents. This is particularly true of teenagers. Some parents seem to have little control over the behavior of their teenage children, particularly after they turn sixteen and get their driver's licenses.

19   On the other hand, many Americans give their young people a lot of freedom because they want to teach their children to be independent and self-reliant. Traditionally, American children have been expected to "leave the nest" at about age eighteen, after they graduate from high school. At that time they are expected to go

---

[5] **conscientious:** showing a lot of care and attention
[6] **nurture:** to feed and take care of a child or a plant while it is growing
[7] **vanished:** disappeared suddenly, especially in a way that cannot easily be explained; stopped existing suddenly

on to college (many go to another city) or to get a job and support themselves. By their mid-twenties, if children are still living with their parents, some people will suspect that something is wrong. Traditionally, children have been given a lot of freedom and equality in the family, so that they will grow up to be independent, self-reliant adults. Today, however, a number of young people are unable to find jobs that support the lifestyle they have grown up with, and they choose to move back in with their parents for a time. These young people are sometimes called "boomerang kids," because they have left the nest once but are now back again.

Four Stages of Marriage Relationships

20 The idea of equality also affects the relationships between husbands and wives. Women have witnessed steady progress toward equal status for themselves in the family and in society at large. According to Letha and John Scanzoni, two American sociologists, the institution of marriage in the United States has experienced four stages of development.* In each new stage, wives have increased the degree of equality with their husbands and have gained more power within the family.

21 **Stage I: Wife as Servant to Husband** During the nineteenth century, American wives were expected to be completely obedient[8] to their husbands. As late as 1850, wife-beating was legal in almost all the states of the United States. Although both husbands and wives had family duties, the wife had no power in family matters other than that which her husband allowed her. Her possessions and any of her earnings belonged to her husband. During the nineteenth century, women were not allowed to vote, a restriction that in part reflected women's status as servant to the family.

22 **Stage II: Husband-Head, Wife-Helper** During the late nineteenth and early twentieth centuries opportunities for women to work outside the household increased. More wives were now able to support themselves, if necessary, and therefore were less likely to accept the traditional idea that wives were servants who must obey their husbands. Even though the great majority of wives chose not to work outside the home, the fact that they might do so increased their power in the marriage. The husband could no longer make family decisions alone and demand that the wife follow them. The wife was freer to disagree with her husband and to insist that her views be taken into account in family decisions.

23 Even though the wife's power increased, the husband remained the head of the family. The wife became his full-time helper by taking care of his house and raising his children. She might argue with him and sometimes change his mind, but his decision on family matters was usually final.

24 This increase in equality of women in marriages reflected increased status for women in the society at large and led to women gaining the right to vote in the early twentieth century. Today, the husband-head, wife-helper marriage is still found in the United States. Economic conditions in the twentieth century, however, carried most marriages into different stages.

25 **Stage III: Husband-Senior Partner, Wife-Junior Partner** During the twentieth century, more and more wives took jobs outside the home. In 1940, for example,

---

* Scanzoni, Letha, and John Scanzoni, *Men, Women, and Change.* New York: McGraw-Hill, Inc., 1981.

---

[8] **obedient:** always doing what you are told to do by your parents or by someone in authority

only 14 percent of married women in the United States held jobs outside the home. By the 2000s, more than 60 percent were employed. When married women take this step, according to the Scanzonis, their power relative to that of their husbands increases still further. The wife's income becomes important in maintaining the family's standard of living. Her power to affect the outcome of family decisions is greater than when her duties were entirely in the home.

26   Although she has become a partner, however, in this stage the wife is still not an equal partner with her husband, since in these marriages the husband's job or career still provides more of the family income. He sees himself as the senior partner and she is the junior partner of the family enterprise. Even though she has a job, it has a lower priority than her husband's. If, for example, the husband is asked to move to advance his career, she will give up her job and seek another in a new location.

27   In the United States today there are still a number of marriages that are the senior-partner/junior-partner type. However, the majority of women have jobs outside the home and some of them earn more money than their husbands do. More and more marriages are what the Scanzonis call Stage IV marriages.

28   **Stage IV: Husband-Wife Equal Partners** Beginning in the late 1960s, a growing number of women expressed a strong dissatisfaction with any marriage arrangement where the husband and his career were the primary considerations in the marriage. By the end of the 1970s, for example, considerably less than half of the women in the United States still believed that they should put their husbands and children ahead of their own careers. In the 2000s, most American women believe that they should be equal partners in their marriages and that their husbands should have equal responsibility for child care and household chores.

29   In an equal-partnership marriage, the wife pursues a full-time job or career which has equal or greater importance to her husband's. The long-standing division of labor between husband and wife comes to an end. The husband is no longer the main provider of family income, and the wife no longer has the main responsibilities for household duties and raising children. Husband and wife share all these duties equally. Power over family decisions is also shared equally.

30   The reality of life in the United States is that although most American women now have an equal say in the decisions affecting the family, they sometimes earn less than men for the same work. Also, most women are still spending more time taking care of the children, cooking, and cleaning than their husbands are. Many women are resentful[9] because they feel like they have two full-time jobs—the one at work and the one at home. In the 1980s, women were told they could "have it all"—fast-track career, husband, children, and a clean house. Now, some women are finding that lifestyle exhausting[10] and unrewarding. Some young women are now choosing to

In an equal-partnership marriage, husbands share household duties such as cooking.

[9] **resentful:** feeling angry and upset about something that you think is unfair
[10] **exhausting:** making someone very tired

stay at home until their children start school, but many others who would like to cannot afford to do so.

31   Juggling two careers and family responsibilities can be as difficult for men as it is for women, especially if there is truly an equal division of duties. American fathers are often seen dropping the kids off at the babysitter's or taking a sick child to the doctor. Some businesses are recognizing the need to accommodate families where both parents work. They may open a day care center in the office building, offer fathers paternity leave to stay home with their new babies, or have flexible working hours. Unfortunately, these benefits are not yet available to all. While young couples strive to achieve equality in their careers, their marriages, and their parenting, society at large still lacks many of the structures that are needed to support them.

The Role of the Family in Society

32   The American ideal of equality has affected not only marriage, but all forms of relationships between men and women. Americans gain a number of benefits by placing so much importance on achieving individual freedom and equality within the context of the family. The needs and desires of each member are given a great deal of attention and importance. However, a price is paid for these benefits. American families may be less stable and lasting than those of some other cultures. The high rate of divorce in American families is perhaps the most important indicator of this instability.

33   The American attitude toward the family contains many contradictions. For example, Americans will tolerate a good deal of instability in their families, including divorce, in order to protect such values as freedom and equality. On the other hand, they are strongly attached to the idea of the family as the best of all lifestyles. In fact, the great majority of persons who get divorced find a new partner and remarry. Studies show consistently that the vast majority of Americans believe that family life is an important value.

34   What is family life? We have seen that only one in four households consists of a traditional family—a father, mother, and their children. Many of these are actually *stepfamilies* or *blended families*. Since most divorced people remarry, many children are living with a stepmother or stepfather. In a blended family, the parents may each have children from a previous marriage, and then have one or more children together—producing "yours," "mine," and "ours." Such families often result in very complicated and often stressful relationships. A child may have four sets of grandparents instead of two, for example. Blending families is not easy, and, sadly, many second marriages fail.

Three generations of a multi-ethnic family

35   In addition to traditional families and blended families, there are a number of single parents, both mothers and fathers (more mothers), raising their children alone. Many of the single mothers are divorced, but some have never married. Indeed, by the mid-1990s, one-third of all new babies were born to single mothers, and this trend continues. Sometimes single parents and their children live with the grandparents for economic and emotional support. There are all sorts of arrangements. In recent years, some gay and lesbian couples have created family units, sometimes adopting children. Some states are considering recognizing same-sex marriages, and others may recognize them as *civil unions*. This is a very controversial issue. There is no doubt, however, that the definition of *family* has become much broader in the 2000s. The majority of Americans would now define a family as "people who live together and love each other."

36   Sociologists and psychologists tell us that the family is the best place for children to learn moral values and a sense of responsibility. Today, the state of the American family is frequently discussed, not only by the experts, but by the press, elected officials, and the general public. Some Americans believe that the institution of the family and *family values* are both in trouble. But if you ask Americans how their own families are, most will tell you they are generally happy with their family life.

Family Values

37   In *Values and Public Policy*, Daniel Yankelovich reports on surveys done on family values. There are eleven points that a majority of Americans agree are family values. Yankelovich classifies six of them a "clearly traditional":

- Respecting one's parents
- Being responsible for one's actions
- Having faith in God
- Respecting authority
- Remaining married to the same person for life
- Leaving the world in better shape

The other five are "a blend of traditional and newer, more expressive values":

- Giving emotional support to other members of the family
- Respecting people for themselves
- Developing greater skill in communicating one's feelings
- Respecting one's children
- Living up to one's potential as an individual

38   The ideal of the American family is group cooperation to help achieve the fulfillment of each individual member, and shared affection to renew each member's emotional strength. Families can be viewed as similar to churches in this regard. Both are seen by Americans as places where the human spirit can find refuge from the highly competitive world outside and renewed resources to continue the effort. Although in many cases churches and families do not succeed in the task of spiritual renewal, this remains the ideal of church and family in America.

Understand Main Ideas

Working with a partner, discuss how the six traditional basic American values affect the American family. Fill in the chart with the value, the advantages and disadvantages to the individual, and the advantages and disadvantages to the family.

Value: _____

Advantage to the Individual	Disadvantage to the Individual

Advantage to the Family	Disadvantage to the Family

Value: _____

Advantage to the Individual	Disadvantage to the Individual

Advantage to the Family	Disadvantage to the Family

Understand Details

Write _T_ if the statement is true and _F_ if it is false according to information in the chapter.

___T___ 1. One American household in four now consists of someone living alone.

___F___ 2. "Baby boomers" are young people who are in their twenties.

___F___ 3. Americans usually consider what is best for the whole family first and what is best for them as individuals second.

___T___ 4. Americans believe that the family exists primarily to serve the needs of its individual family members.

___T___ 5. Most Americans believe that marriages should make both individuals happy and that if they cannot live together happily, it is better for them to get a divorce.

___T___ 6. American parents generally think more about the individual needs of their children than they do about what responsibilities the child will have to the society as a whole.

___F___ 7. Although Americans believe in democracy for society, they generally exercise strict control over their children, particularly teenagers.

___F___ 8. The amount of equality between husbands and wives has remained pretty much the same since Tocqueville visited the United States in the 1830s.

___T___ 9. If an American wife works outside the home, she is likely to have more power in the family than a married woman who does not work.

___F___ 10. In the husband-senior partner, wife-junior partner type of marriage, the husband and wife both work, have equal power and influence in making family decisions, and divide the family duties equally.

___F___ 11. In most American families, the father does just as much housework and child care as the mother.

___T___ 12. Having faith in God and respecting authority are two of the traditional American family values.

___T___ 13. Although one out of every two marriages ends in divorce, Americans still believe strongly in the importance of marriage and the family.

Improve Your Reading Skills: Highlighting and Summarizing

In the American education system, there is a great deal of emphasis on recognizing and remembering main ideas. Highlighting main ideas as you read helps you remember them. In Chapter 3 (pages 60–61), we discussed identifying topic sentences and how they usually contain the main idea of a paragraph. In Chapter 4 (page 79), and Chapter 5 (page 104), you practiced highlighting topic sentences.

Remember that most topic sentences are the first sentence of the paragraph. Therefore, if you just focus on the first sentence of the paragraph in an academic reading, you should have an understanding of the main ideas of the reading. And if you want a summary of the reading, using the first sentence of each paragraph is an easy way to summarize it.

Review the exercises on topic sentences and highlighting main ideas on pages 60–61, 79, and 104. Then go through this chapter and highlight the first sentence of each paragraph. For most paragraphs, this will give you the main idea, and these topic sentences will contain the main ideas of the chapter. You can use this information to write a summary of the chapter in your own words.

Talk About It

Work in small groups and choose one or more of these topics to discuss.

1. What do you think is the ideal number of children to have? What responsibilities should children have in the family?

2. What type of parenting do you think is most effective? How would you discipline and parent your children? Would you give your teenagers the same amount of freedom as you had as a teenager? Why or why not?

3. Which type of marriage is most common in your country? Which of the four types do you think is ideal? Why?

4. How is divorce viewed in your country? If two people are unhappy, should they get a divorce? What if they have children? Under what circumstances would you get divorced?

5. Do you think it's important for one parent to stay home with the children? In your country, who takes care of the children when both parents work? Would you leave your child in a day care center?

6. Should husbands be able to choose to stay at home while their wives go to work? In the United States, these men are sometimes called "househusbands." Are there househusbands in your country?

Build Your Vocabulary

Vocabulary Check Use the words in the box to complete the sentences.

blended	courtship	juggling	refuge
compensate	demographic	nurture	stable
conscientious	exhausting	priority	vanish

1. Many _____ American mothers would like to stay at home with their young children, but they have to work to make ends meet.

2. _____ a career and family responsibilities is very stressful.

3. Many young mothers who work have an _____ lifestyle—they work all day at their jobs and then care of their families and homes.

4. Most Americans would probably agree that fathers, as well as mothers, should be able to _____ their children.

5. Parents who do not have enough time for their children may feel guilty and then try to _____ by giving their children material gifts.

6. Sometimes a demanding career can be a _____, even though a parent would like to have more time to spend with the children.

7. _____ families may be a source of stress, as parents try to cope with raising each other's children, plus their own.

8. In the United States, _____ is the time that young people in love get to know each other and decide if they want to get married.

9. Although marriages are not very _____ in the United States, most Americans still believe that it is an important institution in society.

10. Families have traditionally provided an important _____ from the competitive stresses of American society.

11. _____ studies show that young Americans are now waiting longer to get married and have children.

12. In spite of all its problems, the institutions of marriage and the family will certainly never _____.

More AWL Words Test your knowledge of these additional AWL words in the reading by doing the crossword puzzle below. The clues are on the next page.

accommodate	dramatic	final	labor	potential	role
consist	emphasis	flexible	license	previous	trend
contradictory	expert	generation	obtain	primary	
controversial	factor	institution	policy	restriction	

Across

5. most important
6. an official document
9. exciting and impressive
12. in opposition or disagreement with something else
15. able to change or be changed easily
16. the possibility that something will develop in a certain way
17. to accept someone's opinions or needs
20. to get something you want
21. all people of about the same age

Down

1. causing a lot of disagreement
2. principle, procedure, or way of doing something
3. special attention or importance
4. a rule that limits or controls
7. someone who has special skill or knowledge
8. work using physical effort
10. the last in a series
11. the part someone plays
13. an established social system
14. a general tendency
15. one of several things that influence a situation
18. to be made of
19. happening or existing before now

EXPAND YOUR KNOWLEDGE

Ask Americans

Interview several Americans of different ages and ask them about their families. Ask each one the following questions and record their answers.

1. Who are the members of your family? Name them and indicate their relationship to you (mother, sister, etc.).

2. Who lives in your household? Where do your other relatives live?

3. How often do you see your parents? Your grandparents? Your sisters and brothers? Your aunts, uncles, and cousins? Do you write, e-mail, or telephone any of them regularly?

4. What occasions bring your relatives together (birthdays, holidays, weddings, births, deaths, trips)? Have you ever been to a family reunion?

5. Do you feel you have a close family? Why or why not?

6. Who would you ask for advice if you had a serious personal problem?

7. Who would take care of you if you became ill?

8. What obligations and responsibilities do you feel you have toward your family?

9. What duties and responsibilities do you believe children have toward their family?

(continued)

The American Family **255**

10. On a scale of 1 to 10, with 10 as *most important*, how important are the opinions of the members of your immediate family concerning the following decisions?

_____ Who you marry   _____ What job you take
_____ Where you live   _____ How you spend your money
_____ Where you go to school

Ask Yourself/Ask Americans

Do you agree or disagree with each of the following statements? Put a check under the number that indicates how you feel.

+**2** = Strongly agree

+**1** = Agree

  0 = No opinion

−**1** = Disagree

−**2** = Strongly disagree

	+2	+1	0	−1	−2
1. Arranged marriages are better than marriages where the couple have met and dated on their own.	___	___	___	___	___
2. It is very important for my family to approve of the person I marry.	___	___	___	___	___
3. If my parents disapproved of my choice, I would still marry that person if we were very much in love.	___	___	___	___	___
4. A woman's place is in the home.	___	___	___	___	___
5. Married women with small children should not work.	___	___	___	___	___
6. Men should be able to stay home and take care of the children while their wives work.	___	___	___	___	___
7. Husbands and wives should share equally the work of taking care of the house and the children.	___	___	___	___	___
8. Unhappy couples should stay married for the sake of the children.	___	___	___	___	___
9. Married couples who choose not to have children are selfish.	___	___	___	___	___
10. Equality between a husband and wife causes divorce.	___	___	___	___	___

Read these statements to several Americans and ask them if they agree or disagree. Compare your answers with theirs.

People Watching

It has been said that in most societies children are often spectators watching adults interact. They are learning what it means to be an adult in their society. In American society, however, the adults are usually the spectators who are watching the children.

Observe American adults interacting with children in the following places:

- In restaurants
- On a playground or at a sports event
- At the movies
- On the street
- At home (If you are unable to visit an American home, watch American TV shows that have children as characters.)

Record your observations in your journal. You may wish to write up these observations as a report and present it to the class. What differences did you observe from the way children are treated in other countries?

Father and daughter dancing at a family wedding

Understand the Role of the Elderly in America

The role of the elderly is one that most foreigners cannot understand about American life. Some have heard that all the elderly are in nursing homes, but this is not true. Actually, only one in four Americans spends any time in a nursing home, and the average stay is two years. It is generally the sick and the disabled who require nursing home care at the end of their lives. Americans generally try to live on their own as long as possible, choosing to be independent and self-reliant. The vast majority of the care of the elderly is done by family members. Working mothers with children under eighteen who must care for elderly parents are called the "sandwich generation," because they must be a parent to both their children and their own dependent parents. However, as the baby boomers age, adult children who are taking care of their parents are themselves getting older and older.

A. **To try to understand how Americans feel about being old and what they plan to do with their lives when they retire, ask several Americans who are not yet sixty-five the following questions:**

1. What do you hope to do when you retire?

2. Where do you plan to live?

3. Would you move in with your children? Under what conditions?

4. What do you think life will be like when you are 65 or older?

5. Are you afraid of growing old? Are you looking forward to growing old?

B. Many retirement communities now have different kinds of living arrangements, from independent living in homes and apartments, to assisted living in buildings with private rooms and meals served in a common dining room, to nursing homes that offer full-time care by doctors and nurses.

If you are able to, visit a retirement community for older Americans, or a nursing home. Answer the following questions.

1. Why do you think that many older people choose to live apart from their grown children?

2. Think about the description of the family presented in this chapter. What evidence do you see of the American values of equality in the family and the emphasis on individual freedom?

Proverbs and Sayings

Ask Americans to explain these proverbs and sayings to you. Then ask them for other examples of sayings about men, women, children, or the family. What sayings like these do you have in your language?

1. The hand that rocks the cradle rules the world.
2. As the twig is bent, so grows the tree.
3. That child is a chip off the old block.
4. A man may work from sun to sun, but a woman's work is never done.
5. Behind every successful man, there is a woman.
6. Blood is thicker than water.

Think, Pair, Share

Working mothers often feel that they have two full-time jobs—one outside the home, for which they get paid, and the other inside the home, for which they do not get paid. Most working American women still have the major responsibility for managing the household—cooking, cleaning, shopping, and seeing that the children are cared for—even if their husbands help them with some of the household duties. What do you think husbands with working wives should do around the house?

Write your answer and then discuss it with your partner. Then share your answer with another pair of students.

Use the Internet

Many young people have difficulty meeting others because of their busy lifestyles. Computer dating is becoming increasingly popular and more acceptable in the United States. People can find dates or even a potential husband or wife on the Internet. Men and women answer questions about themselves—their interests, hobbies, likes and dislikes—and they also indicate the qualities they are looking for in a date. Couples are then matched by the computer, and each person receives a list of names of people to contact.

Work with a partner and look at two popular websites, www.match.com and www.eharmony.com. Spend a few minutes learning about each website and how people meet others there. You may want to take the personality quiz on eharmony.

Read some of the profiles that people have written to introduce themselves. Imagine putting an ad on one of the websites. What would be your "catchphrase," and how would you introduce yourself?

Write your ad without your name on it. Collect all the ads from the class and put them in a box. Have each person pick an ad, read it aloud, and guess who wrote it.

A. Choose one of the following writing topics. Then write a short composition about it.

1. Imagine that a foreign exchange student will be living with you for a year. Write a letter to him or her explaining how your family *is* or *is not* a typical family in your country.

2. Write about the person in your immediate or extended family who you admire the most. Tell what makes the person special and what you admire most.

 B. Choose one of these Internet topics to write about.

1. Many Americans have pets that they consider to be part of the family. Some studies have shown that owning a pet lowers a person's blood pressure and helps to reduce stress.

   Learn more about Americans and their pets. Find information on the Internet and write a report about what you find. Or write about a pet you have or have had, or what would be your ideal pet.

2. What kind of companies are good places for working mothers? Search the Internet and write a report about how some American businesses accommodate working mothers.

The family dog enjoys a ride in an antique convertible.

Books to Read

Robert Bly, *Iron John*—Robert Bly, a talented poet and translator, discusses what it means to "be a man" in this inspiring guide.

Maxine Hong Kingston, *The Woman Warrior*—A Chinese woman explains how her identity was formed growing up in California and learning about her culture through family stories and Chinese myths.

Joe Starita, *The Dull Knifes [sic] of Pine Ridge: A Lakota Odyssey*—The stories and struggles of the Dull Knife family, a Lakota Sioux family, over five generations.

Laura Ingalls Wilder, *Little House on the Prairie*—The author's account of growing up on the frontier in Kansas with her family.

Thornton Wilder, *Our Town*—First produced in 1938, this play about small-town America is a classic often performed by American high school students.

Movies to See

Cheaper by the Dozen—While a wife is away publicizing her book, her husband must juggle his new job and take care of their twelve children.

Father of the Bride—In this comedy, a remake of the Spencer Tracy classic, a family plans the wedding of their daughter.

My Big Fat Greek Wedding—A young Greek woman falls in love with a non-Greek and struggles to get her family to accept him, while she comes to terms with her heritage and cultural identity.

My Family, Mi Familia—This film traces the struggles, joys, and successes of an immigrant family over three generations.

When Harry Met Sally—A romantic comedy about two friends who have known each other for years but are afraid that love would ruin their friendship.

Mother and daughter

Beams of light commemorate the Twin Towers following 9/11.

AMERICAN VALUES AT THE CROSSROADS

CHAPTER 12

The sole certainty is that tomorrow will surprise us all.
Alvin Toffler (1928–   )

BEFORE YOU READ

Preview Vocabulary

A. **Read the following sentences from the chapter and notice the words in italics. These key AWL words will help you understand the chapter reading. Use context clues to help you figure out the meanings. Then choose which definition is best for the italicized word.**

_____ 1. Throughout our history we have disagreed about the meaning of these rights and how far they should be extended. But at the same time we have all *internalized* these rights as our own.

   a. made a belief or attitude become part of your character
   b. rejected a belief or attitude as not important

_____ 2. Since the 1960s and the Great Society programs, the government has continued to *undertake* new responsibilities.

   a. start or agree to do something
   b. decide not to do something

_____ 3. Some Americans think that persons found to be acting *on behalf of* international terrorists trying to damage and destroy the United States should have the same rights to a fair trial that ordinary criminals have.

    a. against their interests
    b. as their representatives

_____ 4. Some scholars and commentators believe that the ever-expanding list of rights since the 1960s may *pose a threat* to social order.

    a. cause a problem, danger, or difficulty
    b. protect something from danger

_____ 5. Hard America creates wealth; Soft America *reassigns* it.

    a. makes better products
    b. gives something to someone else

_____ 6. "Once they have paid the mortgage, payments on two cars, taxes, health insurance, and day care, these apparently prosperous two-income families have less *discretionary income* today and less money to save for a rainy day than a single-income family of a generation ago."

    a. money that you can spend in any way you want
    b. money that earns you a great profit

_____ 7. White says that those on either side of the values divide live in "two *parallel* universes. Each side seeks to reinforce its thinking by associating with like-minded people."

    a. unrelated
    b. similar

_____ 8. Many potential voters are not *registered* members of either party, and both parties must try to persuade them to vote for their party's candidate.

    a. recorded
    b. opposed

_____ 9. For a long time, political *analysts* thought this center was socially liberal and fiscally conservative.

    a. people who raise money for their political party candidates
    b. people who make a careful examination of events to make judgments

_____ 10. Most Americans resist being locked into a single-party *ideology* or position.

    a. a set of ideas on which a political system is based
    b. the rules for conducting an election

_____ 11. In spite of the current image of the United States and some of the actions the government has taken, there has been a long historical tradition of *isolationism*.

    a. belief that your country should not be involved in the affairs of other countries
    b. belief that your country should act as a "World Policeman"

_____ 12. Many Americans are very *reluctant* to see the United States become involved in international military actions unless they are convinced that there is some national interest to be protected.

a. fast and enthusiastic
b. slow and unwilling

B. **Read this quotation from the chapter and notice the words in italics. Then use context clues and write the correct word next to its definition.**

"Millions of middle-class Americans are living from *paycheck* to paycheck, struggling to pay their bills, having to borrow money and go into debt. Many families are just one *layoff* or one medical *emergency* away from going into *bankruptcy*. More people this year [2004] will end up bankrupt than will suffer a heart attack or be *diagnosed* with cancer or graduate from college or file for divorce."

_____ 1. a dangerous situation that you must deal with immediately

_____ 2. recognized by signs and symptoms

_____ 3. check that pays someone's salary

_____ 4. stopping a worker's employment because there is not enough work

_____ 5. inability to pay your debts

Preview Content

A. **Read the quotation by Alvin Toffler at the beginning of the chapter. Do you agree with it? Why or why not? What surprising world events have taken place in recent years?**

B. **Discuss these questions with your classmates.**

1. What impact do you think the traditional American values have on Americans today?

2. What are some of the problems Americans face now?

3. What status does the United States have in the world today?

4. What do you think will happen to American values in the twenty-first century?

C. **Read the headings in the chapter and look at the illustrations. Write five topics that you predict will be covered in this chapter.**

1. _____

2. _____

3. _____

4. _____

5. _____

The Role of Values in the National Identity

1   John J. Zogby, an American pollster, says that Americans really know very little about themselves. "Oddly enough for a nation that conducts, reads, argues over, and bashes[1] polls, we still have difficulty understanding who we really are." He notes that the same question is asked by every generation—What really makes us "American"? What is it that we all share? The nation has survived the American Revolution, the Civil War, the Great Depression, the civil rights struggle, assassinations, and several attempts to impeach[2] presidents. "The reason for this survival is simple—we all share a common set of values that make us Americans." Zogby agrees with Ben Wattenberg, an expert on American culture who believes that "values matter most." These values give Americans a unique identity, and whichever political candidate or party can best represent these values wins an election. The values are the basic rights first stated in the Declaration of Independence:

> *We hold these truths to be self-evident, that all men are created equal, that they are endowed by their Creator with certain unalienable rights, that among these are Life, Liberty and the pursuit of Happiness. That to secure these rights, Governments are instituted among Men, deriving their just powers from the consent of the governed.*

2   The rights were then described in the Constitution and in the first ten amendments to the Constitution, the Bill of Rights (see page 143), written to protect the freedom and the rights of the American people. Zogby believes that "unlike any other nation or people, we are defined by the rights we have, not by geography, by the arts and letters, not by our cuisine[3] or sensibilities,[4] not religion or civilization, not by war. . . . Throughout our history we have disagreed about the meaning of these rights and how far they should be extended. But at the same time we have all internalized these rights as our own."

3   The six traditional basic values we have discussed in this book (individual freedom, self-reliance, equality of opportunity, competition, material wealth, and hard work) are still a major force in American society. In this chapter, we will review the six traditional basic values and what challenges they now face.

Individual Freedom and Self-Reliance

4   As has been noted earlier in this book, freedom (sometimes referred to as the "rights of the individual") is the most precious and the most popular of the six basic traditional values of the United States. The traditional ideas of freedom held by the founding fathers and written into the Constitution and the Bill of Rights were dominant until the 1930s. These freedoms included guarantees of the freedom of speech, freedom of the press, and freedom of religion. There were also freedoms

---

[1] **bashes:** criticizes someone or something a lot
[2] **impeach:** to formally accuse a government official of a serious crime in a special government court
[3] **cuisine:** a particular style of cooking
[4] **sensibilities:** ways that people react to particular subjects or types of behavior

guaranteeing a fair criminal trial, that is, the right to a speedy and public trial, the right to a trial by jury, and the right to a defense attorney. In the 1930s, during the Great Depression, the New Deal greatly increased the size and responsibilities of government. Since the 1960s and the Great Society programs, the government has continued to undertake new responsibilities. This has led to a new category of freedoms or rights that are *economic* in nature. For example, the Supreme Court ruled in 1963 that if a person on trial could not afford a defense attorney, the government must provide one for him or her.

Courtroom trial in session

5   Almost all Americans believe that their country should strive for a prosperity shared by all. However, the idea of economic rights has a broader meaning. It means that government should (in one way or another) provide economic benefits for U.S. citizens. It is on this point that Americans differ. Indeed, this difference has been called the *values divide*. On the one hand, conservative, mostly Republican, Americans believe that the government has gone too far in creating and guaranteeing these economic benefits. They argue that the more the government makes itself responsible for providing economic benefits, the more it makes the American people dependent on the government for their standard of living. This in turn takes away the self-reliance of the people—a basic national value that has helped to make the country great.

6   On the other hand, liberal, mostly Democratic, Americans believe that the guarantee of economic rights by the government broadens and improves the traditional idea of freedom. The process of expanding economic rights should, they believe, continue in the twenty-first century. The possible economic rights that are being proposed include the right to medical treatment and basic health insurance; the right to a college education; the right to have a job that provides a standard of living above the poverty level; and, when people are unemployed, the right to receive public assistance (especially for women and children). The debate about the proper balance between self-reliance on the one hand and government-provided economic security on the other will surely be an important debate in the 2000s.

The Call for New Rights

7   Since the 1960s, new rights have expanded in non-economic areas as well. Although liberals see this expansion as positive, conservatives do not. Opponents of these new rights fear that if the new rights are carried too far, they could endanger social order in the United States. For example, the rights of prisoners have expanded since the 1960s. If carried too far, opponents argue, it could make the administration of prisons very difficult, if not impossible. Another example is the issue of the rights of terrorists. Some Americans think that persons found to be acting on behalf of international terrorists trying to damage and destroy the United States should have

the same rights to a fair trial that ordinary criminals have. Opponents argue that it would make protecting the country against terrorists impossible if every terrorist had these rights. It would be very difficult to give large numbers of suspected terrorists the right to a normal criminal trial by jury with defense attorneys provided at court expense, for example. This is why opponents argue that suspected terrorists should be treated as "enemy combatants" and given military trials.

8   Another controversial issue is what the rights of undocumented noncitizens should be. Some Americans believe that those in the United States who are in violation of U.S. immigration laws should have all the rights that citizens have, including a government-paid attorney to defend them. Opponents argue that this only encourages more people to try to enter the United States illegally. One of the most emotional issues concerns the educational rights of these immigrants' children to a college education. Should they be admitted to state-supported universities and have in-state tuition benefits?[5] Liberals generally believe that all children and adults in the United States should be given equal access to education, regardless of their legal status. Conservatives argue that undocumented immigrants may not have paid the taxes that support the education system, and that their children should therefore not be given the educational benefits provided to citizens and legal immigrants.

The García family celebrates graduation day at Seton Hall University.

9   Some scholars and commentators believe that the ever-expanding list of rights since the 1960s may pose a threat to social order. The founding fathers of the nation believed that if freedom is carried to the extreme, it will destroy the social order. That is why the liberty they favored was *ordered liberty*. They knew that the precious gift of liberty could not survive in the midst of anarchy.[6] Finding the proper balance between freedom and social order will be another one of the great challenges for Americans in the twenty-first century.

Equality of Opportunity and Competition

10   As mentioned before, the American ideal of equality of opportunity can be simply stated—all Americans should have an equal opportunity to succeed in life, to gain prosperity, and to pursue happiness. The United States has sometimes failed to honor this value of equality of opportunity, particularly in the case of African Americans who were subjected to slavery and then to segregation and discrimination. But the nation eventually freed the slaves in the 1860s and then

---

[5] **in-state tuition benefits:** greatly reduced tuition costs charged to residents attending a state university operated in their state

[6] **anarchy:** a situation in which there is no effective government in a country or no order in an organization or situation

addressed segregation and discrimination with the Civil Rights Acts of the 1960s.

11   Traditionally, equality of opportunity has not meant equality of results. If a number of people have the same opportunity to succeed, some may succeed more than others. It is not up to society or the government to make sure that every person ends up with the same amount of wealth or prestige. This traditional interpretation was challenged by affirmative action programs giving racial and ethnic preferences following the Civil Rights Acts of the 1960s. One example of this preferential treatment is the practice of giving extra points on university admission applications of blacks, Hispanics, and other minorities. The Supreme Court upheld this practice by the University of Michigan in 2003. Those who support affirmative action argue that it has helped make up for past discrimination against minorities and that it increases the racial and ethnic diversity on college campuses. Those who oppose what they see as preferential treatment believe that everyone should have the same educational opportunities and that no one should get any special advantages. They defend the traditional idea of equality of opportunity and say that they believe in the natural diversity of the United States, not diversity mandated by the government.

The U.S. Supreme Court building in Washington, D.C.

12   The nation often struggles for a balance between the values of equality of opportunity and competition. Michael Barone has written of the need for balance in his book *Hard America/Soft America: Competition vs. Coddling*. Noemie Emery describes Barone's explanation of the division in the United States this way:

> *Hard America values risk, innovation, effort, and enterprise. Soft America values security and equality. Hard America is ruled by the market, while Soft America is directed by government planning. Hard America creates wealth; Soft America reassigns it. Hard America causes undeserved suffering by making no distinction between poverty caused by sickness and poverty caused by laziness. Soft America causes its own suffering by making no distinctions between poverty caused by bad luck and poverty caused by bad habits. . . . But the problem is really striking a balance that gets people to strive without making them desperate—that gives them support without sapping[7] their will.*

Material Wealth and Hard Work

13   Material wealth has traditionally been seen as the reward for hard work. Although most people still believe in the American Dream, many are now having a difficult time attaining or maintaining it. Middle-class families are under

---

[7] **sapping**: gradually taking away something, such as strength or energy

stress. Many of the high-paying manufacturing jobs have moved overseas, and now Americans in the service and technology sectors are worried that their jobs will suffer the same fate. Mortimer Zuckerman wrote in *U.S. News & World Report*, "Millions of middle-class Americans are living from paycheck to paycheck, struggling to pay their bills, having to borrow money and go into debt. Many families are just one layoff or one medical emergency away from going into bankruptcy. . . . More people this year [2004] will end up bankrupt than will suffer a heart attack or be

Even two-income middle-class families struggle to pay their bills.

diagnosed with cancer or graduate from college or file for divorce."

14   The irony is that in most families both the husband and wife are working. Their combined family income is much larger than that of the single-income family a generation ago. Why are they struggling? There are several reasons. Zuckerman says, "Once they have paid the mortgage, payments on two cars, taxes, health insurance, and day care, these apparently prosperous two-income families have less discretionary income today and less money to save for a rainy day than a single-income family of a generation ago. . . . Many in the middle class, those earning $65,000 and less, who make up roughly 80 percent of the people who work, feel they are falling further and further behind, no matter how hard they work." Health care and health insurance have become more and more expensive, taking a larger percentage of a worker's paycheck. The cost of housing has risen dramatically, but middle-class families still want to have a nice home and two late-model cars. They have come to depend on two incomes to pay for this higher standard of living. Also, as manufacturing jobs have disappeared, a college education has become increasingly important and increasingly expensive. Many middle-class families are struggling to pay for a college education for their children, and tuition costs continue to rise sharply. The plight of the middle class is one reason why some are now calling for the government to extend rights to include a right to health care, a right to a college education, and a right to a decent-paying job.

The Values Divide and Those in the Center

15   The disagreement about what rights the government should guarantee has caused the "values divide" or the "culture wars" of the early 2000s. John Kenneth White has written about the split in *The Values Divide: American Politics and Culture in Transition*, with an introduction by John Zogby. White discusses the fact that Republican conservatives and Democratic liberals disagree strongly about the role of the government in solving the country's problems. He says that those on either side of the values divide live in "two parallel universes. Each side seeks to reinforce its thinking by associating with like-minded people." In a series of articles in *The Washington Post* titled

"America in Red and Blue: A Nation Divided," David Von Drehle explored the political split. "This split is nurtured by the marketing efforts of the major parties, which increasingly aim pinpoint messages to certain demographic groups, rather than seeking broadly appealing new themes."

16   Why have the parties targeted certain groups for various political messages? First of all, the use of computers and demographic studies have made it possible to do so. Second, many Americans are only interested in one or two political issues. They respond well to targeted political messages about specific issues that concern them. Third, many potential voters are not registered members of either party, and both parties must try to persuade them to vote for their party's candidate. Neither party can win without securing some of the Independent votes.

17   The conservative Republican and the liberal Democratic Parties each represent about one-third of the voters. In the middle are the other one-third—the Independents who vote according to how they like each candidate and who they believe best represents their personal views, regardless of party. It is important to understand that the silent Independents in the center are becoming an increasingly important political force. Pollster Zogby says that more and more American voters "consider themselves to be in the political center—without any dominant political ideology." For a long time, political analysts thought this center was socially liberal and fiscally conservative. But Zogby's polls reveal that the opposite is true:

> *Indeed, in recent years, many in the center seem to be liberal on issues such as government spending for the poor and middle class, a higher minimum wage, a federal program covering prescription drugs, universal health care coverage, and government regulation of the environment. On the other hand, they lean conservative on the death penalty, late-term abortion, treating juveniles as adults in criminal courts, and teaching traditional values in schools. [That is, they are in favor of all these except late-term abortions, which they are very strongly against.]*

18   Zogby further notes that the same group, or even the same individual, may hold conflicting opinions. Many who usually support the death penalty, for example, may be against it in certain cases. If the conviction was obtained because of racial discrimination or a defense that was not adequate, or DNA evidence indicated that the accused may not be guilty, many would say that the death penalty should not be used. The same contradictions apply to the abortion controversy. Many believe that ending a pregnancy, particularly in the last three months, is really taking a life and should not be permitted, but they still defend the right of women and their doctors to decide what is best. Those who are "pro-life" believe that the government should protect the rights of the unborn fetus. Those who are "pro-choice" believe that a woman should have ultimate control over her own body and the government should not. These contradictions in individuals' beliefs underline the American conviction that people have the right to make their own decisions about each situation they confront. Most Americans resist being locked into a single-party ideology or position. They prefer to reserve the right to examine the issues and decide for themselves, often changing their positions on a case-by-case basis.

The United States in the World

19   In spite of the current image of the United States and some of the actions the
government has taken, there has been a long historical tradition of isolationism.
President George Washington declared in 1796, "It is our true policy to steer clear of
permanent alliances with any portion of the foreign world." The spirit of isolationism
persists even today, as Americans continue to debate their place in the world community.
Many Americans are very reluctant to see the United States become involved in
international military actions unless they are convinced that there is some national
interest to be protected. Americans are also skeptical[8] about international economic
alliances and global agreements, wanting to be sure that their self-interests are protected
before commitments are made to other countries. Many Americans are more interested
in what is happening close to home than what is happening in the rest of the world.
They want to know how events, national or international, will affect them personally.

HOW AMERICANS SEE THEMSELVES IN THE WORLD

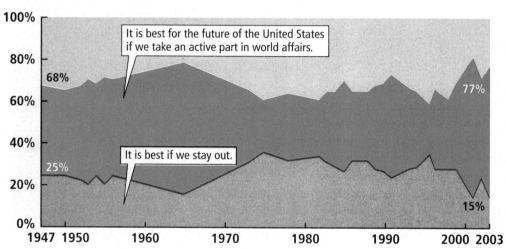

Source: National Opinion Research Center, the Gallup Organization, Program for International Policy Analysis,
TNSSOFRES for the German Marshall Fund, latest that of June

20   Today it would be impossible for the United States to isolate itself from the rest
of the world even if it tried. While some scholars would say that the United States
and its culture played a dominant role in the twentieth century, its role in the twenty-
first is unclear. It is quite possible that the rest of the world will have a greater impact
on the United States than ever before. There are three forces that the United States
has little control over: international terrorism, the global economy, and immigration.

21   First, after 9/11 (the attacks on the World Trade Center and the Pentagon),
Americans became painfully aware that terrorists could attack them inside their own
country. The U.S. government has taken a number of steps to protect Americans
from terrorists, but in a free and open society it is impossible to guarantee that these
attacks will never happen. Terrorists who are willing to kill themselves in an attack are
very difficult to stop. The invasions of Iraq and Afghanistan were meant as *preemptive
strikes* to stop terrorists before they could attack the United States again.

---

[8] **skeptical:** having doubts about whether something is true, right, or good

22   Second, the world economy is growing and changing. Many American companies have discovered that outsourcing jobs is making them more competitive and more profitable. Jobs in the information sector were supposed to take the place of manufacturing jobs that had been outsourced. However, now the middle class sees these information jobs being outsourced to countries such as India and even China. Zuckerman observes that many middle-class Americans "feel that global capitalism has brought into play a vast, new workforce ready and willing to do the jobs of American workers, at a fraction of their pay. Outsourcing has become the symbol of middle-class anxiety."

23   Third, the United States is having trouble controlling the number of illegal immigrants coming into the country, probably more than a million each year. These undocumented workers risk their lives to come into the United States because they cannot make a decent living in their home countries. Although they often take jobs that Americans would rather not do, they are frequently paid in cash and often do not pay taxes or have access to health insurance or other benefits. There are not enough public English classes for them, and providing health care and educational benefits is a problem. Also, many Americans worry about what will happen to the traditional American values as the population of the United States becomes increasingly diverse.

In the midst of an uncertain future, Americans still find refuge and comfort in their families.

24   On the other hand, many recognize that all these new immigrants bring new life and energy into the United States. As the baby boomers get older, immigrants may be an important source of youth and vitality for the nation. Perhaps most importantly, the diversity of ideas and cultures in the United States may be one of its greatest sources of strength in the twenty-first century. Ben Wattenberg, an expert in American culture, believes that the United States is becoming a microcosm of the world—it may be the first *universal* nation, where people from every race, religion, culture, and ethnic background live together in freedom, under one government.

25   The American people and their values have reached another historic crossroads. Will these traditional values endure through this century? One hundred years from now will Americans still have a sense of national identity—of "being American"? What new challenges will this century bring? As Alvin Toffler said, "The sole certainty is that tomorrow will surprise us all."

Understand Main Ideas

Review the predictions that you made on page 265 before reading the chapter.

Throughout the book we have discussed the importance of recognizing main ideas when reading academic material. In Chapter 1 (page 10) we looked at the relationship between the introduction and the conclusion, and how the headings signaled the main ideas. Chapter 2 (pages 35–36) explained how to do a simple outline of main ideas. Chapter 3 (pages 60–61) presented topic sentences and their relationship to main ideas. Chapters 5 (page 104) and 11 (page 252) had exercises on highlighting.

Review these explanations. Then work with a partner and answer these questions.

1. What is the relationship between the opening quotation by Toffler, the introduction, and the conclusion of the chapter reading?

2. What is the purpose of the last paragraph in the first section, *The Role of Values in the National Identity*, paragraph 3, on page 266?

3. What is the main idea of the section *Individual Freedom and Self-Reliance*?

4. What word in the first sentence of the section *The Call for New Rights* ties this section to the previous one?

5. What is the main idea in the section *Equality of Opportunity and Competition*?

6. In the section *Material Wealth and Hard Work*, what is the relationship between these two values?

7. In the section *The Values Divide and Those in the Center*, how would you describe the two groups on the opposite sides of the values divide?

8. What are the three reasons why the Republicans and Democrats try to target Independent voters with specific issues?

9. In the section *The United States in the World*, what are the three forces that the United States has little control over?

Understand Details

Write *T* if the statement is true and *F* if it is false according to information in the chapter.

_____ 1. John J. Zogby believes that Americans have a clear understanding of their national identity.

_____ 2. Today, if you cannot afford a defense attorney, you will have to represent yourself in an American court of law.

_____ 3. A difficult and controversial issue facing the United States today is what rights should be given to undocumented noncitizens.

_____ 4. Everyone agrees that economic rights should be expanded to include health care, a college education, and a good job.

_____ 5. One reason why Americans increasingly worry about their financial security is because of the outsourcing of both manufacturing and information jobs.

_____ 6. In most American families today, only one spouse is working outside the home.

_____ 7. The silent Independents in today's society are becoming an increasingly important force in American politics.

_____ 8. The Supreme Court ruled that the University of Michigan could not give any minorities any preferential treatment in the admission process.

_____ 9. The spirit of isolationism began when the United States first became a nation.

_____ 10. Americans are in complete agreement about what the rights of suspected terrorists should be.

Improving Your Reading Skills: Scanning

Read the following quotations and scan the chapter to find who said each quote. Write the name next to each quotation. (Note: Several sources are quoted more than once.)

_____ 1. "Millions of middle-class Americans are living from paycheck to paycheck, struggling to pay their bills, having to borrow money and go into debt."

_____ 2. "The sole certainty is that tomorrow will surprise us all."

_____ 3. Many middle-class Americans "feel that global capitalism has brought into play a vast, new workforce ready and willing to do the jobs of American workers, at a fraction of their pay. Outsourcing has become a symbol of middle-class anxiety."

_____ 4. "Unlike any other nation or people, we are defined by the rights we have, not by geography, by the arts and letters, not by our cuisine or sensibilities, not religion or civilization, not by war."

_____ 5. The people on either side of the values divide live in "two parallel universes. Each side seeks to reinforce its thinking by associating with like-minded people."

_____ 6. Many American voters "consider themselves to be in the political center without any dominant political ideology."

_____ 7. "This split is nurtured by the marketing efforts of the major parties, which increasingly aim pinpoint messages to certain demographic groups, rather than seeking broadly appealing new themes."

_____ 8. "It is our true policy to steer clear of permanent alliances with any portion of the foreign world."

_____ 9. "Hard America values risk, innovation, effort, and enterprise. Soft America values security and equality. Hard America is ruled by the market, while Soft America is directed by government planning. Hard America creates wealth; Soft America reassigns it."

_____ 10. "Indeed, in recent years, many in the center seem to be liberal on issues such as government spending for the poor and middle class, a higher minimum wage, a federal program covering prescription drugs, universal health care coverage, and government regulation of the environment."

Talk About It

Work in small groups and choose one or more of these topics to discuss.

1. What are the core values in your country? Are they similar to those of Americans?

2. How has your country changed in your lifetime? What changes do you think you will see in the future?

3. What do you think will happen to the balance of power in the world during the next ten years? What role do you think your country will have in the twenty-first century?

4. How does your country view the United States? Americans have been accused of believing that their country is better or more important than any other. Do you think the United States is more important? Explain.

5. What would you do to solve the current problem of undocumented immigrants in the United States?

6. How do you feel about how America handled the problem of terrorism and the invasion of Iraq? Would you have done anything differently?

7. Are you basically optimistic about the future? Why or why not?

Build Your Vocabulary

Scrambled Words Review words used frequently throughout the text. Read these definitions and unscramble the vocabulary words that they define.

_____ 1. **ruectlu**—the ideas, beliefs, and customs that are shared and accepted by people in a society

_____ 2. **oefmred**—the right to do what you want without being controlled or restricted by the government, police, etc.

_____ 3. **drah kwro**—the price you pay for having a high standard of living

_____ 4. **auqytiel**—the state of having the same rights, opportunities, etc., as everyone else

_____ 5. **aaeilmtr thawel**—money and possessions

_____ 6. **lefs-lenaicre**—the state of being dependent on yourself

_____ 7. **pmctioetnio**—a situation in which people or organizations try to be more successful

Vocabulary Check This chapter has a number of words that have to do with the criminal justice system. Circle the eight words and phrases that are related to crime and punishment. Use them to complete the sentences.

conviction	death penalty	jury	opponent
court	defense attorney	justice	outsourcing
criminals	global	microcosm	trial

1. There were also freedoms guaranteeing the right to a speedy and public _____.

2. Americans also have the right to a trial by _____ and the right to a _____ _____.

3. If someone cannot afford an attorney, one will be appointed by the _____. Some Americans believe that suspected terrorists should have the same rights to a fair trial that ordinary _____ have.

4. The administration of _____ may be very difficult.

5. Many who usually support the _____ _____ may be against it if the _____ was obtained because of racial discrimination.

More AWL Words Test your knowledge of these additional AWL words in the reading by completing the crossword puzzle below. The clues are on the next page.

adequate	commitment	evidence	military	reveal	sole
category	define	identity	normal	sector	stress
challenge	distinction	respond	security	survive	target

Across

1. things done to keep a place, person, or thing safe
2. a group of people or things that all have the same particular qualities
4. continuous feelings of worry about your work or personal life
6. a promise to do something or behave in a particular way
7. usual, typical, or expected
10. relating to or used by the army, navy, etc.
11. a clear difference between things
12. enough for a particular purpose
15. facts, objects, or signs that make you believe something is true

Down

1. to continue to exist in spite of difficulties and dangers
3. to describe something correctly and thoroughly
4. a part of an area of activity, especially business or trade
5. to aim an idea or plan at a limited group of people
6. something that tests strength, skill, or ability
8. to react to something that has been said or done
9. the qualities of people or groups that make them different from others
13. the only one
14. to show something that was hidden

EXPAND YOUR KNOWLEDGE

Think, Pair, Share

Review the section *The Values Divide and Those in the Center* and the differences between liberal and conservative views mentioned in the section. Would you say that your views are more liberal or conservative? Are you liberal on some issues and conservative on others?

Write a list of issues in the chart. Indicate whether they are liberal or conservative views. Check those you agree with. (An example has been done for you.) Then share your list with a partner, and then with another pair of students.

Issue	Liberal View	Conservative View	My View
Government spending for the poor and middle class	✔		✔

Ask Yourself/Ask Americans

Do you agree or disagree with these statements? Circle your answers. Then ask an American for his or her opinion. Compare your answers with the American's answers.

1. Nuclear power plants are basically safe and are good sources of energy for the future.   agree   disagree

2. Science and technology do more to improve the overall quality of life than do religion and philosophy.   agree   disagree

3. Protecting the environment is more important than industrial development.   agree   disagree

4. Governments should provide free health care for all the citizens of the country.   agree   disagree

5. Governments should provide a free college education for all citizens of the country.   agree   disagree

6. I expect to have more material possessions than my parents do now.   agree   disagree

7. I am confident that my children will have as good a life as mine or better.   agree   disagree

8. I am basically optimistic about the future.   agree   disagree

Small-Group Project

Work in small groups. Make three predictions about what you think will happen in the future, during your lifetime.

Write your predictions on a piece of paper and give them to your teacher. As your teacher reads the predictions aloud, a classmate can write the predictions on a chart or on the chalkboard. Then the class can vote on which predictions they think are most likely to come true.

Use the Internet

At the end of the 1900s, a number of organizations prepared *time capsules*. A time capsule is a container filled with objects from a particular time, so that people in the future will know what life was like then. You can learn about the one done by *The New York Times Magazine* and displayed at the Smithsonian American Museum of Natural History by visiting the museum website: http://www.amnh.org/exhibitions/timescapsule/.

Read about what was put in this time capsule, and look at other websites about time capsules. Then work in small groups to decide what you would put in a time capsule to be opened in 2100. Prepare a poster with a collage of photos, or bring in actual items for your time capsule. Present your ideas to the rest of the class and explain your reasons for your choices.

A. Choose one of these final projects to write about.

1. Write about some aspect of American culture. Analyze an American movie, a TV show, commercials on TV, advertisements in newspapers or magazines, some current event in the news, the results of interviews or conversations you have had with Americans about their beliefs, or observations you have made about how Americans behave. Choose any aspect of life in the United States that you have observed. Be sure to mention at least two or three of the six values: individual freedom, self-reliance, equality of opportunity, competition, material wealth, and hard work.

2. Or approach the assignment from a different direction. Choose a value and then give specific examples of how you have observed that value existing in American life. Contrast this value with your own culture and how things are done differently. When you have finished writing your analysis, prepare a short speech to report your findings to the rest of the class.

B. Now that you have finished this text, what do you think the *American Dream* is? How can Americans protect it for future generations? How much can and should a nation do to ensure equality of opportunity for its people?

Read the following and write an essay in response.

Theodore H. White, a well-known political analyst, has said that the United States's problem is "trying to do everything for everybody." Ever since the early 1960s, he says, Americans have been making promises—

> . . . *promises to save the cities, promises to take care of the sick, the old, the universities. . . . Many of our problems flow out of American goodwill, trying to do everything for everybody. . . . In the 1960s we exploded with goodwill as blacks, who had been denied equality, rightfully demanded it. We could afford it, and we should have done what we did. But we have ended up pushing equality and other ideas to absurd limits as we sought perfect equality rather than realistic equality of opportunity. . . . We have to choose what we can do; we have to discipline our goodwill.* *

Contrast Theodore H. White's view with that expressed by Martin Luther King Jr. in his "I Have a Dream" speech. In 1963, on the 100th anniversary of the Emancipation Proclamation that freed the slaves in the southern states that had left the Union, there was a huge civil rights march in Washington, D.C. Martin Luther King Jr. delivered his famous speech on the steps of the Lincoln Memorial to several hundred thousand marchers. In the speech he spoke of the journey of African Americans from slavery into freedom, and the need to continue

---

* "America's Problem: 'Trying to Do Everything for Everybody,'" *U.S. News & World Report* (July 5, 1982).

American Values at the Crossroads **281**

the journey so that they could one day have equality with whites and be truly free from prejudice and discrimination.

The "I Have a Dream" speech is one of the finest in the English language and one that you should hear. If you are in the United States, your university or town library probably has a videotape of it, or you may purchase an audiotape or videotape from the King Center in Atlanta, Georgia. The speech concludes with a quote from the Declaration of Independence and an old African-American spiritual (religious song). Here are some excerpts:

Dr. Martin Luther King Jr.

Five score years ago, a great American, in whose symbolic shadow we stand today, signed the Emancipation Proclamation. . . . But one hundred years later, the Negro still is not free. . . . One hundred years later, the Negro is still languishing in the corners of American society and finds himself an exile in his own land. So we have come here today to dramatize a shameful condition.

In a sense, we have come to our nation's capital to cash a check. When the architects of our republic wrote the magnificent words of the Constitution and the Declaration of Independence, they were signing a promissory note to which every American was to fall heir. This note was a promise that all men— yes, black men as well as white men—would be guaranteed the inalienable rights of life, liberty, and the pursuit of happiness.

It is obvious that America has defaulted on this promissory note insofar as her citizens of color are concerned. . . . <u>Now</u> is the time to make real the promises of democracy. . . . <u>Now</u> is the time to make justice a reality for all of God's children. . . .

I say to you today, my friends, even though we face the difficulties of today and tomorrow, I still have a dream. It is a dream deeply rooted in the American dream. . . . I have a dream that my four little children will one day live in a nation where they will not be judged by the color of their skin, but by the content of their character. . . . I have a dream today.

I have a dream that one day this nation will rise up and live out the true meaning of its creed: "We hold these truths to be self-evident, that all men are created equal. . . ." [One day] all of God's children, black men and white men, Jews and Gentiles, Protestants and Catholics, will be able to join hands and sing in the words of the old Negro spiritual: "Free at last! Free at last! Thank God Almighty. We are free at last."

Books to Read

Peter Brimelow, *Alien Nation: Common Sense About America's Immigration Disaster*—A controversial argument for limiting immigration to the United States.

Sheryll Cashin, *The Failures of Integration: How Race and Class Are Undermining the American Dream*—The author, a black Georgetown professor, argues that the continuing segregation in the United States is hurting both blacks and whites.

Richard A. Clarke, *Against All Enemies: Inside America's War on Terror*—The man who was head of counterterrorism for Presidents Clinton and Bush describes America's efforts to fight al Qaeda.

Samuel P. Huntington, *Who Are We? The Challenges to America's National Identity*—In this controversial book, the author, a Harvard professor, questions whether a multicultural nation can retain its national identity.

Aldous Huxley, *Brave New World*—Written in 1931, this classic novel imagines a future world that includes test tube babies, cloning, and drugs that the rulers use to keep the workers happy and completely under their control.

Movies to See

Air Force One—When terrorist hijackers seize the plane carrying the president and his family, the president, an ex-soldier, fights to defeat them.

American History X—A former "neo-Nazi skinhead" tries to prevent his younger brother from going down the same wrong path that he did.

El Norte—After the Guatemalan army destroys their village and kills their family, a teenage brother and sister who have survived travel to Los Angeles to make a new life.

Fahrenheit 9/11—An extremely controversial documentary expressing the views of Michael Moore about what happened to the United States after September 11 and how the Bush administration responded to the attack.

13 Going on 30—A thirteen-year-old girl plays a game on her thirteenth birthday and wakes up the next day as a thirty-year-old woman who takes another look at her choices in life.

ACADEMIC WORD LIST

The reading material in each chapter has been analyzed by comparing it to several vocabulary lists: the 2,000 Most Frequent Word Family List and the Academic Word List. Vocabulary words used in exercises (1) are from the Academic Word List, or (2) are not from either of the two lists but are important to the context of the reading and are useful to know for academic reading in general.

The Academic Word List (AWL) was developed by Averil Coxhead. The list contains 570 word families that were selected by examining academic texts from a variety of subject areas. The list does not include words that are among the most frequent 2,000 words of English. Each word family has a headword (the stem form) and a list of other word forms (or parts of speech) for that headword.

AWL Words Used in Chapter Readings

The number after each AWL headword indicates the chapter in which the word was first used. (Note: another form of the word may have been used, not the stem form.)

abandon 3	area 4	circumstance 4
academy 9	aspect 1	cite 3
access 4	assemble 5	civil 4
accommodate 8	assign 12	classic 1
accompany 5	assume 7	comment 10
accumulate 2	attach 2	commit 10
achieve 2	attitude 3	communicate 5
acquire 2	authority 2	community 1
adapt 5	automate 4	compensate 11
adequate 4	available 5	complex 4
adjust 5	aware 4	compute 5
administrate 6	behalf 12	concentrate 9
adult 2	benefit 2	concept 1
affect 1	bias 8	conclude 5
aid 6	bond 10	conduct 3
alternative 6	brief 9	confine 4
analyze 12	capable 4	conflict 5
annual 9	capacity 3	consent 7
apparent 12	category 1	consequent 3
approach 1	challenge 2	considerable 11
approximate 11	channel 5	consist 4

constant 2	diverse 1	foundation 2	issue 2
constitute 1	document 8	function 3	item 10
construct 5	dominate 1	fund 5	job 1
consume 5	drama 3	fundamental 2	justify 9
context 2	economy 2	furthermore 7	label 10
contradict 3	edit 5	generate 6	labor 2
contrary 10	element 10	generation 2	lecture 10
contrast 3	eliminate 2	globe 2	legal 1
contribute 1	emerge 1	goal 3	legislate 4
controversy 4	emphasis 2	grade 9	liberal 3
convert 2	enable 4	grant 5	license 1
convince 1	energy 2	guarantee 4	likewise 10
cooperate 4	enormous 2	hypothesis 1	link 6
core 9	ensure 2	identify 1	locate 11
corporate 6	environment 5	ideology 12	maintain 1
couple 11	equip 10	ignorance 9	major 1
create 1	establish 1	illustrate 7	margin 7
credit 3	estimate 1	image 4	mature 9
criteria 9	ethic 2	immigrate 1	media 5
culture 1	ethnic 1	impact 4	medical 5
cycle 6	evaluate 9	impose 3	mental 10
data 1	eventual 2	incentive 5	method 9
debate 1	evident 2	incidence 1	military 7
decade 1	evolve 10	incline 8	minor 1
decline 2	exclude 1	income 5	monitor 10
define 2	expand 5	indicate 9	motive 1
demonstrate 4	expert 5	individual 2	negate 5
deny 4	explicit 10	injure 7	network 10
depress 7	export 5	innovate 6	neutral 1
derive 10	expose 10	insight 11	nevertheless 2
design 2	facilitate 8	instance 6	normal 4
despite 8	factor 1	institute 1	nuclear 11
detect 4	feature 4	instruct 8	obtain 9
device 5	federal 8	integrate 9	occupy 6
devote 3	fee 5	intelligence 2	occur 3
diminish 2	file 9	intense 10	option 5
discrete 12	final 4	internal 12	orient 3
discriminate 8	finance 2	interpret 7	outcome 7
display 3	flexible 6	invest 5	output 6
distinct 1	focus 7	involve 10	overall 6
distribute 6	found 4	isolate 12	overseas 10

parallel 12
participate 1
partner 11
perceive 2
percent 1
period 1
persist 3
perspective 9
phase 4
phenomenon 8
philosophy 3
physical 4
policy 6
portion 4
pose 12
positive 5
potential 5
predict 5
predominant 9
previous 3
primary 3
principal 4
principle 7
priority 11
proceed 7
process 1
professional 5
prohibit 8
project 10

promote 2
psychology 10
publish 6
pursue 2
range 10
react 4
refine 6
region 4
register 12
regulate 5
reinforce 4
reject 2
relax 5
reluctance 12
rely 2
require 3
research 3
reside 8
resolve 7
resource 1
respond 5
restrain 7
restrict 5
retain 8
reveal 1
reverse 7
revolution 6
role 1
section 5

sector 9
secure 4
seek 2
select 9
series 7
sex 3
shift 2
significant 1
similar 3
site 5
sole 3
somewhat 8
source 4
specific 1
specify 1
stable 11
status 2
strategy 7
stress 5
structure 3
style 6
submit 6
subsidy 5
substitute 2
sum 3
survey 2
survive 1
symbol 5
tape 3

target 7
task 4
team 6
technical 9
technique 5
technology 5
temporary 6
text 1
theme 2
theory 6
trace 8
tradition 1
transform 9
trend 3
ultimate 6
undergo 5
undertake 12
uniform 2
unique 1
vary 1
version 4
via 10
violate 9
virtual 1
visible 1
voluntary 3
welfare 2
widespread 5

BIBLIOGRAPHY

In addition to these sources, more than 100 websites were researched.

Aaron, Henry J., Thomas E. Mann, and Timothy Taylor, eds. "Introduction." *Values and Public Policy*. Washington, D.C.: The Brookings Institution, 1994.

Adelman, Larry. "Down the Road from the Michigan Rulings: Right Ruling, Wrong Reason." *Washington Post*, 29 June 2003, Outlook section B3.

Alger, Horatio. *Mark the Match Boy, or Richard Hunter's Ward*. Philadelphia: John C. Winston Company, 1897.

Alger, Horatio. *Tony the Tramp, or Right Is Might*. New York: The New York Book Company, 1909.

"America's Immigrant Challenge." *Time* Magazine. Special Issue, Fall 1993, 3–12.

Asnes, Marion. "The Affluent American: A Money Survey Delves into the Changing Definition of 'the Good Life.'" *Money*. December 2003, 40, 43.

Bacon, Perry, Jr. "How Much Diversity Do You Want from Me?" *Time* Magazine. 7 July 2003, 108.

Barone, Michael. "A Tale of Two Nations: Why Coddled Kids Grow Up to Become Supercompetent Adults." *U.S. News & World Report*. 12 May 2003, 24.

Becker, Carl L. *The Declaration of Independence: A Study in the History of Political Ideas*. New York: Vantage Books, 1958.

"Been There, Done That" [Adventure Travel]. *Newsweek*. 19 July 1993, 42-49.

"Best Columns: The U.S.: Orange Alert: Why We're Laughing; Peace Protests: Giving Naivete a Chance; Bush: A Third Kind of President; Affirmative Action: What's Really at Stake. *The Week*. 7 March 2003, 12.

"Best Columns: The U.S.: American Culture: A Dwindling Export." *The Week*. 4 April 2003.

Bohr, Peter. "In the Age of Super-Sizing, Is There Room in America for the Small Car?" *AAA World*. January/February 2003, 30–36.

Bowman, Karlyn, ed. "Men Today/Guy Talk." *The American Enterprise*. September 2003, 60–61.

Brascoupe, Jeremy. "My World: Young Native Americans Today." *Smithsonian National Museum of the American Indian*. Spring 2003, 9.

Brogan, D. W. *The American Character*. New York: Alfred A. Knopf, 1944.

Brogan, Hugh. *Tocqueville*. London: Fontana, 1973.

Brookheser, Richard. "We Can All Share American Culture." *Time* Magazine. 31 August 1992, 74.

Burns, James MacGregor. *Deadlock of Democracy: Far-Party Politics in America*. Englewood Cliffs, N.J.: Prentice-Hall, 1963.

Burns, James MacGregor. *Cobblestone Leadership: Majority Rule, Minority Power*. Norman: University of Oklahoma Press, 1990.

"Campaign Finance Reform: Opinions of People of Faith and the Clergy." A survey by the Gallup Organization for The Interfaith Alliance Foundation August 2001 in *Call for Reform*, published by The Interfaith Alliance Foundation.

Carlson, Margaret. "And Now, Obesity Rights." *Time* Magazine. 6 December 1993, 96.

Carnegie, Andrew. *Autobiography of Andrew Carnegie.* Boston: Houghton Mifflin, 1920.

Carnegie, Andrew. *The Gospel of Wealth and Other Timely Essays.* Cambridge: Harvard University, Belknap Press, 1962.

Cash, W. J. *The Mind of the South.* New York: Alfred A. Knopf, 1960.

Cater, Douglass, ed. *Television as a Social Force: New Approaches to TV Criticism.* New York: Praeger, 1975.

"A Class of Their Own." *Time* Magazine. 31 October 1994, 52–61.

Cloud, John. "Why the SUV Is All the Rage." *Time* Magazine. 24 February 2003, 35–42.

CNN/*USA Today*/Gallup Poll, 2-4 Sept. 2002. "How Important Would You Say Religion Is in Your Own Life: Very Important, Fairly Important, or Not Very Important?"

Cohen, Richard. "Intolerance Swaddled in Faith." *Washington Post,* 1 May 2003, A27.

Cohn, D'Vera, and Sarah Cohen. "Statistics Portray Settled, Affluent Mideast Community." *Washington Post,* 20 November 2001, A4.

Cohn, D'Vera. "Hispanics Declared Largest Minority: Blacks Overtaken in Census Update." *Washington Post,* 19 June 2003, A1, 46.

Corliss, Richard, Jeffrey Ressner, and James Inverne. "Ladies' Night Out" [Movies]. *Time* Magazine. March 2003, 73–75.

Cose, Ellis. "The Black Gender Gap." *Newsweek.* 3 March 2003, 46–55

Counts, George S. *Education and American Civilization.* New York: Bureau of Publications, Teachers College, Columbia University, 1952.

Counts, George S. *Education and the Foundations of Human Freedom.* Pittsburgh: University of Pittsburgh Press, 1962.

Coy, Peter. "Right Place, Right Time." *Business Week.* 13 October 2003.

Cullen, Bob. "New Kids on the Block: As Affluent Schools in the Suburbs Grow More Diverse, They Face the Test That City Schools Failed: Can They Keep Everyone Happy?" *The Washingtonian.* April 2003, 29–34.

Cullen, Lisa Takeuchi. "Now Hiring!" *Time* Magazine. 24 November 2004.

"Daughters of Murphy Brown" [Single Motherhood]. *Newsweek.* 2 August 1993, 58–59.

"The Dawn of Online Home Schooling." *Newsweek.* 10 October 1994, 67.

"Diversity or Division On Campus: Minority Graduation Galas Highlight a Timely Issue." *Washington Post,* 19 May 2003, A1, 8.

"Domesticated Bliss: New Laws Are Making It Official for Gay or Live-In Straight Couples." *Newsweek.* 23 March 1992, 62–63.

Ellison, Christopher G., and W. Allen Martin, eds. *Race and Ethnic Relations in the United States: Readings for the 21st Century.* University of Florida, 1998.

Ellwood, Robert S. "East Asian Religions in Today's America." *World Religions in America: An Introduction,* ed. Jacob Neusner. Louisville, Ky.: Westminster/John Knox Press, 1994.

Emery, Noemie. "America in the Middle: Michael Barone Seeks a Balance." *Weekly Standard.* 17 May 2004, 31–33.

Entine, John, Gary Salles, and Jay T. Kearney. *Taboo: Why Black Athletes Dominate Sports and Why We're Afraid to Talk About It.* New York: Public Affairs, 2001.

Esposito, John L. "Islam in the World and in America." *World Religions in America: An Introduction,* ed. Jacob Neusner. Louisville, Ky.: Westminster/John Knox Press, 1994.

Farrand, Max. *The Framing of the Constitution of the United States.* New Haven: Yale University Press, 1913.

Fetto, John. "Reader Request: Your Questions Answered: Not Only Are Americans Going to School in Record Numbers, They're Also Staying in School Longer." *American Demographics.* April 2003, 8–9.

"50 Years After Brown: Unequal Education." *U.S. News & World Report.* 22, 29 March 2004, 64–70.

"The Fight to Bear Arms." *U.S. News & World Report.* 22 May 1995, 28–37.

Fineman, Howard. "Bush and God: A Higher Calling: How Faith Changed His Life and Shapes His Presidency." *Newsweek.* 10 March 2003, 22–30.

Fineman, Howard, and Tamara Lipper. "Do We Still Need Affirmative Action? Affirmative Action: Race in the Spin Cycle." *Newsweek.* 27 January 2003, 26–29.

Finlely, Bill. "Women's Game Is Looking Good, and Fans Notice." *New York Times*, 20 July 2003, Sports section: 5.

Fox-Genovese, Elizabeth. "Religion and Women in America." *World Religions in America: An Introduction,* ed. Jacob Neusner. Louisville, Ky: Westminster/John Knox Press, 1994.

"Fractured Family Ties: Television's New Theme Is Single Parenting." *Newsweek.* 30 August 1993, 50–52.

Friedan, Betty. *The Feminine Mystique.* New York: W.W. Norton, 1963.

Friedan, Betty. *The Second Stage.* New York: Summit Books, 1981.

Galbraith, John Kenneth. *American Capitalism: The Concept of Countervailing Power.* Classics in Economics Series. Boston: Houghton Mifflin, 1956.

Galbraith, John Kenneth. *The Affluent Society.* Boston: Houghton Mifflin, 1976.

Galbraith, John Kenneth. *The Culture of Contentment.* Boston: Houghton Mifflin, 1992.

Gibbs, Nancy. "The Vicious Cycle." *Time* Magazine. 20 June 1994, 24–33.

Gill, Sam. "Native Americans and Their Religions." *World Religions in America: An Introduction,* ed. Jacob Neusner. Louisville, Ky.: Westminster/John Knox Press, 1994.

Gladwell, Malcolm. "Big and Bad: How the S.U.V. Ran Over Automotive Safety." *The New Yorker,* 12 January 2004, 28–33.

Glazer, Nathan. "Multiculturalism and Public Policy." *Values and Public Policy,* ed. Henry J. Aaron, Thomas E. Mann, and Timothy Taylor. Washington, D.C.: The Brookings Institution, 1994.

Glazer, Nathan, and Daniel P. Moynihan. *Beyond the Melting Pot: The Negroes, Puerto Ricans, Jews, Italians, and Irish of NYC.* Publications of the Joint Center for Urban Studies. Cambridge: M.I.T. Press, 1963.

Goldsborough, James O. "The American Political Landscape in 2004." *San Diego Union,* 1 January 2004.

Gonzalez, David. "What's the Problem with 'Hispanic'? Just Ask a 'Latino.'" *New York Times,* 15 November 1992.

Gonzalez, Justo L. "The Religious World of Hispanic Americans." *World Religions in America: An Introduction,* ed. Jacob Neusner. Louisville, Ky.: Westminster/John Knox Press, 1994.

Greeley, Andrew M. "The Catholics in the World and in America." *World Religions in America: An Introduction,* ed. Jacob Neusner. Louisville, Ky.: Westminster/John Knox Press, 1994.

Greeley, Andrew M. "Religion and Politics in America." *World Religions in America: An Introduction,* ed. Jacob Neusner. Louisville, Ky. Westminster/John Knox Press, 1994.

Green, William Scott. "Religion and Society in America." *World Religions in America: An Introduction,* ed. Jacob Neusner. Louisville, Ky.: Westminster/John Knox Press, 1994.

"The Grid: Mapping Consumer Markets: Sweat Equity: Where Today's Do-it-yourselfers Are Most Likely to Stake a Claim." *American Demographics.* April 2003, 18–19

Hamilton, Anita. "Your Time: Find It on Craig's List." *Time* Magazine. 3 March 2003, 76.

Handlin, Oscar. *Race and Nationality in American Life.* Boston: Little, Brown, 1957.

"Happily Unmarried: How-to from a Guidebook for Couples Living Together Without Saying 'I Do.'" *Time* Magazine. Bonus Section, March 2003, A10.

Harris Interactive. *The Harris Poll* ® #30, 21 May 2003. "Americans Are Far More Optimistic and Have Much Higher Life Satisfaction Than Europeans" by Humphrey Taylor.

Henderson, Neil. "Greenspan Calls for Better-Educated Workforce." *Washington Post,* 21 February 2004, Business E3: 1, 3.

Henry, W. A. "Pride and Prejudice." *Time* Magazine. 28 February 1994.

Hinson, Hal. "Life, Liberty and the Pursuit of Cows: How the Western Defines America's View of Itself." *Washington Post,* 3 July 1994, 1(G), 6(G).

Hofstadter, Richard. *The American Political Tradition and the Men Who Made It.* New York: Vintage Books, 1954.

Hofstadter, Richard. *Social Darwinism in American Thought.* New York: G. Braziller, 1969.

Huffington, Arianna. *Pigs at the Trough: How Corporate Greed and Political Corruption are Undermining America.* New York: Crowne Publishing Group, 2003.

"Income Report: The Near-Affluent, the Affluent, the Upper Echelon: Generosity and Income." *American Demographics.* December 2002/January 2003, 40–47.

"In Search of the Sacred." *Newsweek.* 28 November 1994, 52–55.

Jones, Malcolm. "The New Turf Wars: A Plague of Critics Bushwhacks the Venerable American Lawn." *Newsweek.* 21 June 1993, 62-63.

Joyce, Amy. "Balancing Their Personal Goals: Younger Employees Value Family Time as Highly as Career Advancement." *Washington Post,* 24 October 2004, F5.

Kantrowitz, Barbara, and Pat Wingert. "Education: What's at Stake." *Newsweek.* 27 January 2003, 30–38.

Kegley, Charles, and Eugene Wittkopf. *World Politics: Trend and Transformations,* 3d ed. New York: St. Martin's, 1989.

Kennedy, John F. *A Nation of Immigrants.* New York: Harper & Row, 1958.

"Kids Who Care: Everybody Wins When Students Volunteer to Help Out." *Better Homes and Gardens.* March 1992, 37–39.

King, Martin Luther, Jr. *I Have a Dream.* Littleton, Mass.: Sundance Publications, 1991.

Klein, Joe. "Whose Family? Whose Values? Who Makes the Choices?" *Newsweek.* 8 June 1992, 18–22.

Klein, Joe. "The Education of Berenice Belizaire." *Time* Magazine. 9 August 1993, 26.

Kristol, Irving. "The Rise of the Neocons." *The Week,* 23 May 2003, 13.

Langley, Alison. "It's a Fat World, After All: U.S. Food Companies Face Scrutiny Abroad." *New York Times,* 20 July 2003, Money & Business: section 3: 1, 11.

Lasch, Christopher. *The Culture of Narcissism: American Life in an Age of Diminishing Expectations.* New York: W. W. Norton, 1978.

Leo, John. "On Society: Pushing the Bias Button." *U.S. News & World Report,* 9 June 2003, 37.

Levy, Steven, and Pat Wingert. "The Next Frontiers [Series]: Spielberg Nation: With Digital Camcorders, PCs and Easy-to-use Software, Anyone Can Become a Film Auteur." *Newsweek.* 25 November 2003, 56–58.

Lipset, Seymour Martin. Continental Divide: *The Values and Institutions of the United States and Canada.* New York: Routledge, 1990.

Lipset, Seymour Martin. *American Exceptionalism: A Double-Edged Sword.* New York: W. W. Norton, 1996.

Lowi, Theodore. *The End of Liberalism: Republic of the United States.* New York: W. W. Norton, 1969.

Lowi, Theodore, and Benjamin Ginsberg. *American Government: Freedom and Power.* New York: W. W. Norton, 1994.

Macbay, Harvey. *Swim with the Sharks Without Being Eaten Alive.* New York: William Morrow Company, 1988.

"Malcolm X." *Newsweek.* 16 November 1992, 66–71.

Malcom X and Alex Haley. *The Autobiography of Malcolm X.* New York: Grove Publishers, 1966.

Mansbridge, Jane. "Public Spirit in Political Systems." *Values and Public Policy,* ed. Henry J. Aaron, Thomas E. Mann, and Timothy Taylor. Washington, D.C.: The Brookings Institution, 1994.

Marklein, Mary Beth. "Higher Education: Tribal Colleges Bridge Culture Gap to Future." *USA Today,* 13 April 1998, 4D.

Markon, Jerry. "Virginia Colleges May Bar Illegal Immigrants: Judge's Ruling Is Said to Be U.S. First." *Washington Post,* 26 February 2004, B1.

Marty, Martin E. "Protestant Christianity in the World and in America." *World Religions in America: An Introduction,* ed. Jacob Neusner. Louisville, Ky.: Westminster/John Knox Press, 1994.

Marty, Martin E. "The Sin of Pride: Vision Thing: Why His 'God Talk' Worries Friends and Foes." *Newsweek.* 10 March 2003, 32–33.

Mason, Alpheus T. *In Quest of Freedom: American Political Thought and Practice.* Englewood Cliffs, N.J.: Prentice-Hall, 1959.

Mason, Alpheus T., and Gordon E. Baker, eds. *Free Government in the Making: Readings in American Political Thought.* New York: Oxford University Press, 1949.

Michaud, Anne. "City Population Hits 8.1 Million, Keeps Growing: Reasons: Immigrants, New Housing." *Crain's New York Business.* 29 March–4 April 2004, 1, 24.

Morganthau, Tom. "America: Still a Melting Pot?" *Newsweek.* 9 August 1993, 16–23.

Morin, Richard. "Misperceptions Cloud Whites' View of Blacks." *Washington Post,* 11 July 2001, A1.

Morin, Richard. "Unconventional Wisdom: New Facts and Hot Stats from the Social Sciences: Church Givers vs. Church Goers." *Washington Post,* 4 April 2004, Outlook section: B5.

Morrow, Lance. "Family Values." *Time* Magazine. 31 August 1992, 22–27.

"National Endowment Campaign Launched to Spearhead Native Language Revitalization." *Native Language Network, Newsletter of the Indigenous Language Institute.* Winter/Spring 2002.

Naughton, Keith and Marc Peyser. "The World According to Trump." *Newsweek.* 1 March 2004, 48–57.

Nelan, Bruce W. "Not So Welcome Anymore." *Time* Magazine. Special Issue, Fall 1993, 10–12.

"Networks Under the Gun." *Newsweek.* 12 July 1993, 14–15.

Neusner, Jacob, ed. "Introduction." *World Religions in America: An Introduction.* Louisville, Ky.: Westminster/John Knox Press, 1994.

Nevins, Allan, and Henry Steele Commager. *America: The Story of a Free People.* Boston: Little, Brown, 1942.

"A New Era of Segregation: Classrooms Still Aren't Colorblind." *Newsweek.* 27 December 1993, 44.

Noonan, Peggy. "The Working Spirit: Why We Work So Hard." *O* [Oprah]. May / June 2000, 90.

Paris, Peter J. "The Religious World of African Americans." *World Religions in America: An Introduction.* ed. Jacob Neusner. Louisville, Ky.: Westminster/ John Knox Press, 1994.

"Partnership or Peril? Faith-Based Initiatives and the First Amendment" by Oliver Thomas, First Reports, vol. 2. no. 1, May 200.1 A First Amendment Center Publication, First Amendment Center, Funded by the Freedom Forum (an affiliate of the Newseum).

Peterson, Karen S. "Stay Close By, for the Sake of the Kids: Children of Divorce Suffer When a Parent Moves Away, Study Says." *USA Today,* 7 July 2003, Health & Behavior section: 7D.

Peterson, Peter. *Facing Up: How to Rescue the Economy from Crushing Debt and Restore the American Dream.* New York: Simon & Schuster, 1993.

Poniewozik, James, "Has the Mainstream Run Dry? What Does Mass Culture Without the Masses Look Like?" *Time* Magazine. 29 December 2003–5 January 2004, 148–152.

Popenoe, David. "The Family Condition of America: Cultural Change and Public Policy." *Values and Public Policy*, ed. Henry J. Aaron, Thomas E. Mann, and Timothy Taylor. Washington, D.C.: The Brookings Institution, 1994.

Potter, David M. *People of Plenty: Economic Abundance and the American Character.* Chicago: University of Chicago Press, 1969.

Profile of General Demographic Characteristics for the United States: 2000 Census.

Quinn, Jane Bryant. "Retire Early? Think Again." *Newsweek.* 21 July 2003, 43.

Reeves, Richard. *American Journey: Travelling with Tocqueville in Search of Democracy in America.* New York: Simon & Schuster, 1982.

Reich, Charles A. *The Greening of America.* New York: Random House, 1970.

Reich, Robert. *The Work of Nations: Preparing Ourselves for 21st-Century Capitalism.* New York: Alfred A. Knopf, 1991.

Relin, David Oliver. "More Than 13 million Children in America Are Struggling to Survive: Won't You Help Feed Them?" *Parade* Magazine. 4 April 2004, 7–9.

"A Rich Legacy of Preference: Alumni Kids Get a Big Break on Admissions." *Newsweek.* 24 June 1991, 59.

Riesman, David. *The Lonely Crowd: A Study on the Changing American Character.* New Haven: Yale University Press, 1950.

Riesman, David. *Individualism Reconsidered and Other Essays.* Glencoe, Ill.: The Free Press, 1954.

Roberts, David. "Points of Interest: Whose Rock Is It Anyway?" *Smithsonian.* March 2003, pp. 26, 29.

Roberts, Johnnie L. "Rethinking Black Leadership: The Race to the Top." *Newsweek.* 28 January 2002, 42–45.

Roberts, Sam. *Who We Are: A Portrait of America Based on the Latest U.S. Census.* New York: Times Books, 1993.

Robinson, Joe. "Ahh, Free at la-Oops! Time's Up." *Washington Post,* 27 July 2003, Outlook section: B1–3.

Rosenberg, Debra. "Justice: 25 Years After Bakke: Not Just Black and White." *Newsweek.* 30 June 2003, 37.

Samuel, Terrence. "Born-Again Agenda: The Peak of Political Power." *U.S. News & World Report.* 23 December 2002, 42–43.

Samuelson, Robert J. "Globalization Goes to War." *Newsweek.* 24 February 2003, 41.

"Saving Youth from Violence." *Carnegie Quarterly.* Winter 1994, 1–15.

Scanzoni, John. *Opportunity and the Family.* New York: The Free Press, 1970.

Scanzoni, John. *Sex Roles, Lifestyles, and Childbearing: Changing Patterns in Marriage and the Family.* New York: The Free Press, 1975.

Schickel, Richard. "Ladies Who Lunge." *Time* Magazine. 7 July 2003, 96.

Schlesinger, Arthur M., Jr. *The Disuniting of America: Reflections on a Multicultural Society.* New York: W.W. Norton, 1992.

"Sexism in the Schoolhouse: A Report Charges That Schools Favor Boys Over Girls." *Newsweek.* 24 February 1992, 62.

Sheler, Jeffery L. "All in the Family: As Billy Graham Steps Down, Will His Kids Shape the Future of American Evangelicalism?" *U.S. News & World Report.* 23 December 2002, 36–43.

"The Simple Life." *Time* Magazine. 8 April 1991, 58–63.

Singer, Audrey "At Home in the Nation's Capital: Immigrant Trends in Metropolitan Washington." A report by the Brookings Institution Center on Urban and Metropolitan Policy, June 2003.

Span, Paula. "Marriage at First Sight." *Washington Post* Magazine, 23 February 2003, 16–23, 32–38.

Squires, Sally. "Food Labels Must List Trans Fats: Starting in 2006, Rule Targets Risk Factor for Heart Disease." *Washington Post*, 10 July 2003. A3.

Stampp, Kenneth. *The Peculiar Institution: Slavery in the Ante-bellum South*. New York: Vintage Books, 1956.

Suro, Roberto. "Study of Immigrants Finds Asians at Top in Science and Medicine." *Washington Post*, 18 April 1994, 6(A).

"Survey of the attitudes of the American people on highway and auto safety: Wave five of a periodic tracking survey." Louis Harris and Pete Harris Research Group, Inc., June 2004.

Takaki, Ronald. *A Different Mirror: A History of Multicultural America*. Boston: Little, Brown, 1993.

"Talking Points: Evangelicals: The Hidden Mainstream." *The Week*. 21 March 2003, 16.

"Talking Points: Retro-sexism: The Return of the Real Man." *The Week*. 21 March 2003, 17.

Tocqueville, Alexis de. *Democracy in America*. New York: J. & H. G. Langley, 1845.

Toffler, Alvin. *Power Shift: Knowledge, Wealth, and Violence at the Edge of the 21st Century*. New York: Bantam Books, 1991.

"Trouble at the Top: A U.S. Survey Says a 'Glass Ceiling' Blocks Women from Corporate Heights." *U.S. News & World Report*. 17 June 1991, 40–48.

Turner, Frederick Jackson. *The Rise of the New West*. New York: Harper & Brothers, 1906.

Tyrangiel, Josh. "The Center of Attention" [Yao Ming]. *Time* Magazine. 10 February 2003, 68–71.

Tyre, Peg. "Getting Physical: A New Fitness Philosophy Puts Gym Teachers on the Front Lines in the Battle Against Childhood Obesity." *Newsweek*. 3 February 2003, 46–47.

Tyre, Peg and Daniel McGinn. "She Works, He Doesn't." *Newsweek*. 12 May 2003, 44–53.

U.S. Department of Education, National Center for Education Statistics, *The Condition of Education 2003*, NCES 2003–067, Washington, D.C.: U.S. Government Printing Office, 2003.

Von Drehle, David. "America in Red and Blue: A Nation Divided [Series]: Political Split Is Pervasive: Clash of Cultures Is Driven by Targeted Appeals and Reinforced Geography." *Washington Post*, A1, 10.

Waldman, Steven. "Benefits 'R' Us." *Newsweek*. 10 August 1992, 56–58.

"The War for the West." *Newsweek*. 30 September 1991, 18–32.

"Washington Area School Superintendents Demand Changes in Testing Regulations Affecting LEP and Special Education Students." 2 February 2004, a press release by the Washington Area School Study Council.

Waters, Harry F. "On the Trail of Tears: Ted Turner's Massive, Compelling Chronicle of the Native American Order." *Newsweek*. 10 October 1994, 56–58.

Wattenberg, Ben J. *The Real America: A Surprising Examination of the State of the Union*. New York: Doubleday, 1974.

Wattenberg, Ben J. *The Good News Is the Bad News Is Wrong*. New York: Simon & Schuster, 1984.

Wattenberg, Ben J. *The First Universal Nation: Leading Indicators and Ideas about the Surge of America in the 1990s*. New York: The Free Press, 1991.

Wattenberg, Ben J. *Values Matter Most: How Republicans or Democrats or a Third Party Can Win and Renew the American Way of Life*. New York: The Free Press, 1995.

Weiss, Michael. *Latitudes & Attitudes: An Atlas of Tastes, Trends, Politics and Passions*. Boston: Little, Brown, 1994.

Whelan, David. "In a Fog about Blogs." *American Demographics*. July/August 2003, Media Channels: 22–23.

"When America Went to the Moon." *U.S. News & World Report*. 11 July 1994, 50–60.

White, John Kenneth. *The Values Divide: American Politics and Culture in Transition,* with forward by John Zogby. New York: Chatham House Publishers of Seven Bridges Press, LLC, 2003.

Wilson, James Q. "Culture, Incentives, and the Underclass." *Values and Public Policy,* ed. Henry J. Aaron, Thomas E. Mann, and Timothy Taylor. Washington, D.C.: The Brookings Institution, 1994.

Woodward, Kenneth. "Dead End for the Mainline: The Mightiest Protestants Are Running Out of Money, Members and Meaning." *Newsweek.* 9 August 1993, 46–48.

Woodward, Kenneth. "Angels: Hark! America's Latest Search for Spiritual Meaning Has a Halo Effect." *Newsweek.* 27 December 1993, 52–57.

Woodward, Kenneth L. "Gospel on the Potomac." *Newsweek.* 10 March 2003, 29.

Yankelovich, Daniel. *New Rules: Searching for Self-Fulfillment in a World Turned Upside Down.* New York: Random House, 1981.

Yankelovich, Daniel. "How Changes in the Economy Are Reshaping American Values." *Values and Public Policy,* ed. Henry J. Aaron, Thomas E. Mann, and Timothy Taylor. Washington, D.C.: The Brookings Institution, 1994.

Zakaria, Fareed. "Bush, Rice and the 9-11 Shift." *Newsweek.* 16 December 2002, 35.

Zakaria, Fareed. "The Arrogant Empire: Part Three: America's Global Reach: Where Bush Went Wrong." *Newsweek.* 23 June 2004, 18–33.

Zuckerman, Mortimer B. "A Truly Cruel College Squeeze." *U.S. News & World Report.* 8 March 2004, 80.

Zuckerman, Mortimer B. "America's High Anxiety." *U.S. News & World Report.* 15 March 2004, 83–84.

CREDITS

Photos

Page viii, © Francisco Cruz/SuperStock; page 8, © David Canon/Getty Images; page 9, © Nick Ut/Associated Press; page 20, © Mark Richards/PhotoEdit; page 21, © Chuck Savage/Corbis; page 24, © Statue of Liberty National Monument; page 30, © Statue of Liberty National Monument; page 31, © Rolf Bruderer/Corbis; page 34, Maryanne Kearny Datesman; page 42, © Craig Hammell/Corbis; page 48, © Roxane Fridirici, JoAnn Crandall, Maryanne Kearny Datesman; page 53, © Allen T. Jules/Corbis; page 56, © Stuart Ramson/Associated Press; page 57, © Charles Krupa/Associated Press; page 58, © Jeff Greenberg/PhotoEdit; page 68, © Grace Beahm/Associated Press; page 70, © AP/Wide World Photos; page 74, © Library of Congress; page 77, © Library of Congress; page 81, © American Indian College Fund; page 86, from *Terminator 3: Rise of the Machines*, Arnold Schwarzenegger, 2003, © Warner Brothers/courtesy Everett Collection; page 88 (top), © NASA; page 88 (bottom), © Michael T. Sedam/Corbis; page 89, Courtesy, National Museum of the American Indian, Smithsonian Institution (2002-15323). Photo by Jim DiLoreto, NMNH; page 90, © Maryanne Kearny Datesman; page 95, © Owen Franken/Corbis; page 96, © Ariel Skelley/Corbis; page 98, © Michael Newman/PhotoEdit; page 101, © Image Bank/Getty Images; page 107, © Mary Kate Denny/PhotoEdit; page 109, © Roxane Fridirici; page 111, © Yusrin/Associated Press; page 114, © L. M.Otero/Associated Press; page 119, © Steve Starr/Corbis; page 121, © Library of Congress; page 124, © Mark Peterson/Corbis; page 125, © National Institute of Health; page 135, © Nancy Kaszerman/Corbis; page 138, © National Park Services, National Capital Area; page 142, © Library of Congress; page 145, © Rex Arbogast/Associated Press; page 147, © Stoughton; page 150, © George Nikitin/Associated Press; page 162, © A. Devaney, Inc., N.Y.; page 165, © Library of Congress; page 167, © Library of Congress; page 168, © Library of Congress; page 170, © AFL-CIO News; page 171, © J. Scott Applewhite/Associated Press; page 182, © Michael Newman/PhotoEdit; page 186, © Ken Karp; page 190, © Tom Stewart/Corbis; page 194, © Jose Luis Pelaez, Inc./Corbis; page 196, © Comstock Images/Getty Images; page 199, © Ariel Skelley/Corbis; page 208, © Lalmute E. Druskis; page 212, ©Duomo/Corbis; page 216, © Don Heupel/Associated Press; page 218, © John Russell/Associated Press; page 219, © Kyle Ericson/Associated Press; page 220, © Roxane Fridirici/JoAnn Crandall; page 235, © American Ballet Theater; page 238, © Rhonda M. Sommer; page 242, © Tony Freeman/PhotoEdit; page 244, © JoAnn Crandall; page 247, © Maryanne Kearny Datesman; page 248, © Maryanne Kearny Datesman; page 257, © Maryanne Kearny Datesman; page 260, © JoAnn Crandall; page 261, © Maryanne Kearny Datesman; page 262, © Joseph Sohm/Corbis; page 267, © Taxi/Getty Images; page 268, © Vivian Garcia; page 269, © Susan Walsh/Associated Press; page 270, © WavebreakMediaMicro/Fotolia; page 273, © Peter Langone/Index Stock; page 282, © Bettmann/Corbis

Illustrations

Page 3, © Rob Rogers/United Feature Syndicate, Inc; pages 5, 6, 19, 28, 44, 52, 55, 110, 122, 145, 200, 221, 272, Burmar Technical Corporation; page 99, © The New Yorker Collection 1993, Peter Steiner, from cartoonbank.com; all rights reserved.